T0074175

Integral Communication and Digital Identity

Ozren Rafajac • Alen Jakupović
Editors

Integral Communication and Digital Identity

palgrave
macmillan

Editors
Ozren Rafajac
Polytechnic of Rijeka
Rijeka, Croatia

Alen Jakupović
Polytechnic of Rijeka
Rijeka, Croatia

ISBN 978-3-031-47459-0   ISBN 978-3-031-47460-6   (eBook)
https://doi.org/10.1007/978-3-031-47460-6

This Palgrave Macmillan imprint is published by the registered company Springer Nature Switzerland AG.
The registered company address is: Gewerbestrasse 11, 6330 Cham, Switzerland

Paper in this product is recyclable.

PREFACE

In the information age, the ability to share and process information efficiently becomes the fundamental catalyst for learning and development. The fundamental challenge in the information society revolves around how to optimise information exchange. For this reason, a whole range of new social networks and mobile applications have appeared on the digital market in the last decade, all of which, in their own way, aim to facilitate presentation, collaboration, and feedback. The fact that there are currently at least 31 IT systems on the market that support collaboration and feedback sharing shows that there is an exceptionally high level of interest in these activities. On the other hand, the popularity of the sharing economy, often referred to as the peer-to-peer economy, shows that today's people are willing to share resources and collaborate with complete strangers if there is an IT system that acts like a digital intermediary that improves trust and lowers transaction costs. Today, Airbnb, an online marketplace for short-term accommodations and experiences, has 150 million users and 7 million listings offered by 4 million hosts, while Uber, a leading global ride-sharing marketplace, has 93 million customers and 3.5 million drivers serving its growing user base. Today, the online gaming industry generates higher profits than the film and music industries combined, while various companies such as Meta announce the further development of immersive virtual worlds. At the same time, in the public sector, the strongest economies such as Denmark, Australia, South Korea, and China are developing e-governance systems to improve the experience of public service delivery. Today, there are no students, teachers, creative professionals, entrepreneurs, public relations professionals, human resources managers, marketing experts, salespeople, business leaders, politicians, journalists, or public servants who could do their jobs effectively without digital communication tools that support the communication loop based on encoding, decoding, and feedback. For this reason, the aforementioned target groups are very interested in solutions that can improve these capabilities.

The main problem with current digital solutions that support social networking, electronic collaboration, and feedback sharing is that they are incompatible with each other. When educational and recruitment software are incompatible, educational institutions fail to match educational programmes to market needs, students have difficulty finding jobs, and employers have difficulty finding new employees. Today, if someone is looking for a ride service, they have to create an account with Uber or Lyft, and if someone is looking for accommodation, they have to create a separate account with Airbnb, Vrbo, or TripAdvisor. In a traditional (non-integral) way, the user on each of these platforms is forced to create a user profile and build a reputation from scratch. In other words, this personal data and reputation that the user has built in one IT system cannot usually be transferred and used in another IT system. Another problem arises from the fact that most of the current social networks do not reflect the full picture of the user. Although it is quite clear that networks based on incomplete and incorrect information cannot provide quality, efficiency, and reliability, most social networks and online platforms today only record distorted images or sections of a user's character, showing only individual pieces of the puzzle. The only way to overcome these problems is to design an integral communication framework in which all network elements (e.g., people, organisations, products, services, events, and places) can be described and evaluated in all aspects of their being. Although some exceptions can be found, from the end user's perspective, it is very impractical to manage multiple virtual profiles and accounts. In the near future, every IoT device and AI system will require identification of the individual, which will further increase the pressure on the user to use a unique digital identity. Similarly, it is fairly certain that users will not find it convenient to use different digital profiles in the applications that control their home appliances and personal cars, even if they are produced by different manufacturers. For this reason, there is no doubt that at some point in the near future, everyone's virtual and legal identities will merge into a single digital identity that can be used in the private, educational, business, and public spheres. Unfortunately, there is currently no consensus on how this should or will happen. Although their success is based on managing end-user data, today's social networks are more focused on making profits for their shareholders than on the well-being of their users. Although e-collaboration could greatly improve quality and reduce the global environmental footprint (e.g., e-collaboration improves group communication, negotiation, and resource sharing), most popular digital social networks today do not offer such features. Although there is no direct link between social networking and depression, several independent empirical studies have confirmed that people who limit their time on social media tend to be happier than those who do not. In addition, increasing social complexity creates problems and challenges that cannot be addressed with traditional communication methods and solutions. The latest OECD data on skills mismatch in the labour market for 2023 shows that even in developed countries such as Ireland (30.7%), New Zealand (28.2%), and the United Kingdom (20%), there is a significant proportion of under-skilled workers. As the use of artificial intelligence solutions (e.g., ChatGPT) and cloud computing continue to grow in the near future, the problem of skills mismatch will not be addressed without IT platforms that support vocational education and training. Although ordinary Internet users are hardly aware of this fact, the Internet, along with cryptocurrencies, gaming, and cloud computing, is becoming one of the biggest threats to environmental sustainability when considering overall energy consumption. For this reason, there is an urgent need to develop new approaches to information sharing that reduce the environmental footprint of today's society. All these examples show that nowadays it is necessary to promote the development of communication solutions that can ensure a more precise definition of users and an easier identification of opportunities for holistic development and collaboration, especially among actors who need professional help.

This book explains how taxonomy can be used to describe and connect social actors in an integral way. Integral communication refers to a specific way of openly exchanging information that takes into account all the characteristics and preferences of the interlocutors and allows for an anonymous exchange of feedback that promotes trust and personal development. In this book, the authors propose a new, original way of digital communication using tags that describe all the characteristics and preferences of a particular node in the network. Although most social networks, sharing platforms, and e-government frameworks already use taxonomies and social tagging to define user identity, none of them focus exclusively on tags as a fundamental element of user definition and networking. Furthermore, none of these platforms allow for anonymous sharing of feedback, nor are they focused on personal development of individuals. In face-to-face communication, many people are unwilling to provide negative feedback to avoid potential conflict with those who should receive it. This tactic of non-confrontation creates a false atmosphere in which individuals and groups significantly limit their ability to grow and learn. Only during the anonymous assessment, the evaluators are not afraid to express their critical views freely. The fact that rating is anonymous does not mean that users or group administrators cannot control who can rate and during what time period. Moreover, in all existing communication solutions, tags are used only to describe user activities in general terms, completely ignoring vertical dimensions and user development preferences. Last but not least, today there is an increasing amount of unreliable online information, which, without tools and methods to confirm its accuracy, threatens to turn the information society into a disinformation society. Considering that the total amount of information people are trying to process is increasing exponentially, while their cognitive abilities in information processing remain quite limited, people are forced to develop new approaches and methods for communication and information management. The authors' analysis shows that the presence of an integral set of dynamic data about user characteristics and preferences improves social perceptibility, control over personal data, the ability to collaborate and cooperate, identification of compatible and complementary positions, time and resource efficiency, dynamic exchange of feedback, and trust and security. The authors also point out that the implementation of such solutions is not without potential dangers such as autocratic and unauthorised control, dependence on digital infrastructure, potential crime problems, addictive user behaviour, privacy issues, and filter bubbles.

Thanks to the Internet, people today have the opportunity to openly share all the information they consider important for a better understanding of their personal characteristics and preferences. The role of integral communication is to promote perceptiveness, collaboration, personal development, and organisational learning among all the actors involved. Aside from helping actors present their qualities and preferences, integral communication promotes self-awareness, teamwork, sustainability, trust, organisational learning, and personalised communication with AI machines. Although the idea of integral tagging may sound threatening and undesirable to some readers, mainly due to negative experiences related to social tagging in China (e.g., Social Credit Score or Social Credit System), an empirical study conducted by the authors on a sample of 772 (N) respondents in the Republic of Croatia shows that a significant number of potential users have a positive attitude towards integral presentation, assessment, and development. To follow the path of sustainable development, today's society needs a communication framework that fosters the processes of searching, learning, collaboration, feedback, and resource sharing. Since mindful communication is a fundamental element of any constructive social action, any improvement in the field of communication has a tremendous impact on society as a whole. After reading this book, readers will learn how to harness the power of integral networking and understand why anonymous feedback is a critical element for learning and development.

Over the past two decades, many different books have been published explaining the benefits of feedback. The most important titles, which can be considered as precursors of the present book, are: *360-Degree Feedback: The Powerful New Model for Employee Assessment & Performance Improvement*, written by Edwards and Even (1996), *Thanks for the Feedback: The Science and Art of Receiving Feedback*, written by Stone and Heen (2014), *The Feedback Imperative: How to Give Everyday Feedback to Speed Up Your Team's Success*, written by Crroll (2014), and *The Fearless Organization: Creating Psychological Safety in the Workplace for Learning, Innovation, and Growth*, written by Edmondson (2018), which asserts that the feedback process should proceed without consequences. In the last five years, many other books have been published on feedback, such as *Visible Learning: Feedback*, written by Hattie and Clarke (2018), *Handbook of Strategic 360 Feedback*, written by Church et al. (2019), *Let Talk: Make Effective Feedback Your Superpower*, written by Huston (2021), *Organizational Learning from Performance Feedback: A Behavioral Perspective on Multiple Goals (Elements in Organization Theory)*, written by Audia (2021), and *Digital Feedback Methods*, written by Schluer (2022). Among the literature dealing with digital identity, titles of particular interest include *Digital Identities: Creating and Communicating the Online Self*, written by Cover (2015), *Learning Digital Identity: Design, Deploy, and Manage Identity Architectures*, written by Windley (2023), and *Virtual Identities and Digital Culture*, written by Kannen and Langille (2023). Although all of the aforementioned authors emphasise the importance of sharing feedback and creating a digital identity, in most cases they do not provide an empirical analysis of user attitudes towards integral presentation, evaluation, and development, nor do they provide guidance on how to design a web and mobile application for integral presentation and feedback sharing.

In this book, the subject of integral communication is treated in four chapters. The first chapter, entitled "Introduction to Integral Communication", defines the basic concepts of integral communication, the purpose of integral information exchange, and the integral communication methodology that enables the implementation of integral ecosystems. The second chapter, titled "The Power of Integral Networking", analyses the existing challenges and benefits of integral networking and provides key guidelines for designing integral networks in the civic, educational, business, and public sectors. In addition, this chapter presents the results of an empirical study of potential users' personal attitudes towards integral communication. "Integral Communication Framework" is the title of the third chapter, which defines the conceptual model of the integral communication platform, the methodology of mapping and visualising integral information, and provides the SWOT analysis of the integral communication framework. The fourth chapter, titled "Perspective on Integral Communication", extends the discussion of personal development and organisational learning in the IoT ecosystem.

The Integral Communication Framework (ICF) offers today's society the opportunity to structurally transform its communication, collaboration, and learning processes. Using keywords that can be translated into multiple languages, evaluated, and enriched with metadata, the integral communication methodology creates a whole range of opportunities to enhance live conversations and digitally supported interactions that improve personal development and organisational learning. Communication frameworks that enhance human perceptiveness and efficiency are extremely important factors in creating an environmentally sustainable future. This book is aimed at four different types of readers. The first group includes human resource managers, marketers, salespeople, public relations professionals, entrepreneurs, politicians, public officials, executives, and managers of private and public organisations who can use the integral communication framework to improve the efficiency and organisational intelligence of their organisations. The second audience includes scientists, innovators, software engineers, and developers of various measurement tools, learning games, and instruments that can be used in integral assessment. The third group includes teachers, professors, counsellors, and various types of professionals (e.g., psychiatrists, psychotherapists, and psychologists) who can use this book and the integral communication framework to enhance their professional activities and share various learning materials or links. The fourth audience includes students and all other ordinary people who can use the integral communication framework for their personal growth and pursuit of their personal interests. After reading this book, anyone interested will be able to try the integral communication framework developed by the authors and their team of collaborators.

Rijeka, Croatia
Ozren Rafajac
Alen Jakupović

Contents

About the Authors

Ozren Rafajac, PhD Graduated from the Faculty of Economics of the University of Rijeka in 2004 (International Trade), he holds a master's degree from the Faculty of Tourism and Hospitality Management of the University of Rijeka (Master of Sciences in the field of Social Sciences, Management; 2008) and PhD from the Faculty of Economics and Tourism "Dr. Mijo Mirković" (Doctor of Science in the field of Social Sciences, Economics; 2013). Since 2004 he has been working at the Polytechnic of Rijeka, first as a research assistant in the scientific project "Management in Entrepreneurial Economy" (0081002) and now as a professor of professional studies, where he teaches human resources management, business communications, sales management, and digital marketing. From 2006 to 2007, he participated in the INTERIM project, funded by the INTERREG IIIB CADSES programme of the European Union. From 2018 to 2021, he participated in the project "Development of the International Educational Programme Veleri-OI IoT School" (UP.03.1.1.02.0027), funded by the European Social Fund, Efficient Human Resources. Since 2019, he has been an external assistant professor at the Faculty of Maritime Studies at the University of Rijeka, where he teaches e-business and cloud computing. His research interests focus on HR management, organisational intelligence, e-business, organisational development, communication, tourism, and sales management. He is active in the fields of e-business, marketing, management consulting, and sailing (Yachtmaster up to 100 GT). He is a co-founder of the start-up company METREAN Llc.

Alen Jakupović, PhD Graduated from the Faculty of Education in Rijeka in 1997 (teacher of mathematics and informatics), he holds a master's degree from the Faculty of Organization and Informatics in Varaždin (Master of Sciences in the field of social sciences, information sciences, 2006) and doctorate degree from the Faculty of Humanities and Social Sciences in Zagreb (doctorate in the field of social sciences, information and communication sciences, 2010). From 1998 to 2008 he worked in an information and programming technology company as a programmer, project designer, project manager, sales representative, financial advisor, and company manager. Since 2008 he has been working at the Polytechnic of Rijeka, where he has taught several courses in programming and project design. From 2014 to 2018 he worked as an external associate professor at the Faculty of Educational Sciences, Juraj Dobrila University in Pula. Since 2012, he has been an external associate of the doctoral studies Department of Informatics, University of Rijeka. He was appointed to the teaching grade of a college professor with tenure and associate professor. He has participated in various professional and scientific projects. His scholarly and professional interests include development of metrics and methodologies for information systems development, artificial intelligence (knowledge representation formalism), intelligent systems development, information and business systems dependability, and ICT in education. He is also active in business, as a consultant for the implementation of information technology and designer of information systems, and is a co-founder of a start-up company METREAN Llc.

ABBREVIATIONS

AEP	Application Enabled Platform
AI	Artificial Intelligence
AR	Augmented Reality
BYOD	Bring Your Own Device
CCT	Cognitive Communication Trap
CI	Communication Intelligence
CRM	Customer Relationship Management
CVE	Collaborative Virtual Environment
CX	Customer Experience
DADE	Distributed Agile or Adaptive Development Environment
DSR	Design Science Research
DPC	Data Protection Commission
ERP	Enterprise Resource Planning
EU	European Union
GDPR	General Data Protection Regulation
GIS	Geographic Information System
GPS	Global Positioning System
HCI	Human-Computer Interaction
HRI	Human-Robot Interaction
HRIS	Human Resource Information System
HR	Human Resources
IC	Integral Communication
ICF	Integral Communication Framework
ICT	Information and Communication Technologies
IM	Instant Messaging
IoT	Internet of Things
IT	Information Technology

LMS	Learning Management System
MBO	Management by Objectives
NFT	Non-Fungible Token
OI	Organisational Intelligence
PIAV	Personal Interests, Attitudes, and Values
QR code	Quick Response Code
RFID	Radio-Frequency Identification
SCD	Social Coordination Dynamics
SCS	Social Credit System
SWOT	Strengths, Weaknesses, Opportunities, and Threats
TPB	The Pirate Bay
TV	Television
UPC	Universal Product Codes
U.S.	United States
VALS	Values and Lifestyles
VR	Virtual reality
Web3D	Navigate Websites Using 3D
WebRTC	Web-Based Communication in Real-Time

LIST OF FIGURES

Integral Communication Framework

Perspective on Integral Communication

LIST OF TABLES

The Power of Integral Networking

Integral Communication Framework

Introduction to Integral Communication

Ozren Rafajac and Alen Jakupović

INTRODUCTION

Since its beginnings, mankind has been continuously improving its communication skills. All of this is happening simply because of the need for
people to collaborate and share information about locations, ideas, expertise, preferences, and any other topic that can help them improve their
efficiency and the quality of their well-being. Whether it is defined as
meaningful interaction between communicators or as a process of sharing
information based on common symbols, there is no doubt that communication is a fundamental element of almost any (constructive) social activity.
While in general even the absence of good communication is a type of
communication, communication in its basic sense is the process that connects group members and enables them to coordinate their activities
(Shakin, 2012). The word communication is derived from the Latin word
communis, which means common (Lunenburg, 2010). Every form of
communication consists of two phases – transmission and feedback. In the
transmission phase, information is exchanged between two or more

---

O. Rafajac (✉) • A. Jakupović
Polytechnic of Rijeka, Rijeka, Croatia
e-mail: ozren.rafajac@veleri.hr; alen.jakupovic@veleri.hr

© The Author(s), under exclusive license to Springer Nature
Switzerland AG 2024
O. Rafajac, A. Jakupović (eds.), *Integral Communication and
Digital Identity*, https://doi.org/10.1007/978-3-031-47460-6_1
1

people. According to Gutierez (2017), feedback is the reaction of the audience. In the context of this research, feedback is defined as information about a characteristic or experience that helps to improve the performance and quality of the recipient. It is extremely valuable information that promotes personal development and organisational learning. Communication can be either verbal, nonverbal, or visual (Poyatos, 1992). Communication that is either written or spoken is verbal communication (Nwabueze & Mileski, 2018). On the other hand, various types of body language such as posture, facial expressions, eye contact, and communication through objects such as clothing, accessories, and hairstyles are all forms of nonverbal communication (Subapriya, 2009). Visual communication is the exchange of ideas and information in a form that is visible to the human eye and includes pictures, symbols, illustrations, and other types of visual information (Knox, 2007). Communication skills and techniques represent specific methods of presenting, sharing, filtering, and handling different types of information. To improve their communication skills, today's people and organisations are constantly trying to invent new ways to communicate. Social perceptual skills are the skills that help people recognise, interpret, and respond to cues given by others in social interactions (Romanczyk et al., 2005). For the purposes of this study, perceptivity is defined as the ability to correctly interpret the physical, emotional, cognitive, mental, verbal, and nonverbal characteristics of other social actors. Why is this ability so important? By gaining better insight into what group members feel, know, think, have, and want, leaders can more accurately determine strategies and actions to accomplish complex tasks. According to Yarbrough (2017), social actors tend to imitate gestures of other social actors they like, and they do so unconsciously. This means that mirroring nonverbal signs and verbal expressions can improve understanding, empathy, and communication. Thus, the ability to adapt to the communication style of the interlocutor and the ability to easily show preferences are important functions of cognitively aware infocommunicative devices (Navarretta, 2018). The ability to see different perspectives expands knowledge, reduces egocentrism, and increases the chance of making wise decisions.

After reading this chapter, the reader will be able to:

- Recognise why it is important to improve communication and collaboration skills.
- Discuss current communication trends.

- Define the purpose of integral communication.
- Explain the fundamentals of integral communication methodology.
- Highlight important issues about integral communication that need closer examination.

BACKGROUND

In today's society, timely, accessible, easily understood, and reliable information is becoming a fundamental resource for shaping sustainable social relationships. Although modern technologies offer almost unlimited possibilities for information exchange, individuals and organisations in today's world still face a variety of communication problems. According to the most recent data available for all EU Member States, the number of marriages has recently decreased and the number of divorces has increased (Eurostat, 2021). Although the concept of the family unit is in flux, it is obvious that many people have problems maintaining a long-term relationship. Of course, every relationship has its ups and downs, and there can be many different reasons why one of our relationships comes to an end. When today's experts educate others on how to build and maintain healthy and stable relationships, active communication is among their first suggestions. A good communicator is not the one who is constantly talking, but the one who is asking *deep questions* (i.e., questions that require critical thinking) and actively listening. Although this and similar advice for better communication do not seem so difficult to apply, in practice things usually become much more complicated. People's cognitive limitations combined with information overload and personal differences such as character, preferences, and value systems make things even more complicated. The difficulties of finding compatible partners, friends, and people (with complementary interests) with whom we can build long-term, quality relationships is something we all face on a daily basis. The same is true for all economic activities. Everyone knows that motivated employees and satisfied customers are essential components of good and sustainable management, and that the best strategy to achieve this is intensive communication. However, practice shows that a large part of employees are not motivated. According to the latest Gallup study conducted in 142 countries, only 13% of workers worldwide are engaged at work, 63% are disengaged, meaning they lack motivation, while 24% are actively disengaged, meaning they are unhappy and unproductive at work (Crabtree, 2013). In rough numbers, this means that 900 million workers worldwide are disengaged and 340 million are actively disengaged (Crabtree, 2013). Although a number of different reasons can be found for workers' lack of engagement in the workplace, most of them stem from poor communication. Without effective information sharing and active listening, it is very difficult to ensure that employees' personal goals are aligned with organisational goals. This is not news. There are numerous studies in the literature explaining that effective communication is key to employee motivation and high performance (Rajhans, 2009; Semren, 2017). To be effective in their business, management must actively communicate with many different stakeholders. For example, if a company does not communicate with an educational institution that trains its future employees about the skills and knowledge needed in its business processes, there is a high likelihood that its educational programmes will not be aligned with actual market needs. This lack of communication is confirmed by studies showing that a growing number of employers believe that graduates do not have sufficient skills to be effective (Cukier et al., 2015).

In addition, more and more organisations today are using various tools (e.g., surveys) to help their managers monitor customer satisfaction and organisational climate. Customer satisfaction is an effective response of varying intensity, with a timed determination point and limited duration, directed at key aspects of product acquisition and/or consumption (Giese & Cote, 2000). When successfully managed, customer responses are an extremely valuable asset that companies can use to improve the quality of existing products and processes, develop new products, and build long-term relationships with end users. Although surveys are useful, they are extremely time-consuming and require expertise to interpret. For this reason, solutions that simplify the exchange of feedback and the management of human resources are urgently needed. Organisational climate represents the perception of the work environment by the employees of the organisation (Zhang & Liu, 2010). Apart from the positive correlation between organisational climate and managers' communication skills (Alipour, 2011), empirical results show that there is a positive and significant relationship between organisational climate and organisational performance (Guzley, 1992; Putter, 2010; Umoh et al., 2013; Berberoglu, 2018). Most management decisions, including those related to organisational climate, are usually based on the periodic collection, analysis, and interpretation of performance measures that form the basis for decision making. Over time, people's interests, experiences, and preferences change. To be optimally informed, managers need communication techniques and tools that can regularly capture these changes.

COGNITIVE COMMUNICATION TRAPS

In the information society, the ability to efficiently share and process information becomes the fundamental catalyst for personal and organisational development. The fact that someone tries to communicate does not guarantee that the communication will take place, nor that the message will be understood. Empirical findings show that when communication is poor, an organisation's global competitiveness is severely limited (Nwabueze & Mileski, 2018). Individuals and organisations that have highly developed communication skills tend to be more successful in collaborating and achieving desired goals than those with poorly developed communication skills (Tucker et al., 1996). This also means that all those who are not able to apply the most sophisticated methods of communication and information processing are in a kind of cognitive trap from which it is not easy to get out. The cognitive communication trap (CCT) is a condition in which social actors fail to process information that could improve their efficiency and well-being. Such traps can arise for many different reasons. The most obvious cause is cognitive bias. According to Hallman (2022), there are at least fifty systematic errors in cognitive processes, such as: fundamental attribution error (e.g., when social actors judge others based on their personality or basic character, but judge themselves based on the situation), anchoring (e.g.., When social actors rely heavily on the first piece of information in making decisions), framing effect (when social actors draw different conclusions from the same piece of information depending on how it is presented), false consensus (when social actors believe that agreement on a conclusion is greater than it actually is), etc. This tendency of the human brain to simplify information processing through its own mental shortcuts can often lead to irrational interpretations and judgments. Cognitive communication traps can occur because of cognitive biases, lack of knowledge about information processing, and/or because information processing would require too much time and energy. When an organisation's management is unfamiliar with its customers' preferences and when policymakers are unaware of what their constituents think about certain policy issues, they fall into the cognitive communication trap. With more than 5.7 billion people connected to mobile services in 2022, our society should be on the cusp of a whole new age of communication and collaboration (GSMA, 2022), but this is not yet the case. Despite the fact that 80% of these devices are smartphones (Deloitte, 2017), which provide tremendous help in processing information, nowadays companies still have problems finding suitable employees, while ordinary people still have difficulties finding partners, jobs and all other things that could improve their well-being. Despite the fact that our society has already developed many different technological solutions that try to connect people at different levels, the authors of this book try to emphasise that there is a need for a new communication methodology that improves the efficiency, sustainability and quality of human interactions.

Increasing social complexity creates problems and challenges that cannot be overcome with traditional communication methods and solutions. Apart from positive effects such as price reduction, increased efficiency and greater choice, rapid technological progress, when applied without critical thinking, usually brings with it a host of negative side effects. Mental illnesses such as depression, suicide, crime, structural unemployment, and environmental degradation are all related to poor communication skills and abilities. This means that tons of waste, chemicals, and harmful gas emissions that irrevocably destroy our natural environment are not only related to consumer culture and planned obsolescence that ensure high profits at the expense of the biological environment, but also to the communication and cooperation skills of all members of modern society. To achieve its goal of long-term sustainability, contemporary society must rethink and redesign its communication and cooperation processes. The most recent WHO (2022) report estimates that 5% of adults worldwide suffer from depression and that over 700,000 people die by suicide each year. Although these people should receive adequate psychological help, about 75% of people in low- and middle-income countries do not receive treatment (WHO, 2022). Without urgent action, the amount of global waste will increase by 70% by 2050 (The World Bank, 2018). Another challenge resulting from rapid technological progress is structural unemployment, which occurs because workers lack the necessary job skills or live too far from regions where jobs are available and cannot move nearby (Kenton, 2019). Between 2007 and 2013, the number of people in Europe who were unemployed for more than a year doubled (EC, 2019). At its peak, this sharp increase in long-term unemployment affected about 12 million people, or 5.1% of the labour force in the EU (2019). In 2014, on average, 29% of the adult European labour force was affected by skills shortages, and one in five workers in the EU considers it very likely that some of their skills will become obsolete in the next five years (Cedefop, 2015).

The last decades have been marked by an ongoing debate between those who claim that new communication technologies have a negative impact on interpersonal relationships and those who disagree with this view. While the first group claims that the Internet, virtual reality, and social networks are a surrogate for human relationships and interactions that are leading our society toward dehumanisation, excessive control, and lack of privacy, the second group claims that it is not the technology itself that is the problem, but the way the technology is used. In many cases, proponents of the first camp have good points. Many of the problems currently facing our society are due to technological solutions that were intended to solve other problems. Although computers and robots reduce the need for hard physical labour, excessive looking at screens and sitting in front of computers has a negative impact on human health. Rapid technological development reduces the ability of individuals to maintain a long-term job and thus a stable income, which in turn leads to problems in family relationships. People who spend too much time on social media, online games, and virtual reality may actually become antisocial and anxious (Gioia et al., 2022). Despite these dangers, proponents of the second camp believe that new communication technologies can help people improve their perceptiveness, sustainability, and personality (Ahn et al., 2014). This trend is called digital humanism and is based on the idea that new technologies extend and develop new tools of social cognition that help individuals take perspectives of others that would be impossible to understand without the help of such technologies (Żuromski et al., 2018). Proponents of digital humanism believe that it is possible to optimise the time and energy that social actors invest in communicating and searching for content. To be able to qualitatively distinguish different solutions, including the integral communication framework elaborated in later chapters, readers should first understand the meaning of integral communication, learn how this type of communication relates to the latest communication trends, and what the methodology of integral communication looks like.

The main objective of this book is to improve the organisational intelligence of individuals and organisations of today. To achieve such a complex goal, it was necessary to identify the appropriate methodology, analyse the attitudes of potential users, design a framework, and analyse the opportunities and risks in implementing integral communication. This chapter introduces the reader to the basics of integral communication. The main goal of this chapter is to find a communication methodology that enhances organisational learning and personal development. To achieve this goal, five key problems have been identified. The first problem is that humans have cognitive limitations when processing a large amount of information. Unfortunately, the amount of information that people attempt to exchange during various social activities is constantly increasing. Therefore, one of the biggest challenges in the network society is information overload (Roetzel, 2018). In recent decades, the total amount of online information available has increased so much that social actors often cannot find and follow all the information they find relevant and interesting. Even when they do their best, ordinary people invest a lot of time and energy in these tasks. As the amount of information they are exposed to on a daily basis continues to increase, it becomes increasingly difficult for individuals to judge the accuracy and truthfulness of information. It is not always possible to verify the reliability of certain information on one's own, and even when it is possible, it is an extremely costly process. When it is not possible to independently determine the veracity of information, people have two choices: to believe or not to believe those who convey information (Blöbaum, 2016). Up to a point, it is normal and reasonable to believe others, but when the total amount of information people consider trustworthy exceeds that whose accuracy they can independently confirm, a space for manipulation and poor decision-making is created. Without appropriate methods and technologies that seek to valorize information in a transparent way, the information society could easily become a misinformation society. The second problem is that every technology has both positive and negative effects. The invention of the commercial aeroplane has greatly increased transatlantic travel, but it has also increased pollution. The Internet and mobile devices have significantly increased the availability of information, but also the amount of time social actors spend looking at screens and searching for content (Rahaman, 2017). Without further optimization of the time and energy spent on information exchange, it is not possible to create a sustainable society and Internet. The third problem is that analysing unstructured data is expensive and time-consuming. Today, experts believe that between 80% and 90% of data is unstructured (Hollander, 2022). The problem of unstructured communication becomes apparent whenever a group refuses to introduce structural patterns into its communication. The fourth problem is that people differ not only in horizontal aspects of their personalities (e.g., certain interests) but also in vertical or developmental aspects (e.g., their ability to achieve a certain result). The problem is that there are still no widely used communication tools that measure and use the vertical or developmental dimension of social actors in addition to the horizontal dimension. The fifth problem is that sustainable behaviour requires collaboration among social actors who do not know (and/or trust) each other. Without communication solutions that ensure a higher level of trust between actors who do not know each other, building their collaboration will remain very difficult. To solve the problems identified, today's society needs to adopt a holistic communication methodology based on an automated exchange of information about the characteristics and preferences of different types of users. This chapter is based on two main hypotheses:

Hypothesis One: Integral communication improves social perceptiveness.
Hypothesis Two: Integral communication improves collaboration.

All of the previously mentioned examples suggest that people should develop new communication solutions that improve their ability to perceive, collaborate, and understand. Although many different barriers can be identified that prevent people from collaborating and cooperating much more effectively, one of the most important is the lack of communication solutions that enable such behaviour. Although face-to-face communication will always retain its fundamental quality, improving people's ability to recognize different perspectives (e.g., feedback) and their ability to present themselves in all aspects of their personality (through an integral communication interface) will greatly improve people's communication and collaboration skills.

CONTEMPORARY COMMUNICATION TRENDS

In recent decades, scientists, entrepreneurs, and enthusiasts in the field of information and communications technology (ICT) have created a whole new set of products, services, and ways to improve communication and collaboration. All of this is happening because of our need for collaboration and efficient information sharing. Since the advent of the Internet, there has been increasing discussion about the network society, which is a social structure composed of networks supported by microelectronic information and communication technologies (Castells, 2012). The fundamental factor that distinguishes a network society from traditional social networks lies in the application of information and communication technologies that help social individuals to create and maintain widely distributed and flexible networks in which new forms of social relationships emerge. Because they are not limited by time and place, these virtual IT networks provide a space for substantial improvement in all economic, social, and political relationships. However, in addition to the positive effects, the development of communication technologies also brings some dangers. The fundamental problem is the fact that technology is greatly changing human behaviour patterns. The problem derived from this relates to the fact that without solutions that enable open sharing and evaluation of information, it will become increasingly difficult for today's social actors to distinguish true and reliable from false and unreliable information (e.g., fake reviews, hoaxes, and fake news). Since machine learning software is already capable of creating genuine-looking text (Yao et al., 2017), audio files (Mukhopadhyay et al., 2015), images, and videos (Qi et al., 2019), without appropriate solutions to help evaluate information and its evaluators and sources, the problem of misinformation will continue to grow (Kumar & Shah, 2018). History shows that people use a technology first and only then think critically about its value. According to a Common Sense Media report (2022), teens spend an average of 1 hour and 27 minutes per day scrolling social media, an increase of 17 minutes from 2019, with girls more likely than boys to use social media daily (68% vs. 57%).

Despite the development and popularity of social networks, our society does not yet fully appreciate and utilise the potential of IT in education, politics, and business. Although the transformation process towards a network society has already begun, today's society is still on the threshold of Internet networking. Here are some examples. To attract new users and keep existing users active, many social networks nowadays develop algorithms to keep their users in the so-called filter bubble. The main problem with these filter bubbles is that they reduce the chance of users seeing an opposing viewpoint, which in turn increases polarisation and supports beliefs regardless of whether they are correct (Pariser, 2012; Papa & Photiadis, 2021). It is a well-known fact that the way a piece of information is conveyed has an impact on the interpretation of the information. This assertion is supported by Valenzuela et al. (2017), who show that message frames can have an impact on behaviour (e.g., a morality frame increases message sharing, while a conflict frame decreases it). Numerous

TV channels, websites, and social networks disseminate information for profit in ways that often do more harm than good (e.g., clickbait). This claim is supported by several authors. While Konrath (2013) argued that social networks and media promote narcissism and reduce empathy, Michel et al. (2019) identified advertising as one of the main sources of human dissatisfaction. Clearly, the ideas people share with each other help shape their worlds, and individuals are forced to find their own optimal balance between different, often conflicting, personal goals. McNamee et al. (2019) findings show that prolonged social media use (more than 4 hours per day) is associated with poorer emotional health and behavioural difficulties, but that limited social media use (less than 3 hours per day) has some positive effect on peer relationships. The main challenge is to reduce the total amount of information processed by social actors without losing useful and important information. The authors of this book propose that the next level of interconnectedness is achieved through an integral communication framework that enhances human perceptual capability and collaboration (e.g., electronic collaboration can ensure significant energy savings). Perception is the ability to understand inner qualities or relationships (Merriam-Webster, 2020a). In this book, integral perceptual capacity is understood as the ability to understand the widest possible range of properties, characteristics, and relationships that arise between different entities in real and virtual social interactions. It is achieved through digital technology that helps people to present their characteristics and preferences. Integral networking means purposefully linking subjects based on a wide range of personal characteristics and preferences. Personalised communication is designed to help people optimise their everyday and business activities. While automation of production and service processes is a key feature of Economy 4.0, personalization will be a key feature of Economy 5.0, and this will happen through an integral communication framework that enables automation of communication processes and organisational learning. In other words, to enter Economy 5.0, people need a solution that optimises the time and energy they spend on digital communications. According to a recent study by market research firm Nielsen, adult Americans spend more than 11 hours per day watching, reading, listening to, or simply interacting with media, and that's an increase of 9 hours and 32 minutes over the past four years (Fottrell, 2018). As shown in Figs. 1 and 2, the majority of the U.S. adult population uses the TV services, web, and apps.

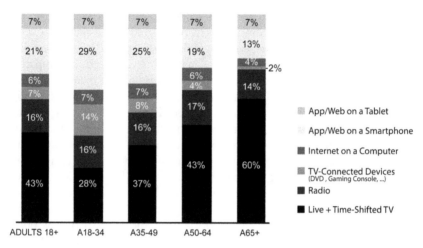

Fig. 1 Share of daily time spent by platform – Based on Total U.S. Population. (Source: Fottrell 2018; Nielsen 2018)

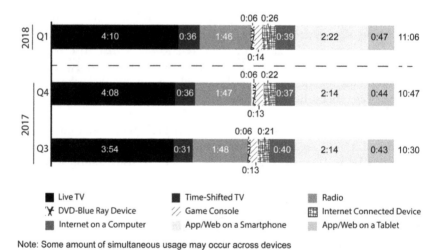

Note: Some amount of simultaneous usage may occur across devices

Fig. 2 Average time spent per adult 18+ per day (based on total U.S. population). (Source: Fottrell, 2018; Nielsen, 2018)

While younger adults spend more time using apps and the Internet on smartphones, older users consume more TV services. For most users, search tools were the entry point or first step to online shopping, but nowadays people's IT communication habits are changing rapidly. In addition to the extremely popular ecosystems such as Facebook, YouTube, Instagram and Twitter, new communication applications are constantly emerging that are redefining the communication habits of modern people. In the United States, Meta Platforms has launched the fastest-growing app in history (overtaking ChatGPT's record), gaining over 100 million users in its first five days (Siladitya, 2023). It is called Threads and aims to focus on public dialogues rather than private communication (Isaac, 2023).

Digitally supported communication and e-collaboration are particularly popular in China. According to iResearch (2018) China Internet Traffic report, the share of Internet search tools decreased from 33% in 2012 to 25% in 2017, while the share of e-commerce increased from 23% in 2012 to 32% in 2017, while social network traffic increased from 4.1% in 2012 to 10% in 2017. Since their appearance in 2007, smart mobile devices have been continuously changing users' habits of creating and sharing Internet content. The lower prices and overall convenience compared to desktop computers make smartphones very popular in communication. It was no surprise when Dischler (2015), the vice president and manager of Google, said that in ten countries, including the U.S. and Japan, more searches were conducted via mobile devices than desktop computers. Although the data displayed is constantly changing across markets, Fig. 3 shows the relative share of mobile and desktop Internet access time per industry in the U.K. for 2017. According to Hollander (2018), consumers in China download more apps than consumers in other markets and spend significantly more time in apps than consumers in other markets. A good example of how witty, personalised, and upbeat content presentation and sharing can attract a large number of users is a fast-paced short video sharing app called TikTok, which currently has 732 million users worldwide who spend an average of 89 minutes per day using the app (Ingham, 2021). The success of TikTok's personalization algorithm shows that the key aspect of electronic collaboration is the ability to track the performance of others (and showcase one's own performance) within specific genres or subnets that connect people with similar interests (Pitre, 2023). Interestingly, consumers in China spend the most time in communication apps (see Fig. 4).

Interestingly, consumers in China spend the most time in communication apps (see Fig. 4). This is especially true for the WeChat app, which is a small ecosystem of over half a million micro apps (e.g., mini-programmes)

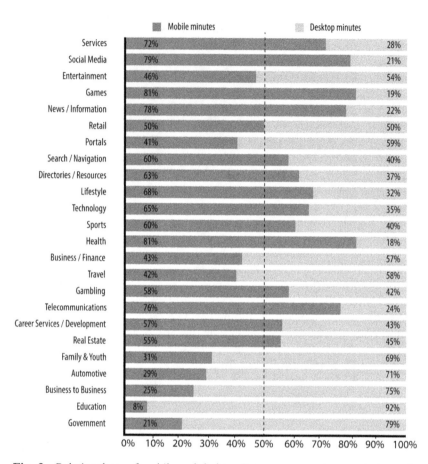

Fig. 3 Relative share of mobile and desktop Internet access time per industry in the UK for 2017. (Source: ComScore, 2017)

integrated into the social messaging platform (Cheng et al., 2020). This platform is used for a variety of activities, from chats and phone calls to paying grocery bills and making medical appointments. In addition, an experimental application of mutual evaluation in social relationships has already been released in China (Ma, 2018). The purpose of this system, called the Social Credit System (SCS) is to reinforce honesty in various types of activities to reward desirable behaviours and sanction undesirable ones (Creemers, 2015). According to Donnelly (2022), 80% of provinces,

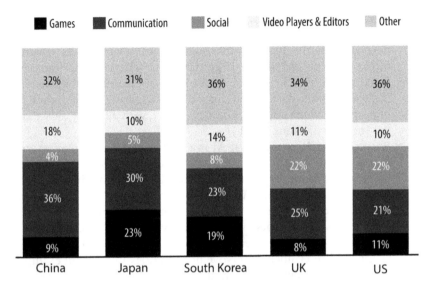

Fig. 4 Time spent in apps, by category (on Android operating system). (Source: Hollander, 2018)

regions, and cities in China have adopted or are in the process of adopting some version of the system. It seems that, in China at least, the age of integral communication has already begun. What is problematic in the case of China is that this rating system is under the direct control of the government, which can and will use it to sanction its own citizens. There is no doubt that any technology can be used for positive and negative purposes. Like any other technology, integral communication methodology should be used on a voluntary basis with an appropriate level of privacy and user rights. When the risks of unwanted use are minimised, integral communications enables a variety of opportunities for personal and organisational improvement, such as enhancing collaboration, increasing trust and quality, reducing operational costs, etc. The Forbes Communications Council (2018) recently presented a list of the latest trends in communications, which has been expanded to include some additional trends that the authors believe are of particular interest:

- **Cloud Services:** Storing and sharing data in clouds has become more convenient than traditional storage and sharing methods.

Cloud technology uses a minimum of network resources and processing power on our personal network devices. This cloud technology becomes the best possible solution when companies transfer media content and set up large databases. The latest technology, based on highly efficient use of the radio spectrum, enables virtual reality on mobile devices and smart objects such as glasses, sharing of high-quality video content, and networking with all other devices in the Internet of Things (IoT).

- **Artificial Intelligence (AI):** AI is a sophisticated computer system that is able to operate under complex circumstances and conditions by learning from its own experience in gathering information. Although some types of AI are already being used in virtual social networks, search engines, and autonomous transportation, what we see today is just the beginning of the evolution of artificial intelligence. An artificial intelligence chatbot called ChatGPT, developed by OpenAI and launched in November 2022, is an excellent example of how AI can help people find smart solutions. In the next few decades, nearly one in two companies will decide to redesign their processes to include and ensure human support for scalability and precision. Today's society needs communication frameworks with user-friendly interfaces that enable efficient information exchange between humans and AI devices.

- **Improved Storytelling:** Storytelling is becoming one of the key differentiators between brands that are perceived and those that aren't. The market will become increasingly noisy, and brands that create human connections through the art of storytelling will rise. In today's world, anyone with access to the Internet can tell their story, and many will take advantage of this opportunity.

- **Better Content and More Content Creators:** Nowadays, there are more and more solutions based on user-generated content. Youtube and TikTok are good examples. Using the latest technology, nowadays almost anyone can create high-quality animated films, videos or images that can be used for education and entertainment. All these people are trying to find new creative ways to make money and/or express their attitudes and feelings.

- **Internet of Things:** The Internet of Things (IoT) is a network of various physical devices with built-in electronics, software, sensors, and actuators that enable these devices to connect, collect, and exchange data. To make the most of the capabilities of AI devices (e.g., robots) in an IoT environment, people need to move their personal data to the cloud and work to share information efficiently with various IoT devices.

- **Rise of Video Communications:** Everything seems to be shifting to video. Real-time web-based communications (WebRTC) is an innovative concept that enables video conferencing and collaboration between people via user-friendly devices with video cameras and Internet browsers. With these relatively simple tools, users can communicate remotely and do many different things, such as chat, screen sharing, content sharing, audio and video communication, etc.
- **Virtual Reality, Augmented Reality and Metaverse:** Virtual reality (VR) is an artificial, computer-generated simulation or replica of a real environment or situation. Augmented reality (AR) is a technology in which computer-generated augmentations are superimposed on an existing reality to make it more meaningful through interaction with it. Such software can be used, for example, to provide virtual walks to potential buyers of yachts that have not yet been built, to discover landscapes on distant planets, to provide additional information about the facilities and objects encountered while walking through a city or manufacturing plant, etc. According to Mystakidis (2022), the metaverse is an interconnected network of social, networked immersive environments that enable real-time and dynamic interactions with digital artefacts. It is a new concept of the Internet where users can interact in 3D spaces.
- **Blockchain and Non-Fungible Tokens:** Blockchain is a shared, immutable database that facilitates the process of recording transactions and tracking assets (Gupta, 2018). Because it offers a new level of efficiency and trust, blockchain technology will be used in a variety of different business and social activities (e.g., contracts, payments, document management systems, logistics, etc.) in the coming decades. An NFT (non-fungible token) is a digital asset or virtual collectible that represents real and virtual objects such as art, music, gaming items, and videos. By making it easier to trade and define ownership of various things such as artwork, clothing, shoes, collectibles, and even real estate, the blockchain and NFTs will help the digital economy take off.
- **Promotion of the Bring Your Own Device strategy:** Bring Your Own Device (BYOD) is a trend where employees are allowed to use their own personal devices for work. One of the first companies to

adopt this strategy was Cisco. Networking different devices allows companies to save on their budgets by requiring fewer offices and devices, while allowing employees to work from their own offices.

- **Increasing transparency in the use of personal data:** With the General Data Protection Regulation and other laws, today's society is trying to regulate how companies do business and how they use customer data in marketing and advertising. As a result, modern businesses are being forced to redesign their own communications strategies. Today, personal data must be processed in a fair and secure manner and only for specific purposes on a lawful basis. This also means that everyone has the right to know, access and rectify their personal data processed by third parties or delete personal data that has been processed without right (Rihter, 2011).

- **Digital innovations that improve trust and integrity:** Public and private organisations are developing new personalised strategies for communicating and interacting with their own users and customers. Users expect timely and accurate information, as well as tools (such as social media) that enable a personalised approach. Unfortunately, today there are a large number of individuals and organisations that do not behave responsibly and honestly. In order to reduce the negative consequences of such socially undesirable activities, new communication tools need to be developed that are able to detect such characteristics and help these individuals and/or organisations improve their behaviour.

- **Enhancement of communication abilities:** Today, more and more organisations are trying to educate their own members about the importance of dialogue and discussion in creating learning organisations (Senge, 2006). Debate is a combative and victorious form of communication in which opposing views are presented and defended. Although debates are common and sometimes necessary, the problem is that they focus on winning rather than learning. To solve this problem, individuals and organisations tend to engage in various discussions. Discussion is a sophisticated form of debate in which any disagreement is supported by rational arguments to reach a "neutral" conclusion (UNC, 2023). Although extremely useful for representing different points of view and challenging those of others (Hastwell, 2023), the problem with discussion is that it tends to avoid areas of strong conflict and difference (UNC, 2023). To solve this problem, social actors promote dialogue. In dialogue, individuals freely and creatively explore issues, listen to each other, and put aside their own views in search of truth (Arnold, 2013). Since the main purpose of dialogue is to increase overall knowledge about a given topic, it helps to eliminate misunderstanding and conflict. An organisational climate that supports dialogue includes: Asking questions, encouraging others to express their ideas, asking for feedback, and looking for common ground. A balance between dialogue and discussion helps teams reach joint decisions and take the right actions (Senge, 2006). Promoting dialogue and discussion in a relatively small group of people is not a particularly difficult task. However, as a group grows larger, it becomes increasingly difficult to communicate. The best way to overcome this problem seems to be the development of IT platforms that support group communication. One of the most recent innovations in communication is the introduction of the hashtag, a word or phrase preceded by a hash sign (#), which is used on social networks, websites, and applications to identify messages about a particular topic. Using unique tags to describe topics and objects on the web creates a space for dialogue and discussion among all individuals and organisations using such a methodology. The following chapters describe specific examples of how tags can be used in various forms of cooperation and collaboration.

- **The rise of open networks:** Open networks are networks that can be accessed by anyone who is willing to comply with the prescribed conditions of cooperation. According to Raymond (2001), the architecture of open networks can be classified in two basic models: Cathedral and Bazaar. Within the cathedral network, specific benefits of every level (e.g., Profits) are mainly distributed between members of that level, while everyone else shares the same core benefit (e.g., web portal, web-shop). An example is eBay. Within Bazaar networks, there are no special benefits between different organisational levels and users. This type of open network can be associated with Linux operating systems, Wikipedia, TPB network, etc. In the last two decades, the open networking model has become a dominant organisational strategy. This assertion is confirmed by the market value of the most popular open networks such as Google, Uber, Amazon, and Facebook compared to companies that prefer relatively closed organisational models. The main reason for such a shift is the fact that shared knowledge and other benefits of collaboration spread much faster in open organisational models than in closed organisational models. Therefore, in the near future, members of today's society will certainly see the further development of open (electronic) cooperation networks that will reduce costs and improve quality in various areas of life.

- **Improvement of organisational intelligence:** Organisational intelligence (OI) implies effective information flow that improves the quality of all activities, relationships, and processes within an organisation. Organisational intelligence refers to the ability of an organisation to mobilise all of its available intelligence and focus that intelligence on accomplishing its mission (Erçetin et al., 2016). It is a systematic process of planning, collecting, analysing, and sharing information that helps organisations reduce uncertainty and optimise response time (Anunciação & Nunes, 2016). Organisational intelligence is closely related to a learning process that involves the development of adaptive behaviour using organisational memory (Erçetin et al., 2016). The development of information and communication technologies has created many different ways to improve organisational intelligence. Nowadays, enterprise resource planning (ERP) and customer relationship management (CRM) systems are becoming the norm in modern organisations. Until recently, most organisations focused only on optimising their own internal operations, but today they are looking for ways to optimise and improve their collaboration with all stakeholders, including customers, business partners, and public agencies. To consolidate or expand their position in the marketplace, modern companies must develop new models of communication and collaboration (e.g., partner sales) in an environment that enables personal development and organisational learning.
- **Data growth:** The total amount of information in a networked society is constantly increasing, and this growth is further accelerated by the development of new IoT solutions. Without tools that enable automated filtering, analysis and processing of important data for today's humans, it will become increasingly difficult to manage the growing complexity in the information domain. According to Statista's (2022) report, the total volume of data/information created, captured, copied, and consumed worldwide was 64.2 zettabytes in 2020. The forecast states that the amount of data/information will triple between 2020 and 2025, and storage capacity will increase by 19.2%. To reduce humanity's ecological footprint and improve

information management (e.g., web search, information sharing, and information analysis), all important information such as digital identities of subjects and objects in digital interaction must be properly structured.

• **Mnemonics:** From the time when it was originally developed as a learning technique to support the retention or retrieval of information (remembering) to the present days when it is transformed into various methods of information transfer and sharing, mnemonics does not lose its popularity. Although the main reasons for using mnemonics have changed, the basic principle is the same: how to reduce the total amount of information to a minimum that still allows efficient encoding by other communicators? As later analysis shows, the ability to compress information is an extremely important element in improving communication efficiency.

Despite the latest technologies, the communication skills of today's people and managers are in many cases underdeveloped. Apart from the popularity of social networks, which are mainly focused on fun, messaging, and dating, electronic communication and electronic collaboration in the business and political spheres lag significantly behind. One of the main causes of this situation is the lack of communication platforms designed to improve people's communication and collaboration skills. If today's society wants to become environmentally sustainable, it should develop communication frameworks that improve efficiency, adaptability, resource sharing, and evaluation of various social interactions. One of the main problems of this research is that people still have not developed a communication framework that could help them share their information and preferences automatically, or at least with minimal expenditure of time and energy. Over the past decade, there has been a steady increase in the number of authors suggesting that people should develop holistic communication tools and techniques. Until recently, however, most authors who have written about the need for integral communication (IC) were focused on marketing and corporate communications. Although the models of IC are rooted at the advertising agency level, according to Holm (2006), these techniques have not arrived at the management level, whose communication skills have remained inadequate, mainly due to outdated traditions. Resistance to change in organisational policies, lack of motivation, additional workload, training costs, lack of personnel, and fear of losing control are among the most important reasons why organisations have problems adopting new information and communication technologies (Delaney & D'Agostino, 2015). However, it is undeniable that even in those rare cases where personal communication and analytical skills are excellent, it is very difficult for modern managers without advanced communication platforms and software to be adequately informed about all the important changes taking place inside and outside their organisations. Of course, not all companies are equally advanced. The most successful multinational companies are well aware that effective information management, including knowledge sharing, is an extremely important and strategic activity (Kalla, 2005). However, most managers of small and medium-sized enterprises (SMEs), which account for 99% of all companies in the EU, rarely collect enough data to personalise their communication strategies and market offerings.

Purpose of Integral Information Exchange

Whether described as a synergy of persuasive voices (Thorson & Moore, 1996) or a catalyst for the growth of e-business management (Oladele Jo, 2011), integral communication is becoming an extremely important competitive advantage in the network society. Integral communication represents an automated exchange of all information that interacting subjects consider important for a better understanding of their personal characteristics and preferences. The goal of integral communication is to improve the organisational intelligence of individuals and organisations. Achieving such a complex goal is not possible without a whole set of additional goals such as improving social perceptiveness, collaboration, personal development, sustainability, trust, and organisational learning. Currently, there are more and more authors such as Leonard (2004), Brown and Riedy (2006), and Östmar (2014) who recognize that integral communication should be applied in a broader socioeconomic context. The question, then, is not whether social actors should communicate integrally, but how they should do so. As with all other social activities and processes, in practice there are multiple optima and more possible solutions. Since people do not operate with only one worldview, Brown (2005) proposes a methodology that allows for the simultaneous integration of multiple worldviews. Along the same lines, Collins (2005) defines integral communication as a skill, an art, a state of mind, and a state of being that fosters dialectical tensions in our exchanges by allowing different concepts, inclinations, emotional states, and spiritual insights to coexist so that new and unexpected synergies emerge in a neutral field. Despite the fact that electronic collaboration technologies sometimes present obstacles to communication, it is possible to overcome the obstacles and achieve success and the desired quality of the team outcome if virtual teams adapt their communication to be more focused, clear, precise, neutral, concrete, concise, persuasive, considerate, and complete (DeLuca et al., 2006). Through the use of semantic networks, geographic information systems (GIS), and interactive 3D content embedded in web pages (Web3D), e-collaboration technology can significantly improve participant awareness in globally distributed organisations (Sultanow et al., 2011). According to Silic et al. (2014), the unified communication and collaboration platform is the perfect choice for organisations that want to increase employee productivity and reduce costs. Although there are a number of new communication platforms (e.g., Skype, Twitter, and Facebook) that claim to support communication and collaboration needs in distributed agile or adaptive development environments (DADE), it is quite clear that not all of these platforms are equally effective in supporting communication and collaboration. For example, instant messaging (IM) is undoubtedly an extremely useful tool for maintaining team cohesion and supporting team communication, but Zhang and Liu (2010) noted that the informality of this medium in interacting with different cultures and the loss of productivity due to the disruption of IM can still cause problems. Moreover, IM is only one possible feature of the tool designed to optimise collaboration in the e-environment. For this reason, today's information technology experts argue about the need for communication technology assessment tools capable of evaluating the usefulness of a particular social technology in the context of communication and collaboration (Gill, 2015).

Thanks to the development of the Internet and other communication technologies, today's social actors have the ability to communicate and exchange virtually unlimited amounts of information at extremely high speed and very low cost. According to recent statistics, nearly 4.33 billion people were active Internet users in 2021, while 5.43 billion were mobile phone users (GSMA, 2022). The mere fact that a technology exists does not mean that people will make the best use of it. Although the socioeconomic system depends on the natural environment, current patterns of communication, organisation and behaviour still undermine the capacity of future ecosystems. In everyday life, most products that people own and use are not used optimally (e.g., the average family car spends 80% of its life in a parking lot). The same is true for communication devices (e.g., most hardware in PCs has become obsolete since cloud technology came along). Since any product that is not used optimally represents a potential economic loss and an environmental problem, today's society needs to move to a circular economy model, which is a production and consumption system that generates as little loss as possible (Stanik, 2014). To follow the path of long-term sustainability, social actors must change not only the way they use technology and organise production and distribution, but also their entire mindset, including their cultural norms and personal value systems. In other words, to become more environmentally sustainable than they are today, people must abandon the culture of consumption and the mechanistic paradigm and replace it with the culture of sharing and the holistic paradigm. Reducing the amount of time and energy that society invests in its communication and collaboration processes becomes a cornerstone for all other types of sustainable behaviour. The goal of integral communication is to promote this organisational and cultural transformation of society by using a specific set of dynamic, efficient, adaptable, and user-friendly IT interfaces that enable integral mapping. As explained in the following chapters, integral mapping is the process of assigning uniform tags to people, organisations, events, places, products, and services. In addition to functions that enhance information sharing, collaboration, and learning, integral communication promotes the exchange of feedback that directly encourages people to rethink their own character, value system, personal goals, and/or patterns of behaviour.

To address complex challenges such as pollution, corruption, and economic segregation, social actors must constantly improve the way they communicate and share information. Any reduction in the cost and effort of sharing information frees up resources to address new challenges and problems. Therefore, improving communication is a fundamental factor for sustainable socioeconomic development. In this research, communication intelligence means timely, meaningful, practical, efficient and reliable information exchange. It is important to emphasise that communication intelligence is a broader and more fundamental concept than organisational intelligence. This means that it is possible to communicate intelligently even within systems that have low levels of organisational intelligence. Intelligent organisations are those that enable optimal use of resources by promoting the efficiency of information sharing to create new value for their owners, members, users, and stakeholders. In addition, organisational intelligence implies open knowledge and information sharing that promotes synergy among members. Intelligent organisations are those in which all members can achieve their goals with the least number of rules and constraints. In addition, intelligent organisations are those that ensure high levels of satisfaction, support, and engagement among their members and users. Improving organisational intelligence requires the acquisition of competencies in many different areas, such as organisational structure, organisational culture, interpersonal relationships, knowledge management, and strategic planning, which simply cannot be achieved without effective and meaningful communication. For this reason, one of the biggest challenges for today's leaders and managers is to improve the qualitative level of communication (with their employees, partners, customers, users and all other stakeholders). Despite the widespread availability of personal computers, cell phones, and the Internet through which they can easily share information and collaborate, average members of modern society still face significant communication problems. It is undeniable that there are many different reasons why this is the case, ranging from individuals not having the appropriate skills to the cultural, social and political norms that do not promote open communication, sharing and collaboration. The current or traditional communication methodology is a very limiting factor for personal and organisational development. When relying on traditional communication methods, liars and deceivers easily find new victims, communication noise is created through which recognition does not reach those who deserve it, team members do not understand the goals that leaders set for them, and due to lack of time and cognitive skills in processing a large amount of information, many important facts remain under the radar of social actors, who thus miss opportunities to improve collaboration. On the other hand, digital communication frameworks that improve social perception and the quality of communication enable new insights that promote collaboration and cooperation. The exponential growth of data, as well as the proliferation of different (often unreliable) sources of information, can drive up the cost of data processing and analysis so much that it does more harm than good. When making decisions based on a large amount of disparate information that they cannot personally review and evaluate, social actors try to optimise the decision-making process by relying on their own experience, intuition, and the various authorities they trust. The complexity is further increased when the authorities that people trust turn out to be unreliable. For example, Myllylahti and Treadwell (2021) found that trust in the news in New Zealand is high by international standards, but a large proportion (47%) of citizens do not trust the news. According to Hanitzsch et al. (2017), the decline in trust in the media is related to low trust in other social institutions. To deal with false news and disinformation, today's society must find a way to circumvent the subjectivity and moral instability of information authorities (e.g., politicians, journalists, etc.) through technological solutions that can provide a higher level of trust and objectivity. If members of the modern information society continue to make their consumption, political, organisational, and economic decisions based on unreliable information and unreliable sources, this will lead to a further decline in cooperation and trust. For the disinformation society to become an information society, it is necessary to design and implement a holistic communication methodology that allows for automated identification of characteristics and preferences of various social actors. To further strengthen trust, the integral communication framework should be supported by blockchain technology, which uses tokens to enable digital signatures.

Integral communication is based on the following principles:

- **Holistic approach and systems thinking:** The holistic approach to communication implies that social actors should be represented or defined by the widest possible range of information describing their personal characteristics and preferences. The implementation of holistic communication helps social individuals improve their communication skills in complex social systems. This means that any information someone provides to others can be used to improve many different social processes in both private and public settings. Whether it's finding a tennis partner, recruiting, sales, procurement, resource sharing, or politics, integral communication enables quality improvements and cost reductions. The efficiency and adaptability of any socioeconomic system is highly dependent on its inherent capabilities and knowledge in reducing operational costs. Considering that the external experience space does not exist independently of the actors and their interaction processes, our society needs to replace the old linear economic paradigm focused on competition and making profits with a holistic and qualitative economic paradigm focused on: dynamic balance between cooperative and collaborative attitudes; simplification of complex procedures; achieving the desired level of quality; implementation of holistic thinking that entails personal responsibility and preservation of diversity that ensures adaptability (Rafajac & Saftić, 2015, p. 179).

- **Cooperation and collaboration:** One of the greatest misconceptions of modern society, arising from the application of dialectical logic, is that competition is always good and desirable. However, our everyday reality is quite different. Competition is desirable only in certain situations and under controlled conditions, while in most other situations it usually creates more problems than benefits. Despite the fact that competition is particularly important in the development and improvement of living systems, cooperation is a fundamental element of our reality. By ignoring the benefits of cooperation, even when it could lead to significant savings, many people today achieve a much lower quality of life than they could. For example, a person attempting to purchase something independently in the market will usually pay a significantly higher price than people willing to shop in a group. Although not always free, possible, or easy, cooperation and collaboration are the driving forces behind most human actions. Therefore, proponents of the integral communication model create and use various IT platforms that encourage and facilitate cooperation (e.g., It means to work with other people by achieving your own goals as part of a common goal.) and collaboration (e.g., It means to work with someone to achieve a single common goal.) among different types of users.
- **Personal mastery:** Personal mastery is a prerequisite for organisational development, and both happen best in an environment that leaves an open space for experimentation and error. Personal mastery is a process of inner work on ourselves that involves not only acquiring new skills and knowledge, but also recognising the impact that our personal patterns of thinking, feeling, and behaving have on others we encounter (Senge, 2006). This means that the willingness to receive feedback is the fundamental element of personal development. The exchange of feedback should be done in a way that minimises the possibility of personal conflict and increases the capacity for learning and personal development. In any society, the process of personal mastery, including self-actualization and even transcendence of personal needs, is achieved through communication and collaboration. Communication tools and techniques that improve people's ability to give, receive, and analyse feedback make it easy to identify personal attributes that need improvement and provide direct links to materials and people that can help with these goals. While direct interaction will always remain important, the processes

of personal development and counselling, when supported by digital tools, create many new opportunities that cannot be achieved in other ways. Relatively low operating costs, efficient information management, and a high degree of privacy are among the main advantages of online counselling. Earlier assertions are supported by findings of many different authors. Amichai Hamburger et al. (2014) suggest that online therapy should utilise online resources, including online information retrieval techniques, while Mallen et al. (2005) suggest that clients readily accept online counselling services. Depression is a common mental disorder and a leading cause of disability worldwide (WHO, 2018a, b). The World Health Organisation estimates that depression affects 300 million people worldwide (WHO, 2018a). For all these reasons, Norcross et al. (2002) predict that online counselling will increase in the future. Apart from treating milder forms of mental disorders, online counselling can be used in many other areas, such as education, career counselling, finance, health, marriage and family, etc. As several practical examples show (e.g., www.chess.com.), the easiest way to motivate personal coping is through a combination of games, assessments, educational materials, and personal progress reports. Another good example of how feedback can have a positive impact on promoting ethics and trust while reducing corruption and selfishness is a seller rating model on existing web shop platforms (e.g., eBay, Amazon, etc.).

- **Total Quality Management:** Total Quality Management (TQM) is the long-term focus on continuous quality improvement to meet and exceed customer expectations. This concept is important for private and public organisations alike, as it reduces costs, increases productivity and customer satisfaction, ensuring loyalty and long-term sustainability. In today's society, quality management is a prerequisite for long-term sustainability. Zero defects in production are achieved through preventive measures, and the most efficient way to achieve this is based on an effective flow of information. Although total quality management has already proven its effectiveness in practice, many private and public organisations use this concept only as a matter of form and/or to meet the standards required by law, while the quality of their products and/or services falls far short of their users' expectations. If they really care about customer satisfaction, organisations should adopt some kind of communication methodology that allows personalised communication and continuous evaluation of products and services. The last chapter expands the debate on quality, which is no longer a luxury, but a strategic goal for society that wants to ensure long-term sustainability.

• **Reducing collaboration costs:** Nowadays, more and more people are realising that being open about one's qualities, characteristics, and preferences improves their ability to communicate and lowers the cost of cooperation. One of the main reasons that people today do not collaborate more and better than they currently do is that there are no communication platforms designed for this purpose. Similarly, large organisations cannot create opportunities to improve mutual relationships without dynamic mapping of employees and users. Apart from capturing the characteristics and preferences of users and automatically identifying compatible and complementary positions, improvements and savings can be achieved through an open exchange of information, the introduction of electronic contracts, the implementation of a group decision-making system and an electronic evaluation system that facilitates quality management and development.

• **Overcoming communication barriers:** Language barriers are a major obstacle to the development of communication and collaboration between people. Although some communication platforms such as Facebook and Google do their best to solve this problem, these solutions are not always practical and convenient, which means that it is necessary to keep developing new and better ways of communication between users who do not use the same language. Another obstacle in communication is that training is an expensive and time-consuming process. Before the invention of integral communication tools that provide an integrated representation of personal characteristics and preferences, as well as automatic identification of compatible and complementary positions, it was necessary to spend a lot of time and energy collecting and processing such information. Today, integral communication tools effectively solve this problem, especially when communicating with robots and other AI devices.

• **Organisational learning:** Although all organisations are capable of learning, true learning organisations are only those that place the process of organisational learning at the centre of all their activities. To achieve this, organisations must figure out how to foster the engagement and learning capacity of people at all levels (Senge, 2006). The fundamental difference between learning organisations and all others is the speed of organisational learning. The purpose of integral communication is to accelerate the process of organisational learning through the intelligent use of available information (about products, services, organisations, employees, and users) that helps organisations improve communication and collaboration processes. Organisational learning is the acquisition of knowledge or skills through study, experience, or the open sharing of useful information. Moreover, organisational learning is a dynamic process that in many cases is never fully completed.

Integral communication is based on the idea that social actors differ in many different horizontal and vertical aspects that change dynamically over time and/or through interaction with other actors. Because it is a new method of communication that opens up many new possibilities, integral communication is becoming increasingly popular among numerous researchers in the information sciences, social sciences, humanities, and engineering.

METHODOLOGY OF INTEGRAL COMMUNICATION

This research is based on the integral approach, which aims to integrate all practices, methods and experiences available to man. In other words, the methodology of integral communication is the result of extensive research in many different areas of formal, natural, social, and applied sciences, including systems theory, philosophy, sociology, psychology, ecology, economics, and computer science. Despite the author's modest contribution, the methodology presented is but a continuation of the basic research that has been or is still being done by many prominent systemic and holistic scientists such as von Bertalanffy (1971), Wilber (1996), Bausch (2001), Hutchins (2001), Senge (2006), and many others. The idea that everything around us, including ourselves, is highly interdependent and interconnected is one of the basic elements of holistic and integral thinking. Although the assertion of interdependence is evidenced all around us, the need for comprehensive social change and restructuring can easily be seen and understood in the realm of ecology. Most contemporary researchers agree that our society will almost certainly face a serious environmental and socioeconomic crisis if it fails to improve its outdated patterns of organisation and communication. On the other hand, if people are to behave sustainably (with minimal ecological footprint), they need a new communication framework that supports such behaviour. Furthermore, the exponential growth of information also requires effective solutions in the areas of collection, search, and information management. In other words, the increase in social complexity requires the introduction of a new communication methodology that ensures a dynamic balance between efficiency and adaptability. One of the most prominent proponents of the integral approach is Wilber (1996), who has proposed the so-called "All Quadrants, All Levels" (AQAL) model, in which he attempts to explain that everything around us can be interpreted from at least four different perspectives: the individual subjective, the individual objective, the collective subjective, and the collective objective.

As shown in Fig. 5, everyone around us, including ourselves, is evolving at different stages, at different speeds, and in several different directions. The main question is: How can this knowledge be used to improve communication and competitiveness? Given that people differ horizontally in their interests and vertically in their developmental levels, the best strategy for improving mutual communication and understanding is to develop and apply personalised communication tools that can recognise these differences and similarities and use them to qualitatively improve communication skills. The integral approach to communication can save a lot of time and optimise the use of available resources. By encoding information in a way that is understandable and easily accessible to those for whom it is intended, communication is improved and significant optimization of resources is made possible. The basic problem with the most common psychographic assessment tools, such as VALS (Values and Lifestyles) and PIAV (Personal Interests, Attitudes, and Values), is that they provide only shallow value profiles, treating value systems as horizontal personality types rather than as a line of development with many vertical levels (Leonard, 2004).

Decades of research in developmental psychology have identified at least eight lines of development that evolve relatively independently of one another (Gardner, 2006). Some of these lines include the visual, cognitive, linguistic, moral, musical, psychosexual, emotional, and interpersonal. According to Gardner (2006), these lines can range from bodily-kinesthetic intelligence to intelligence of self-understanding. Each person can be described by a developmental psychograph that identifies interests, strengths, and weaknesses. Figure 6 shows an example with five lines and three stages. The person shown in Fig. 6 has extremely high cognitive intelligence but very low emotional intelligence. Any complete

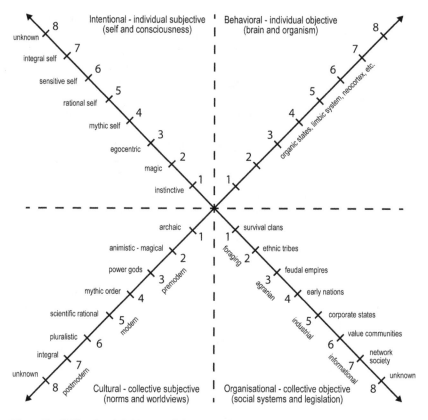

Fig. 5 Wilber's AQAL model applied to human functioning. (Source: Wilber, 1996)

psychographic assessment should include these developmental factors. Multiple lines of intelligence or development lose much of their explanatory power when removed from their organic context. However, when held within their own evolutionary framework, each lineage consists of a series of levels, structures, and directions that can be used to enhance specific communication (Leonard, 2004, p.95).

The biggest challenge of integral communication strategy is figuring out how to speak effectively to developmental audiences. To be more effective in communicating with their audience, modern communicators need an application or tool that can automatically segment their audience

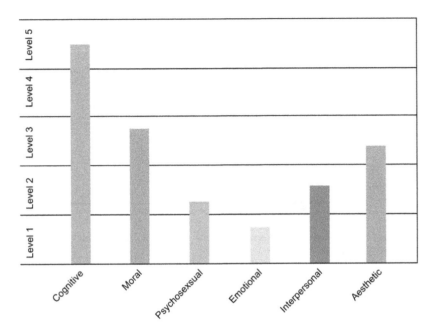

Fig. 6 An example of a developmental psychograph. (Source: Leonard, 2004)

into different horizontal and vertical spheres and suggest the best communication strategies. Since individuals differ in their character, interests, and level of development, success in direct communication is possible only up to a certain level. After that, people still have the ability to communicate, but only through abstract symbols (see Fig. 7).

Even though each individual (e.g., holon) has his or her own centre of gravity, some of his or her specific lines of development are at a similar level of development as those of others, and these lines usually provide expanded fields for direct mutual understanding (see Fig. 8).

One of the most prominent proponents of the integral approach is Wilber (1996), who proposed the so-called All Quadrants, All Levels (AQAL) model, in which he attempts to explain that everything around us can be interpreted from at least four different perspectives: (1) individual subjective, (2) individual objective, (3) collective subjective, and (4) collective objective perspective. As shown in Fig. 5, everyone around us, including ourselves, is evolving at different stages, at different speeds, and

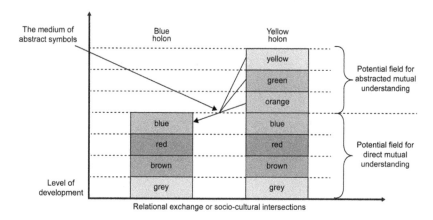

Fig. 7 The fields of direct and abstracted socio-cultural intersections. (Source: Edwards, 2003)

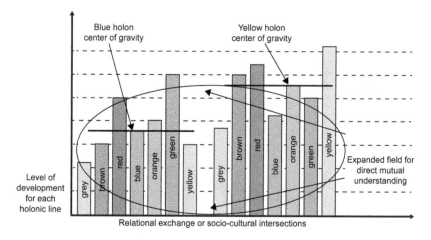

Fig. 8 Expanded field for direct communication between complex human holons. (Source: Edwards, 2003)

in several different directions. The main question is: How can this knowledge be used to improve communication and competitiveness? Given that people differ horizontally in their interests (characters) and vertically in their developmental stages, the best strategy for improving their communication and understanding is to develop and apply personalised communication tools that can recognise and leverage these differences and similarities. The holistic approach to communication can save a lot of time and optimise the use of available resources. Adapting communication frequencies means: translating into another language; putting into simpler terms; expressing in other words; changing from one form, function, or state to another; and involves articulating a message within the acceptable developmental level of the target audience. The integral communication methodology is based on the idea that the personalised and automated exchange of a large amount of different information, distributed horizontally and vertically, in terms of different evaluation methods, allows a significant improvement in communication.

SOLUTIONS AND RECOMMENDATIONS

Social actors face numerous problems in communication and data processing. For this reason, today more than ever, it seems necessary to develop methods and technological solutions that allow effective information exchange and evaluation. Most information can be evaluated in two basic ways: by objective facts (e.g., empirical tests, etc.) or by subjective opinions (e.g., personal experiences). Since some types of information (e.g., character traits, etc.) can only be fully assessed through interpersonal interaction, both methods play an important role in human organisations. To manage the information overload more efficiently, individuals and organisations today need a new communication framework that helps them filter and share information they find useful in a simple but sophisticated way. As the sharing and sifting of digital content continues to increase, social actors need a communication solution that facilitates these processes and avoids duplicate data entry. Without a communications solution that enables consistent information exchange between humans and artificial intelligence (AI) devices, government agencies and private companies will be unnecessarily forced to invest significant resources in personalising their products and services. Although the capabilities of modern society in analysing unstructured data are increasing, processing such data is expensive and requires very powerful resources. Only when data is properly structured can people and organisations harness the power of accessible, searchable, available, and relevant information. Effective communication requires a high degree of flexibility and the ability to take different perspectives. While identifying commonalities among group members facilitates building a group identity and achieving common goals, ignoring differences among group members leads to problems with motivation and work organisation. This means that information about similarities and differences between people are both fundamental elements of successful communication. To successfully meet the challenges of sustainable development, our society needs communication solutions that support collaboration and resource sharing among people and organisations that do not necessarily know each other personally. Technical solutions that enhance trust and reveal opportunities for collaboration among social actors who do not know each other personally are thus the key catalysts of sustainability. Due to their cognitive and resource constraints in information processing, social actors need to adopt the integral communication methodology that enables efficient identification of the characteristics and preferences of all other actors with whom they are trying to communicate. Preliminary research findings suggest that dynamic integral mapping of people, organisations, products, services, events, and places can significantly improve social perceptiveness and collaboration. Integral communication implies an (automatic) exchange of all information that interacting subjects consider important for a better understanding of their personal characteristics and preferences. The integral communication framework is intended to enhance the human potential for perceptivity, learning, and collaboration in the IoT environment. The research conducted suggests that this type of communication framework will be most useful in recognition of personal characteristics and interests, hiring, shopping, selling, sharing resources, team building, collaboration, motivation, education, recreation, negotiation, personal relationships, professional orientation, psychological help, etc. Integral communication represents a specific methodology that favours synergy between the different types of communicators. By fostering purposeful dialogue and automatically sharing relevant information, integral communication improves mutual understanding, collaboration, cooperation and competitiveness. The main problem in collaboration is to find compatible partners, friends, and people (e.g., actors with similar interests) with whom it is possible to build long-term relationships in different areas of life, such as family relationships, education, and leisure. The same applies to all economic activities. The authors found a solution to this problem in the development of an integral communication framework that has three main goals: self-improvement, relationship improvement, and qualitative improvement of collaboration. Despite the fact that it already has the technology and resources needed to improve the quality of communication and collaboration, today's society has not yet fully internalised the idea of integral development. Integral development means progress in all quadrants and at all levels. Integral communication tools can easily find different points of compatibility and friction in different types of interpersonal relationships, completely transforming the experience of communication, learning and collaboration. The holistic paradigm implies that effective human resource management should not only provide for improvements in the workplace, but also for the overall well-being of workers. To improve the employability of its members, a modern society needs new skills anticipation and matching systems that show job seekers – both younger and older – the types of skills and related qualifications for which there is current and expected future demand in the labour market (Cedefop, 2015). To more easily find personal interests, acquire better products and services, work on personal development, and reduce their environmental footprint, modern people need communication tools that facilitate the exchange of personal information and feedback.

FUTURE RESEARCH DIRECTIONS

There is no doubt that people must continue to try to improve their communication skills. Improving electronic collaboration and trust between social actors who do not know each other are important prerequisites for sustainable social development. Moreover, in the near future, social actors will need to find the most appropriate way to communicate with various AI machines and IoT devices. For all these reasons, nowadays there are more and more researchers and scholars trying to find answers to the following questions:

- How to communicate with AI machines and IoT devices?
- How to improve communication between social actors who do not speak the same language?
- How to improve trust between people who do not know each other?
- How to develop communication tools that promote personal mastery?
- How to improve organisational learning capabilities?
- How to improve electronic collaboration?
- How to improve personal presentation?
- How to reduce the cost of communication and collaboration?

- How to improve trust between social actors who do not know each other?
- How to manage quality efficiently?
- What do users think about integral communication?
- How to motivate social actors to participate in integral communication?
- How to ensure privacy and security in integral communication?

In addition to this book, which attempts to provide answers to the above questions, the authors are currently developing an Internet platform and mobile application that will enable the practical application of integral communication between modern individuals and organisations.

CONCLUSION

Integral communication implies an automated exchange of information that improves perceptiveness and collaboration. Since efficient exchange of feedback is a fundamental part of learning and quality management, individuals and organisations today need a communication framework that enhances this process. With the help of IT systems that enable the continuous exchange, evaluation, and analysis of information about different social actors in real time, decision makers can much better perceive changes in their environment. In order to cope with modern challenges (such as environmental protection, lifelong learning, involuntary unemployment, stress and other psychological problems, etc.), members of the network society need holistic communication solutions that will improve their ability to share important information, learn and collaborate. By using algorithms and interfaces that enable dynamic identification, assessment, and development of user characteristics and preferences, integral communication qualitatively improves information sharing and facilitates the identification of opportunities for organisational learning. Today's society needs new communication and cooperation strategies that meet modern challenges. If it is to fit optimally into its environment, modern society needs a communication framework that promotes efficient resource sharing, collaboration and quality management. An intelligent society is the one that succeeds in reducing costs and improving the quality of life for all its members. To successfully meet the challenges of sustainable development, today's society needs communication methods and practical solutions that support collaboration and resource sharing among social actors who do not necessarily know each other personally.

Key Terms and Definitions

Cognitive communication trap: A condition in which social actors do not process information that could improve their efficiency and welfare. Such traps can arise for many different reasons.

Communication intelligence: A process of timely, meaningful, practical, efficient and reliable sharing of information.

Digital humanism: The belief that IT technologies can help social actors improve their well-being.

Feedback: A piece of information about a characteristic or performance that helps to improve the understanding and quality of the person who receives it. It is extremely valuable information that promotes personal development and organisational learning.

Integral communication: A process of automated exchange of all properties and preferences that improves perceptivity and collaboration. It implies the exchange of all information that the interacting subjects consider important for a better understanding of their personal characteristics, attitudes, and preferences. The fourth chapter explains why integral communication improves personal development and organisational learning.

Integral communication methodology: A methodology that promotes synergy between different types of communicators.

Integral perceptual capacity: The ability to understand the widest possible range of properties, characteristics, and relationships that arise between different entities in real and virtual social interactions.

Integral mapping: The process of assigning consistent identifiers to people, organisations, events, places, products, and services.

Organisational intelligence: A capability for effective information sharing that improves the quality of all activities, relationships, and processes within an organisation. It is the ability of an organisation to recognise and use all available attributes and preferences of its members to accomplish its mission.

Social perceptiveness: The ability to correctly interpret the physical, emotional, cognitive, mental, verbal, and nonverbal characteristics of other social actors.

REFERENCES

Ahn, S. J., Bailenson, J. N., & Park, D. (2014). Short- and long-term effects of embodied experiences in immersive virtual environments on environmental locus of control and behavior. *Computers in Human Behavior, 39*, 235–245. https://doi.org/10.1016/j.chb.2014.07.025

Alipour, F. H. (2011). The relationship between organizational climate and communication skills of managers of the Iranian Physical Education Organization. *Procedia – Social and Behavioral Sciences, 30*, 421–428. https://doi.org/10.1016/j.sbspro.2011.10.083

Amichai Hamburger, Y., Brunstein Klomek, A., Friedman, D., Zuckerman, O., & Shani Sherman, T. (2014). The future of online therapy. *Computers in Human Behavior, 41*, 288–294. https://doi.org/10.1016/j.chb.2014.09.016

Arnold, K. (2013). *What's the Difference Between Dialogue and Discussion?* Extraordinary team. Retrieved January 20, 2020, https://extraordinaryteam.com/dialogue_discussion/

Anunciação, P. F., & Nunes, S. (2016). Organizational urbanism. In *Handbook of research on information architecture and management in modern organizations* (pp. 458–486). https://doi.org/10.4018/978-1-4666-8637-3.ch021

Bausch, K. C. (2001). *The emerging consensus in social systems theory.* Kluwer Academic/Plenum Publishers.

Berberoglu, A. (2018). Impact of organizational climate on organizational commitment and perceived organizational performance: Empirical evidence from public hospitals. *BMC Health Services Research, 18*, 399. https://doi.org/10.1186/s12913-018-3149-z

Blöbaum, B. (2016). *Trust and communication in a digitized world: Models and concepts of trust research.* Springer International Publishing Switzerland.

Brown, B. C. (2005). Integral communication for sustainability. *Kosmos – An Integral Approach to Global Awakening, 4*(2), 17–23. Retrieved May 10, 2021, from http://nextstepintegral.org/wp-content/uploads/2011/04/Communicating-Sustainability-Barrett-Brown.pdf

Brown, C. B., & Riedy, C. (2006). Use of the integral framework to design developmentally-appropriate sustainability communications. In W. Leal Filho (Ed.), *Innovation, education and communication for sustainable development* (pp. 661–668). Peter Lang Scientific Publishers.

Castells, M. (2012). *The rise of the network society: Second edition, with a new preface.* Wiley-Blackwell.

Cedefop. (2015). *Skills, qualifications and jobs in the EU: The making of a perfect match? Evidence from Cedefop's European skills and jobs survey* (Cedefop reference series; No 103). Publications Office. https://doi.org/10.2801/606129

Cheng, K., Schreieck, M., Wiesche, M., & Krcmar, H. (2020). Emergence of a post-app era – An exploratory case study of the WeChat mini-program ecosystem. *WI2020 Zentrale Tracks*, 1444–1458. https://doi.org/10.30844/wi_2020_n1-cheng

Collins, T. L. (2005). *Integral communication. Essays by T. Collins Logan.* https://www.tcollinslogan.com/essays/all-essays/index.html

Common Sense Media. (2022). *The common sense census: Media use by tweens and teens, 2021.* Retrieved November 2, 2022, from https://www.commonsensemedia.org/sites/default/files/research/report/8-18-census-integrated-report-final-web_0.pdf

ComScore. (2017, September 12). *The global Mobile report.* Retrieved April 10, 2022, from https://www.comscore.com/Insights/Presentations-and-Whitepapers/2017/The-Global-Mobile-Report

Crabtree, S. (2013, October 8). *Worldwide, 13% of employees are engaged at work.* Gallup.com. Retrieved May 3, 2019, from https://news.gallup.com/poll/165269/worldwide-employees-engaged-work.aspx

Creemers, R. (2015, April 25). *Planning outline for the construction of a social credit system (2014–2020).* Retrieved June 11, 2022, from https://chinacopyrightandmedia.wordpress.com/2014/06/14/planning-outline-for-the-construction-of-a-social-credit-system-2014-2020/

Cukier, W., Hodson, J., & Omar, A. (2015). *Soft skills are hard: A review of literature.* Retrieved July 11, 2022, from https://www.ryerson.ca/content/dam/diversity/reports/KSG2015_SoftSkills_FullReport.pdf

Delaney, R., & D'Agostino, R. (2015). *The challenges of integrating new technology into an organization* (Thesis). Mathematics and Computer Science Capstones, 25. Retrieved July 11, 2022, from http://digitalcommons.lasalle.edu/mathcompcapstones/25

Deloitte. (2017). *Global mobile consumer trends, 2nd edition. Mobile continues its global reach into all aspects of consumers' lives.* Deloitte Touche Tohmatsu Limited. Retrieved June 11, 2021, from https://www2.deloitte.com/content/dam/Deloitte/us/Documents/technology-media-telecommunications/us-global-mobile-consumer-survey-second-edition.pdf

DeLuca, D., Gasson, S., & Kock, N. (2006). Adaptations that virtual teams make so that complex tasks can be performed using simple E-Collaboration Technologies. *International Journal of e-Collaboration, 2*(3), 65–91. https://doi.org/10.4018/jec.2006070104

Dischler, J. (2015, May 5). *Building for the next moment.* Inside AdWords. Retrieved July 5, 2022, from https://adwords.googleblog.com/2015/05/building-for-next-moment.html

Donnelly, D. (2022, September 22). *China social credit system explained – How it works?* Horizons. Retrieved August 10, 2022, from https://nhglobalpartners.com/china-social-credit-system-explained/

EC. (2019). *Evaluation of the council recommendation on the integration of the long – Term unemployed into the labor market.* European Commission. Retrieved

August 1, 2022, from https://ec.europa.eu/social/BlobServlet?docI d=21016&langId=en

Edwards, M. (2003). *Through AQAL eyes – Part 5: Matter, membership and mutuality*. Integral World. Retrieved July 1, 2022, from http://www.integralworld. net/edwards9.html

Erçetin, Ş. Ş., Potas, N., & Koç, İ. (2016). Organizational intelligence scale for business organizations in chaotic situations. In *Advances in religious and cultural studies* (pp. 133–152). https://doi.org/10.4018/978-1-5225-0148-0.ch011

Eurostat. (2021). *Marriage and divorce statistics*. Statistics Explained. Retrieved May 11, 2022, from https://ec.europa.eu/eurostat/statistics-explained/index.php?title=Marriage_and_divorce_statistics#Fewer_ marriages.2C_more_divorces

Forbes Communications Council. (2018, July 12). *Council post: Seven communications trends worth knowing about*. Forbes. Retrieved March 5, 2022, from https://www.forbes.com/sites/forbescommunication-scouncil/2018/07/12/seven-communications-trends-worth-knowing-about/#56ab73414b19

Fottrell, Q. (2018, August 4). *People spend most of their waking hours staring at screens*. MarketWatch. Retrieved May 7, 2022, from https://www.market-watch.com/story/people-are-spending-most-of-their-waking-hours-staring-at-screens-2018-08-01

Gardner, H. E. (2006). *Multiple intelligences: New horizons in theory and practice*. Basic Books.

Giese, J. L., & Cote, J. A. (2000). Defining consumer satisfaction. *Academy of Marketing Science Review, 1*, 1–27.

Gill, A. Q. (2015). Distributed agile development. *International Journal of e-Collaboration, 11*(1), 57–76. https://doi.org/10.4018/ijec.2015010104

Gioia, F., Colella, G. M., & Boursier, V. (2022). Evidence on problematic online gaming and social anxiety over the past ten years: A systematic literature review. *Current Addiction Reports, 9*(1), 32–47. https://doi.org/10.1007/ s40429-021-00406-3

GSMA. (2022). *The mobile economy 2022*. GSMA. Retrieved October 7, 2022, from https://www.gsma.com/mobileeconomy/wp-content/ uploads/2022/02/280222-The-Mobile-Economy-2022.pdf

Gupta, M. (2018). *Blockchain for dummies*. Wiley.

Gutierez, A. (2017). *Effective communication in the workplace: Learn how to communicate effectively and avoid common barriers to effective communication*. CreateSpace Independent Publishing Platform.

Guzley, R. M. (1992). Organizational climate and communication climate. *Management Communication Quarterly, 5*(4), 379–402. https://doi. org/10.1177/0893318992005004001

Hallman, C. (2022). *50 cognitive biases to be aware of so you can be the very best version of you.* TitleMax. Retrieved October 10, 2022, from https://www.titlemax. com/discovery-center/lifestyle/50-cognitive-biases-to-be-aware-of-so-you-can-be-the-very-best-version-of-you/

Hanitzsch, T., Van Dalen, A., & Steindl, N. (2017). Caught in the nexus: A comparative and longitudinal analysis of public Trust in the Press. *The International Journal of Press/Politics, 23*(1), 3–23. https://doi.org/10.1177/1940161217740695

Hastwell, C. (2023, June 13). *The difference between debate, Discussion and dialogue.* Great place to work. Retrieved August 15, 2023, from https://www.greatplacetowork.com/resources/blog/the-difference-between-debate-discussion-and-dialogue

Hollander, R. (2018, February 9). *Consumers in China are spending the most time in apps.* Business Insider. Retrieved November 5, 2022, from https://www.businessinsider.com/consumers-in-china-are-spending-the-most-time-in-apps-2018-2

Hollander, G. (2022, October 18). *What is structured data vs. unstructured data?* Intelligent Information Management Resources. Retrieved October 19, 2022, from https://resources.m-files.com/blog/what-is-structured-data-vs-unstructured-data-3

Holm, O. (2006). Integrated marketing communication: From tactics to strategy. *Corporate Communications An International Journal, 11*(1), 23–33. https://doi.org/10.1108/13563280610643525

Hutchins, E. (2001). Distributed cognition. In N. J. Smelser & P. B. Baltes (Eds.), *The international encyclopedia of the social and behavioral sciences* (pp. 2068–2072). Pergamon.

Ingham, T. (2021, April 14). *TikTok users watch the app for an average of 89 minutes per day – And there's 732M of them worldwide.* Music Business Worldwide. Retrieved August 20, 2023, from https://www.musicbusinessworldwide.com/tiktok-users-watch-the-app-for-an-average-of-89-minutes-per-day-and-theres-732m-of-them-worldwide/

iResearch. (2018, November 21). *Q3 2018 China's internet traffic measuring report.* Retrieved August 9, 2021, from http://www.iresearchchina.com/content/details8_49828.html

Isaac, M. (2023, July 4). Meta's 'twitter killer' app is coming. *The New York Times.* Retrieved August 20, 2023, from https://www.nytimes.com/2023/07/03/technology/meta-app-twitter.html

Kalla, H. K. (2005). Integrated internal communications: A multidisciplinary perspective. *Corporate Communications: An International Journal Corp Communications, 10*(4), 302–314. https://doi.org/10.1108/13563280510630106

Kenton, W. (2019, July 10). *Structural unemployment.* Investopedia. Retrieved August 22, 2021, from https://www.investopedia.com/terms/s/structural-unemployment.asp

Knox, J. (2007). Visual-verbal communication on online newspaper homepages. *Visual Communication, 6*(1), 19–53.

Konrath, S. (2013). The empathy paradox: Increasing disconnection in the age of increasing connection. In R. Luppicini (Ed.), *Handbook of research on Technoself: Identity in a technological society* (pp. 204–228). IGI Global). https://doi.org/10.4018/978-1-4666-2211-1.ch012

Kumar, S., & Shah, N. (2018). *False information on web and social media: A survey.* Social and Information Networks. Cornell University. Retrieved November 11, 2022, from https://arxiv.org/abs/1804.08559

Leonard, A. B. (2004). *Integral communication* (Thesis). University of Florida, Gainesville, F. Retrieved August 22, 2019, from https://www.scribd.com/document/150568634/Integral-Communication-by-Adam-B-Leonard

Lunenburg, F. C. (2010). Communication: The process, barriers, and improving effectiveness. *Schooling, 1*(1), 1–11. Retrieved May 20, 2022, form http://www.nationalforum.com/Electronic%20Journal%20Volumes/Lunenburg,%20Fred%20C,%20Communication%20Schooling%20V1%20N1%202010.pdf

Ma, A. (2018, October 29). *China has started ranking citizens with a creepy 'social credit' system – Here's what you can do wrong, and the embarrassing, demeaning ways they can punish you.* Businessinsider. Retrieved May 22, 2022, from https://www.businessinsider.com/china-social-credit-system-punishments-and-rewards-explained-2018-4

Mallen, M. J., Vogel, D. L., & Rochlen, A. B. (2005). The practical aspects of online counseling: Ethics, training, technology, and competency. *The Counseling Psychologist, 33*(6), 776–818. https://doi.org/10.1177/0011000005278625

McNamee, P., Mendolia, S., & Yerokhin, O. (2019). *Social media extensive use and emotional and Behavioural outcomes in adolescence: Evidence from British longitudinal data.* IZA – Institute of Labor Economics. Retrieved November 2, 2022, from https://docs.iza.org/dp12834.pdf

Merriam-Webster (2020a). *Perception.* Merriam-Webster. Retrieved January 10, 2020, from https://www.merriamwebster.com/thesaurus/perception

Michel, C., Sovinsky, M., Proto, E., & Oswald, A. J. (2019). Advertising as a major source of human dissatisfaction: Cross-national evidence on one million Europeans. In *The economics of happiness* (pp. 217–239). https://doi.org/10.1007/978-3-030-15835-4_10

Mukhopadhyay, D., Shirvanian, M., & Saxena, N. (2015). All your voices are belong to US: Stealing voices to fool humans and machines. *Computer Security – ESORICS, 2015*, 599–621. https://doi.org/10.1007/978-3-319-24177-7_30

Myllylahti, M., & Treadwell, G. (2021). In media we trust? A comparative analysis of news Trust in New Zealand and other Western media markets. *Kōtuitui: New Zealand Journal of Social Sciences, 17*(1), 90–100. https://doi.org/10.1080/1177083x.2021.1948873

Mystakidis, S. (2022). Metaverse. *Encyclopedia, 2*(1), 486–497. https://doi.org/10.3390/encyclopedia2010031

Navarretta, C. (2018). Mirroring and prediction of gestures from Interlocutor's behavior. In *Topics in intelligent engineering and informatics* (pp. 91–107). https://doi.org/10.1007/978-3-319-95996-2_5

Nielsen. (2018). *The Nielsen total audience report: Q1 2018*. Nielsen. Retrieved July 8, 2020, from https://www.nielsen.com/wp-content/uploads/sites/2/2019/04/q1-2018-total-audience-report.pdf

Norcross, J. C., Hedges, M., & Prochaska, J. O. (2002). The face of 2010: A Delphi poll on the future of psychotherapy. *Professional Psychology: Research and Practice, 3*, 316–322.

Nwabueze, U., & Mileski, J. (2018). Achieving competitive advantage through effective communication in a global environment. *Journal of International Studies, 11*(1), 50–66. https://doi.org/10.14254/2071-8330.2018/11-1/4

Oladele Jo, K. (2011). Integrated marketing communication: A catalyst for the growth of E-business management. *The Social Sciences, 6*(2), 64–73. https://doi.org/10.3923/sscience.2011.64.73

Östmar, M. (2014). *Integral communication*. Mattiasostmar. Retrieved April 10, 2019 from https://mattiasostmar.wordpress.com/integralintroduction/integral-communication/

Papa, V., & Photiadis, T. (2021). Algorithmic curation and users' civic attitudes: A study on Facebook news feed results. *Information, 12*(12), 522. https://doi.org/10.3390/info12120522

Pariser, E. (2012). *The filter bubble: What the internet is hiding from you*. Penguin.

Pitre, J. (2023). TikTok, creation, and the algorithm. *The Velvet Light Trap, 91*, 71–74. https://www.muse.jhu.edu/article/881100

Poyatos, F. (1992). *Advances in non-verbal communication: Sociocultural, clinical, esthetic and literary perspectives*. John Benjamins Publishing Company. https://doi.org/10.1075/z.60

Putter, L. (2010). *Organizational climate and performance* (Thesis). Delft University of Technology. Retrieved March 2, 2019, from http://resolver.tudelft.nl/uuid:76a393e1-2528-46a7-838a-6e770d60b655

Qi, P., Cao, J., Yang, T., Guo, J., & Li, J. (2019). Exploiting multi-domain visual information for fake news detection. In *2019 IEEE International Conference on Data Mining (ICDM)*. https://doi.org/10.1109/icdm.2019.00062

Rafajac, O., & Saftić, D. (2015). How to reduce costs? – Discussion about a need for a new economic paradigm. In S. Blažević, D. Dinković, K. Černe, & S. Stjepanović (Eds.), *Economics in crisis, the crisis of economics: Conference* proceedings of the 6th international conference the changing economic landscape: Issues, implications and policy options (pp. 179–192). Juraj Dobrila University of Pula, Faculty of Economics and Tourism.

Rahaman, M. (2017). The effects of mobile phone use on human behaviors: A study of developing country like Bangladesh. *International Journal of Information Technology and Computer Science, 9*(11), 48–56. https://doi. org/10.5815/ijitcs.2017.11.05

Rajhans, K. (2009). Effective organizational communication: A key to employee motivation and performance. *Interscience Management Review*, 145–149. https://doi.org/10.47893/imr.2009.1040

Raymond, E. S. (2001). *The cathedral & the bazaar musings on Linux and open source by an accidental revolutionary* (1st ed.). O'Reilly Media.

Rihter, A. (2011). *Protection of privacy and personal data on the Internet and online media.* Council of Europe. Retrieved June 10, 2021, from http:// assembly.coe.int/CommitteeDocs/2011/RihterviepriveeE.pdf

Roetzel, P. G. (2018). Information overload in the information age: A review of the literature from Business Administration, business psychology, and related disciplines with a bibliometric approach and framework development. *Business Research, 12*(2), 479–522. https://doi.org/10.1007/s40685-018-0069-z

Romanczyk, R. G., White, S., & Gillis, J. M. (2005). Social Skills versus skilled social behavior: A problematic distinction in autism spectrum disorders. *Journal of Early and Intensive Behavior Intervention, 2*(3), 177–193. https://doi. org/10.1037/h0100312

Semren, A. (2017). *The relationship between organizational communication and motivation of employees* (Thesis). Modul University. Retrieved May 28, 2022, from https://www.modul.ac.at/index.php?eID=dumpFile&t=f&f=9388&token=9192b4f8701bef9beac51a8c7d18fe03190f4284

Senge, P. M. (2006). *The fifth discipline: The art & practice of the learning organizations* (2nd edn, 1990 first edition). Doubleday.

Shakin, S. (2012). Essentials of effective and interpersonal communication skills to Manage and Lead dynamic businesses with maintaining public relations. *International Journal of Research in Management, 2*(3), 63–70. Retrieved July 20, 2022, from https://rspublication.com/ijrm/may%2012/8.pdf

Siladitya, R. (2023, July 10). *Threads now fastest-growing app in history—With 100 million users in just five days.* Forbes. Retrieved August 19, 2023, from https:// www.forbes.com/sites/siladityaray/2023/07/10/with-100-million-users-in-five-days-threads-is-the-fastest-growing-app-in-history/?sh=27f14d4b49ab

Silic, M., Back, A., & Sammer, T. (2014). Employee acceptance and use of unified communications and collaboration in a cross-cultural environment. *International Journal of e-Collaboration, 10*(2), 1–19. https://doi.org/ 10.4018/ijec.2014040101

Stanik, R. (2014, June 2). *The economy: Resource efficient, green and circular.* Retrieved June 20, 2022, from https://www.eea.europa.eu/signals/signals-2014/articles/the-economy-resource-efficient-green

Statista. (2022). *Volume of data/information created, captured, copied, and consumed worldwide from 2010 to 2020, with forecasts from 2021 to 2025.* Statista. Retrieved October 25, 2022, from https://www.statista.com/statistics/871513/worldwide-data-created/

Subapriya, K. (2009). The importance of non-verbal cues. *ICFAI Journal of Soft Skills, 3*(2), 37–42. Retrieved October 15, 2022, from https://www.researchgate.net/publication/349525878_The_importance_of_non-verbal_cues_The_second_Tutor

Sultanow, E., Weber, E., & Cox, S. (2011). A semantic e-collaboration approach to enable awareness in globally distributed organizations. *International Journal of e-Collaboration, 7*(1), 1–16. https://doi.org/10.4018/jec.2011010101

The World Bank. (2018, September 20). *Global waste to grow by 70 percent by 2050 unless urgent action is taken.* World Bank Report. https://www.worldbank.org/en/news/press-release/2018/09/20/global-waste-to-grow-by-70-percent-by-2050-unless-urgent-action-is-taken-world-bank-report

Thorson, E., & Moore, J. (1996). *Integrated communication: Synergy of persuasive voices.* Lawrence Erlbaum Associates.

Tucker, M. L., Meyer, G. D., & Westerman, J. W. (1996). Organizational communication: Development of internal strategic competitive advantage. *Journal of Business Communication, 33*(1), 51–69. https://doi.org/10.1177/002194369603300106

Umoh, I. G., Edwinah, A., & Harcourt, W. (2013). Organizational climate and corporate performance: The Nigerian experience. *European Journal of Business and Management, 5*(21), 119–129.

UNC. (2023). *Difference between dialogue, discussion, & debate.* The University of North Carolina. UNC Greensboro. UTLC. Retrieved August 10, 2023, from https://utlc.uncg.edu/teaching/dialoguediscussiondebate/

Valenzuela, S., Piña, M., & Ramírez, J. (2017). Behavioral effects of framing on social media users: How conflict, economic, human interest, and Morality Frames Drive News Sharing. *Journal of Communication, 67*(5), 803–826. https://doi.org/10.1111/jcom.12325

von Bertalanffy, L. (1971). *General system theory: Foundations, development, applications.* Allen Lane The Penguin Press.

WHO. (2018a, March 22). *Depression.* World Health Organization. Retrieved May 22, 2022, from https://www.who.int/en/news-room/fact-sheets/detail/depression

WHO. (2018b, April 9). *Mental disorders.* World Health Organization. Retrieved May 22, 2022, from https://www.who.int/en/news-room/fact-sheets/detail/mental-disorders

WHO. (2022). *World mental health report: Transforming mental health for all.* World Health Organization. Retrieved January 20, 2023, from https://www. who.int/publications/i/item/9789240049338

Wilber, K. (1996). *A brief history of everything.* Shambhala.

Yao, Y., Viswanath, B., Cryan, J., Zheng, H., & Zhao, B. Y. (2017). Automated crowdturfing attacks and defenses in online review systems. In *Proceedings of the 2017 ACM SIGSAC conference on computer and communications security.* https://doi.org/10.1145/3133956.3133990

Yarbrough, M. (2017). *The surprising truth about why we tend to imitate others.* Medium. Retrieved May 28, 2022, from https://medium.com/the-mission/ the-surprising-truth-about-why-we-tend-to-imitate-others-b15831070cd9

Zhang, J., & Liu, Y. (2010). Organizational climate and its effects on organizational variables: An empirical study. *International Journal of Psychological Studies, 2*(2), 189–201.

Żuromski, D., Fedyniuk, A., & Marek, E. M. (2018). Can new technologies make us more human? An inquiry on VR Technologies in social cognition. *Frontiers in Psychology, 9.* https://doi.org/10.3389/fpsyg.2018.00705

The Power of Integral Networking

Ozren Rafajac and Alen Jakupović

INTRODUCTION

This chapter explains the attitude of users towards integral networking and offers practical guidelines for its implementation. Integral networking represents a specific type of group interaction supported by an integral communication framework. Integral communication is a process of automated exchange of all characteristics, attitudes, and preferences that can improve perceptivity and collaboration among different social actors. The integral communication framework is an information system based on integral tags that supports personalised communication. The unique value of the integral communication framework presented in this book comes from its simplicity and broad applicability. To engage in integral communication, ordinary users need only write or select tags and place them in various user maps. This means that integral networking is accessible to anyone who knows how to use a smartphone. It is a well-known fact that social actors communicate through a process of encoding and decoding. In the most general sense, a good communicator is the one who finds the

O. Rafajac (✉) • A. Jakupović
Polytechnic of Rijeka, Rijeka, Croatia
e-mail: ozren.rafajac@veleri.hr; alen.jakupovic@veleri.hr

© The Author(s), under exclusive license to Springer Nature Switzerland AG 2024
O. Rafajac, A. Jakupović (eds.), *Integral Communication and Digital Identity*, https://doi.org/10.1007/978-3-031-47460-6_2

49

optimal way to reach others and register their feedback. Despite the fact that this enables mutual understanding, learning and collaboration, obtaining feedback from larger groups of people is usually a very costly and complex process. In addition, the quality of feedback can vary. Although in some cases it is important to distinguish between different types of feedback givers, since those with higher levels of knowledge and motivation are likely to provide more accurate information, in the long run all types of feedback can be considered useful. It is a fact that many people simply do not have enough time, experience or interest to give their feedback. For this reason, any type of feedback nowadays becomes a valuable resource for personal and/or organisational development (Bracken, 2019). The main goal of active listening is to understand the speaker's perspective (regardless of whether someone agrees with it). Understanding others includes recognising their characteristics, attitudes, and preferences.

> *Contrary to popular belief that listening is a passive approach, clinical and research evidence clearly shows that empathic listening is an extremely effective tool for individual personality change and group development. Listening changes people's attitudes toward themselves and others; it also brings about changes in their core values and personal philosophy. People who have been listened to in this new and special way become more emotionally mature, more open to their experiences, less defensive, more democratic and less authoritarian.* (Rogers & Farson, 1957, p. 1)

According to Mishra (2020), empathetic listening is one of the most important components of communication for influential leadership. Because open dialogue has an extremely positive impact on relationship development and organisational learning, there is growing interest among various professionals and leaders in methods and techniques that can enhance their dialogue skills and abilities (Ballantyne, 2004). To promote efficient and constructive exchange of information, ideas, and feedback, modern professionals seek communication tools that enhance their ability to manage groups and listen actively. Integral networks enhance the ability to collaborate, promote self-reflection, identification of diverse perspectives, personal development, and organisational learning, all of which are important elements of sustainable development. Unlike other social networks, integral networking focuses on personal development and organisational learning. This means that users of the system have the opportunity to communicate and collaborate effectively across a very wide range of private, public, and business activities, while also gathering signals and guidelines about what they should improve. This chapter explains the attitudes of potential users toward the various features of integral networking. After reading this chapter, the reader will be able to:

- Identify the benefits of integral networking.
- Discuss the dimensions of integral networking.
- Identify user attitudes toward integral networking.
- Follow the guidelines for creating integral networks.

BACKGROUND

Despite the enormous development in technology and science, today's man is still far behind in the areas of communication and collaboration. The increasing complexity of societal problems that can only be solved through a variety of interactions has put pressure on many sectors, organisations, and institutions, making the need for collaboration more urgent (Kwibisa & Majzoub, 2018). Although it is possible to identify multiple reasons why people collaborate so poorly, some of the most important stem from the natural selection process from Darwin's theory that was incorporated into the neoliberal economic paradigm that promoted selfishness and competition as the fastest paths to social well-being. Once such a system became universally accepted, the door was opened to numerous social problems, ethical failures, and low morals. Although in recent decades more and more people have begun to realise that only cooperation and collaboration can ensure long-term sustainability, there are still too many corrupt individuals and organisations willing to do almost anything for profit and personal gain, even if it is at the expense of nature and everyone else. Those with the lowest incomes are even forced to do this to survive. Today, the carbon footprint of ICT is about the same as the aviation industry's fuel emissions (Jones, 2018). Some researchers predict that by 2025, the IT industry could consume 20% of all electricity produced and emit up to 5.5% of global carbon emissions (Jones, 2018; Kettle, 2021). If social actors want to create a sustainable future on planet Earth, which will soon have 11 billion inhabitants, it is extremely important to review their current communication and collaboration patterns and introduce new ones that ensure higher levels of trust, integrity, quality, adaptability, and efficiency. In addition to holistic presentation, effective feedback exchange is a critical element of personal development and collaboration. Intelligent information sharing requires the identification and visualisation of various relationships that indicate the quality of connections in information networks. According to Chakkol et al. (2017), the personality traits of the most effective people in terms of collaborative work are: strategic and adaptive orientation, effective information sharing, and prioritisation of shared values. This means that integral networking should enhance these skills to promote collaboration. According to Charles Eames, the quality of connections is the key to quality itself (Böhm & Kamali, 2014). Fortunately, some innovations such as tagging and blockchain have emerged in the last two decades that will significantly improve human collaboration capabilities. Nowadays, collaborative tagging, which helps to connect social actors with similar interests, is becoming more popular (Papadopoulos et al., 2011). In collaborative tagging, many users add metadata in the form of keywords to shared content (Golder & Huberman, 2006). This practice of creating and managing labels (or "tags") that categorise content with simple keywords is known by several names, such as content tagging, collaborative tagging, social tagging, and folksonomy (Getting, 2017). Nowadays, there are more and more authors who recognise the informational value of social tagging networks (Nam & Kannan, 2014). While Samuel (2019) claims that tags have decentralised and democratised the organisation of information, Zacharias et al. (2010) claim that social tagging fosters relationships between users. The main difference between social tagging and integral tagging is that the latter enables dynamic tag evaluation. Integral networking is based on the idea that integral tagging of products, services, places, events, people, and organisations is the simplest and most effective way of networking in the IoT environment. Simplicity comes from the use of a unified set of tags, while effectiveness comes from synergistic effects in linking nodes that have compatible and complementary characteristics. Integral mapping implies the dynamic definition of specific features or tags for each node in the integral communication network. To ensure accuracy of user maps and objectivity in measuring vertical lines or development dimensions, all tags should be evaluated through testing, including the subjective opinions of users who have interacted with the subject and/or object being evaluated. Integral networks represent a set of interconnected nodes (e.g., people, organisations, products, services, places, and events) within the ICF that have complementary and compatible tags indicating some potential for collaboration. For people and organisations, the potential for collaboration exists when they are willing to share resources, buy and sell a product, work together as a team, create and read specific content, develop complementary business ideas, seek advice, interact politically, etc.

CHALLENGES IN INTEGRAL NETWORKING

Building a new kind of networks, especially those that foster new patterns of communication and collaboration, is no easy task. Products and services can become popular only if there are social actors willing to use them. Although this is one of the possible solutions to achieve environmental sustainability and inclusive development, these goals will not be achieved if users are not willing to apply integral networking in their daily activities. For this reason, the basic elements of integral networking should be free and voluntary. Human history has repeatedly confirmed that creating an environment that fosters creativity and free expression is a crucial element for rapid social development. In other words, open solutions with few rules are more successful than closed solutions with many rules. The main objective of this book is to improve the organisational intelligence of individuals and organisations of today. To achieve such a complex goal, it was necessary to identify the appropriate methodology, analyse the attitudes of potential users, design a framework, and analyse the opportunities and risks in implementing integral communication. This chapter introduces the reader to the possibilities of integral networking and analyses the attitudes of potential users toward integral networking. In addition, this chapter attempts to identify the benefits of integral networking, specific dimensions and activities in which it can be applied, and guidelines for its implementation. To achieve these goals, five key problems have been identified. The first problem stems from the fact that many social actors are not yet familiar with the concepts of integral communication and integral networking. Without a public debate that weighs all the pros and cons of integral communication, it is difficult to expect broader implementation. The second problem is that social actors will engage in integral networks only if they can identify direct benefits and other value elements. These elements may be technical, economic, service, or social in nature and vary in tangibility (Anderson & Narus, 1998). According to Kliatchko (2020), integrated marketing communication is all about people, and the same is true for integral networking. The third problem is related to the fact that integral communication frameworks should be designed in accordance with the preferences of potential users (Kelly et al., 2011; Xu & Dukes, 2019). One of the most important contributions of the market system is the idea that it is pointless to develop solutions for which there is no demand. The fourth problem arises from the fact that integral networking requires the exchange of information between different types of users (with different problems and needs). All designers know that it is very difficult to satisfy everyone. Therefore, it is necessary to constantly monitor and analyse the user experience (Knight, 2018), which is especially true for the mobile user experience in targeted interactions (Botha, 2014). The fifth problem arises from the fact that the available literature dealing with user attitudes toward integral networking is still insufficient. Fortunately, there are many related studies that analyse certain aspects of integral networking. For example, Kuyyogsuy (2019) analysed students' attitudes toward peer feedback and concluded that students have positive attitudes toward using peer feedback. Fenwick et al. (2019) analysed mental health professionals' attitudes toward feedback and found that transformational leadership and leader-member interactions were directly and positively related to professionals' attitudes toward feedback. Although their study was conducted on a relatively small group of students in 2007 and 2008, Normore and Blaylock's (2009) study shows the increase in positive feelings toward the benefits of collaborative tagging. According to Allam et al. (2012), the main benefits of social tagging are perceived enjoyment, perceived ease of use, content generation, information discoverability, and information retrieval. In their study of attitudes toward a 360-degree feedback system, Maurer et al. (2002) found that the more explicit or different the peer ratings were compared to self-ratings, the more positive respondents' attitudes toward the system were, but that other variables, such as supportive work context and personal beliefs about the ability to self-improve, were equally (or possibly more) important to respondents' attitudes toward the feedback system and subsequent participation in development activities. In addition, Umoh and Etuk (2016) found that female students' participation in social networking was higher than that of their male peers, but that male students showed more positive attitudes toward integrating social networking into teaching and learning. Despite the fact that various aspects of integral connectivity are increasingly being researched, the results are not always clear. Therefore, more research is needed. Everyone knows that without an open dialogue, it is almost impossible to identify all aspects of a given activity. For this reason, there is a need for additional public discussion of the various aspects and benefits of integral networking. To address the identified issues, it was necessary to identify the main benefits of integral networking, specify the dimensions and activities in which it can be applied, and analyse the attitudes of potential users. This chapter is based on the three main hypotheses:

Hypothesis One: The members of a network society want to present themselves integrally in an online environment so that other members can find them for collaboration.
Hypothesis Two: The members of a network society want to apply integral assessment in their interaction with other members.
Hypothesis Three: The members of a network society want to engage in integral development.

The findings presented in this chapter will help researchers, managers, and decision makers understand what different types of audiences think about integral communication. In addition, this chapter discusses the benefits of integral networking that can be used to better manage organisations, particularly in the areas of human resource management (HR), customer relationship management (CRM), and total quality management (TQM).

BENEFITS OF INTEGRAL NETWORKING

Integral networking creates synergy across a very wide range of activities. In the following section, only the most important benefits of integral networking are explained. Other benefits of integral networking, such as improved mental health, easier resource sharing, and improved public service delivery, are presented in the discussion of the dimensions of integral networking. Figure 1 shows the key benefits of integral communication.

The key benefits of integral networking are:

Better personal presentation experience In the network society, most people feel the need to present themselves to highlight their qualities and preferences. The integral communication framework allows users to present all their personal qualities in one place. The integral communication tool provides a comprehensive image or integral user map that presents key information about a person, organisation, product, service, location, or event in the simplest way possible. By using dynamic and customizable interfaces that allow users to input a variety of characteristics, knowledge,

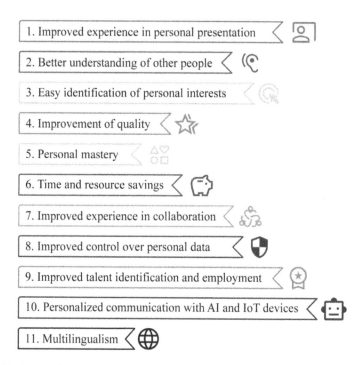

1. Improved experience in personal presentation

2. Better understanding of other people

3. Easy identification of personal interests

4. Improvement of quality

5. Personal mastery

6. Time and resource savings

7. Improved experience in collaboration

8. Improved control over personal data

9. Improved talent identification and employment

10. Personalized communication with AI and IoT devices

11. Multilingualism

Fig. 1   Integral communication benefits. (Source: Made by authors)

skills, and other useful information and tags, integral mapping helps users improve their image and visibility in different languages.

Better understanding of other people People are complicated. If someone cannot rely on the experiences of others who have dealt with a person before, he or she may not know what to expect from that person. Integral communication framework helps people understand themselves and others with whom they interact. When people rely on traditional forms of communication, it takes a lot of time and energy to understand others. Wrong conclusions and assessments can be very costly and dangerous. Therefore, feedback from those who have interacted with a person before is one of the most important pieces of the puzzle. Also, it is difficult to understand people because they are often unable to communicate clearly and express exactly what they want, but also because people's motives and goals often change. As soon as they fulfil one wish, people want something new. A communication framework that synthesises all the important information about people greatly facilitates and accelerates this complex process. Whether the goal is to motivate employees, advance their careers, improve the customer experience, and/or add value by personalising products and services, it is always important to collect the most accurate and relevant data possible about interlocutors. Although customer relationship management (CRM) tools have already proven their usefulness for sales management, the main problem with these tools is that customers have no control over their personal data. In contrast, in ICF, customers are directly asked to present themselves and decide what personal information they want to share with others. In practice, user data is collected in three ways:

1. **Self-description**: In this case, users describe themselves independently and decide what information they want to present.
2. **Feedback**: In this case, users can be described and rated by those they have interacted with.
3. **Testing and activity recording**: In this case, users receive personal tags through online testing and / or automatic recording of activities (e.g., previous purchase).

Combining different approaches improves the accuracy of the information. A better understanding of other people is useful not only in business, but also in private relationships (e.g., with friends, parents, the partner, etc.).

Easy identification of personal interests By using an integral communication framework, users define not only who they are, but also what they want (to be, to know, to work, and to have), which provides insight into their developmental dimension. Recognising the developmental dimension is extremely helpful for counselling services and developing sustainable educational programmes (Remtulla, 2012). Integral information sharing enhances social perception and provides valuable insights in recognising compatible and complementary positions. In this way, users can improve their experience and reduce the cost of various activities such as education, shopping, recruitment, travel, and so on. For example, even if there are no products they are looking for at a price they are willing to pay, the user will receive a notification when a product or service matches the user's price criteria.

Improvement of quality Quality management is one of the most important tasks of modern society. As the environmental footprint of today's society continues to grow, resource sharing frameworks and independent quality auditing tools are becoming extremely helpful in improving environmental sustainability. In a competitive and profit-driven society, the phenomenon of planned obsolescence represents the intentional production of goods and services with short lifespans that encourage consumers to make frequent repeat purchases (Slade, 2007). Although this strategy brings short-term profit and power to manufacturers, in the long run it is completely unsustainable and harmful to the natural environment. Independent communication frameworks through which buyers can rate the attributes of products, services, events, and places will not only help improve user satisfaction and quality, but also reduce overall waste (Aladeojebi, 2013; Valant, 2016). By rating people, products, services, events, and physical places (e.g., children's playground, public park, etc.), users help each other make better decisions about which social actors to engage with, which places and events to visit, and which products and services to purchase.

Personal mastery By facilitating the location of individuals and organisations that provide training, guidance, and expertise in various areas, and by facilitating insight into the competencies needed in specific groups, integral networking greatly enhances personal and organisational development. In addition to tests designed to measure users' knowledge in the various areas of their interest, the integral network provides automatic access to educational materials that enable users to improve their scores on these tests. In addition, integral networking promotes qualitative evaluation and provides information about the user's position within a particular group in comparison to an ideal group member, which in turn provides an excellent basis for personal development. Using reports that show how close they are to an ideal group member, users get a clear idea of the skills and activities they should improve.

Saving time and resources Integral networks enable people to save time and resources in a variety of activities. Talent scouting, recruiting, human resource management, consulting, procurement, sales, training, marketing, customer relations, and quality management are just a few of the activities where integral networking provides significant savings. By simplifying the aforementioned processes and reducing their costs, modern organisations save time and other resources that can be invested in new creative projects. By working together, users strengthen their bargaining power so that they can demand higher quality at a lower cost than the price they would pay if they were not connected as a group of users. Integral networks enable their users to share their characteristics and preferences with others to enhance their ability to pursue their personal goals and interests. By automatically identifying personal characteristics and preferences, integral networks can improve relationships between different types of users. In addition, automatic identification of compatible and complementary users will play an important role in reducing the ecological footprint. All of this happens simply because personal mapping of team members and users provides insight into their shared values and preferences. In addition, identifying complementary and compatible positions among integral network members opens up a new set of opportunities for conversation and collaboration. Of course, an integral communication platform is not omnipotent. In all human activities, including communication, various types of human error must be taken into account. Whether due to subjectivity, cognitive limitations, and/or privacy issues, all user-provided data is not completely reliable until it has gone through a series of independent assessments. Since the responsibility for entering and analysing data rests with the users, who are only partially rational and limited by their personal abilities, it is to be expected that the full potential for cooperation will not always be exploited. Fortunately, the number of missed opportunities for cooperation will nevertheless be significantly lower than for those who do not use the integral communication framework. Of course, the improvement of relationships does not only take place in a virtual environment, but also in real life. This is because integral information sharing improves people's ability to identify interests, skills, and other characteristics of their audience, friends, and/or partners. Combined with features such as e-chat, e-voting and e-schedule, group management and e-wallet, the integral communication framework becomes an important driver of collaborative and cooperative behaviour.

Better collaboration experiences Because it enables a better understanding of users by identifying their characteristics, interests, and reliability, integral networking greatly improves collaboration among members of modern organisations and their ability to manage diverse user groups. The interests, needs, desires, and attitudes of the members of any organisation are constantly changing. To track these changes, managers need tools that make it easy to identify this information. There are at least three reasons why integral networking improves collaboration:

1. **Coordination**: Social tagging improves the identification of content and activities that are particularly interesting and desirable to members of a group. Integral tagging can be used to coordinate a large number of different activities (e.g., identifying people who need psychological help or a relative number of people who support a particular organisational decision).
2. **Organisational Learning**: Integral networking promotes teamwork and organisational learning. In addition, this type of networking allows the right people to be promoted to the right jobs that match their attributes and competencies. Anyone who wants to explore information bases, conduct market research, and/or analyse the characteristics of different social groups needs tools that facilitate the automated sharing of respondents' personal data. The introduction of integral digital identity will help researchers shorten their surveys and improve data analysis.
3. **Dynamic Reporting**: Dynamic reports on the characteristics and preferences of members of different groups, the products and services they create, and the policies they implement promote dialogue and provide tangible resources that can be used in discussing important issues.

Better control over personal data One of the basic requirements for successful electronic collaboration is the ability to have control over the personal data exchanged. Nowadays, very few people know exactly what data is stored about them. For this reason, users should be given the opportunity to view their own profile and change or delete the information collected about them (Treiblmaier & Pollach, 2007). Integral networking is based on the idea that users should independently decide what personal information they want to share with other users. In the context of integral networking, users can decide for themselves what characteristics and preferences they want to present to other social actors. In addition, users in the ICF can choose whether their evaluations of other subjects and objects in the network should be anonymous or public. In both cases, the system must ensure that it is a genuine and relevant user who has expressed his opinion in this way.

Better talent identification and employment The main reasons that talent recruitment and identification are increasingly implemented through integral communication frameworks are: low selection cost, greater choice, and simplicity. After creating an ideal group member (e.g., a virtual employee who meets all job requirements) and inviting potential candidates to join, employers gain effective insight into the list of best potential candidates. By joining this group, potential applicants will gain clear insight into their position compared to the ideal member and the areas in which they need to improve to get closer to the required characteristics, which will greatly facilitate their own career planning. Aside from this initial selection process on the vertical dimension of personal attributes, employers can conduct specific tests that further reduce selection costs. In addition to measurement tools, ICF allows managers to link to educational materials and workshops that help applicants meet the required conditions. Career management is not only the responsibility of the individual, but also the strategic responsibility of the organisations in which the individual is employed. Integral communication framework that provides insights into employee characteristics and preferences greatly simplifies this complex, two-way process.

Personalised communication with AI and IoT devices One of the latest trends in communication is the use of machines and tools that have AI properties. If every AI device or robot were forced to independently collect information about the people they communicate with (e.g., information about who they are and what they are interested in), it would be very cumbersome and inefficient. On the other hand, if users' characteristics and preferences are stored in the cloud and/or on smartphones, AI devices can easily access this data to improve the user experience. Personalised communication requires platforms that can collect, centralise, and use all information efficiently and securely (Tileagă & Oprişan, 2021). Today, Salesforce and Oracle are global leaders in customer experience (CX), but there are many other companies developing human-robot interaction (HRI) solutions, such as Samsung Electronics, Ubtech, Agility Robotics, PSYGIG, Inc. and Shadow Robot Company.

Multilingualism Although the actual number depends on where the line is drawn between language and dialect, there are about 7,000 spoken languages in the world today (Leben, 2018). Communication tools that allow people to understand each other and share information, even if they do not speak the same language, are very useful for collaboration. A good example of the importance of developing communication tools that enable multilingual information sharing is the fact that the Google translation service translated approximately 148 billion words in 2018 (Wolverton, 2018). It can be concluded that the automated exchange of a large amount of information on a multilingual platform is the future of communication.

In addition, in practice, there are many other reasons that drive individuals and organisations to use the integral communication networks, such as: negotiation, marketing and sales, entertainment, web search, and so on. Like all other communication platforms, the integral communication networks can be used for some socially undesirable activities. Therefore, it is necessary to detect and prevent such behaviour as early as possible (see SWOT analysis in chapter "Integral Communication Framework").

DIMENSIONS OF INTEGRAL NETWORKING

Integral networking can be viewed and analysed in four basic dimensions: personal, business, educational, and public. The following sections explain how integral communication can be applied in each of these dimensions and the benefits that can be derived. Figure 2 shows potential applications of integral communication.

Personal Dimension

The personal dimension of integral communication and networking refers to physical persons. It is the broadest user group, encompassing all those end users who choose to apply integral communication in their daily activities. Physical users of integral communication networks gain access to a wide range of benefits in the areas of personal presentation, networking, personalised search, learning, personal development, self-reflection, collaboration, resource sharing, and shopping. The personal dimension of integral networking involves the creation of an integral personal map that contains specific tags describing personality, interests, knowledge, skills, goals, preferences, and any other information by which a person wishes to be identified within an integral communication network. In addition, in the profile area, each user specifies his or her network name, contact information, location and profile picture, and, if necessary, adds additional

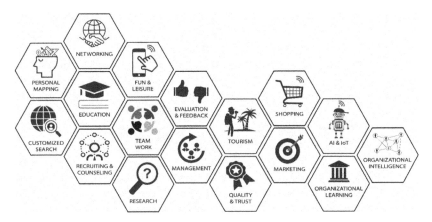

Fig. 2 Potential application possibilities of integral communication. (Source: Made by authors)

information required to carry out commercial activities. Each (integral) personal map consists of 4 basic dimensions and an unlimited number of groups and subgroups with tags. Each tag can have multiple sub-tags or metadata assigned to it. These four basic dimensions represent the four basic perspectives by which each user can be identified. This means that all users within an integral network can be identified by what they are, know, work, and own. There are several types of personal maps. The one that describes the current state, the one that describes the future or desired state (e.g., the preference map), the one that describes the past state, personal maps in groups that show the characteristics of the user that are important to that group, and so on. By facilitating the sharing of personal information and preferences, the integral map acts as a dynamic information filter, allowing users to find and/or search for information that matches their personal interests. Personalised communication optimises the time and energy people invest in realising their wants and needs. Integral mapping improves an individual's ability to define, locate, and track specific interests and preferences. Personalised search functionality allows users to find and rank their specific points of interest with minimal effort. For example, after creating their own integral maps, tourists can automatically identify and locate places, people, organisations, events, and any other content in that destination that relates to their interests, even if they are visiting the destination for the first time in their lives. After registering and creating personal maps, all users, including tourists from the previous example, have the ability to recognise compatible and complementary tags from other users in their vicinity, even if their personal integral maps are written in a foreign language. The difficulty of finding compatible partners, friends and associates (with similar interests) with whom one is willing to collaborate or build long-term relationships is something that all people face on a regular basis. With the integral communication methodology, users can automatically identify all other users with whom they share compatible and complementary positions. After collecting feedback from various interactions, the system learns about potential outcomes and additionally improves the accuracy of its suggestions. There is no doubt that these findings will be of particular benefit to each individual and to socioeconomic development in general.

Integrity is given when all things that people feel, think, say and do are in harmony with each other. Unfortunately, nowadays many people, organisations and especially politicians show a very low level of integrity. To improve trust and quality, our society needs solutions that improve the tagging and evaluation of organisations, including their members, products, services, events and places. In addition to public presentation and networking, individuals can use integral communication to improve their character and personal relationships. The three main areas in which integral networking improves end-user experiences are:

1. **Information management**: Integral tagging and networking will make it easier for people to present themselves to others and identify compatible subjects and objects.
2. **Cooperation**: By automatically identifying complementary positions, end users can easily find potential mentors, buying groups, peers, and organisations that provide information and activities that match users' wants and needs. For example, purchasing cooperatives can offer their members significant advantages (e.g., time savings, greater bargaining power, higher discounts, etc.).
3. **Personal development**: By automatically identifying horizontal and vertical dimensions of skills and talents needed in different groups (e.g., the skills needed for a particular job can be represented by tags with numbers indicating the level of development required), users can easily identify the dimensions in which they should improve. Users willing to learn can access various open and closed groups where they can find posts and educational content intended for

members of those groups. Even those who are not focused on learning and self-development can learn from anonymous feedback they receive in various interactions.

E-cooperation enables a wide range of socio-economic benefits. Although a competitive strategy may look like a good decision in the short run, in the long run, people who do not cooperate usually pay a much higher price and get lower quality than what they could achieve through cooperation. If they want to get the highest quality at the best prices, people should use integral communication in electronic cooperation networks. Since most of their activities take place online, managing such groups is not excessively expensive. User trust and reliability of information are achieved through (anonymous) evaluation of people, organisations, products, services, places and events. Sanctioning unacceptable behaviour is relatively easy to implement, since anyone who (frequently) violates the rules of cooperation is forced to leave the group. Such e-cooperative networks are based on integral information exchange and continuous feedback, but are managed by professionals who care about the interests and specific goals of these groups. Feedback provides indications of the overall quality of the various user features and shows how and where specific features or relationships can be improved. Within an integral network, all users can be evaluated in the three specific ways (Fig. 3):

1. **Personal tags**: Personal tags are all tags that users place in their personal map and that their friends suggest.
2. **Group tags**: These are tags that are relevant to a specific group and can only be evaluated by members of that group who have been authorised by the administrator for this activity.
3. **Automated tags assigned by assessment instruments**: Measurement tools (e.g., speech recognition tool) and tests (e.g., maths test, games) can add new tags and/or score existing tags.

Integral networking offers new opportunities for personal development. An environment in which each individual has the opportunity to present, measure, and improve his or her personal qualities creates fertile ground for overall socioeconomic development. Although motivation is always a product of various intrinsic and extrinsic factors, persistence in personal improvement is most easily achieved through solutions that facilitate the solicitation of feedback and the measurement and visualisation of

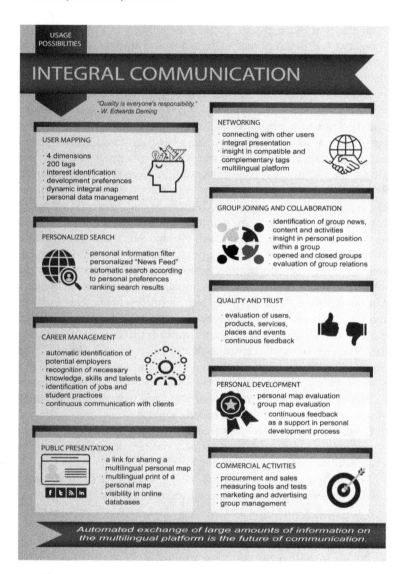

Fig. 3   Usage possibilities of integral networking in personal dimension. (Source: Made by authors)

personal improvement. Constructive feedback plays a very important role in personal coping. It represents helpful and useful information that should be given in a way that breaks down defences and motivates the recipient to make positive changes. The main advantage of integral frameworks and apps over traditional face-to-face communication is that they allow for immediate and balanced feedback. By allowing all members of a group to give their opinions and comments anonymously, they ensure a balance of feedback that is very difficult to achieve in other ways.

In face-to-face communication, many people are unwilling to give constructive feedback to avoid possible conflict with those who are supposed to receive these – sometimes negative – comments (Senge, 2006). This tactic of non-confrontation creates a false atmosphere in which individuals and groups significantly limit their ability to grow and learn. As long as there is a third party (e.g., a group administrator) who can prevent potential abuse (e.g., all tags must be officially approved), anonymity in the evaluation ensures that strengths and weaknesses can be identified without fear that someone will become offended and vindictive over a negative comment. For this reason, an integral communication framework (ICF) acts as a facilitator that enhances users' abilities to communicate, collaborate, and develop personally. The ICF allows its users to receive anonymous feedback from a team as a whole, which is a completely different experience than receiving feedback directly from a specific team member.

One of the main goals of integral mapping is to describe users as accurately as possible. For this reason, each user can be evaluated not only by their peers and group members, but also with various tests and measurement tools that provide additional results and increase objectivity. In addition to increasing trust, these tests and tools, when accompanied by educational materials, can be used for both play and learning. Whether they indicate this in their development map (e.g., a wish list map) or join a group that provides such information and tests, regular users should be able to find someone in their integral network who has roughly the same skills and is interested in collaborating or doing a particular activity (e.g., playing tennis) at a particular time and place. The public presentation of the physical persons is achieved by their visibility in the online search and by a link to share the personal map (e.g., named sports) in different foreign languages. Although natural persons can use integral networking for many different activities, such as: Group shopping, fun, sports, testing, dating, job search, and education, as well as for managing specific user groups (e.g., hiking group, art group, fan club, etc.), the focus is always on improving perceptual ability and personal development.

Business Dimension

Effective leadership means, above all, communicating effectively (Luthra & Dahiya, 2015). As continuous dialogue and feedback sharing provide extremely valuable insights into what employees, partners, and customers feel, know, work, have, and want, more and more leaders and managers are frustrated to find that it is extremely difficult to conduct these activities with large groups of people. Collecting and analysing data about the characteristics and attitudes of large numbers of people and conducting sessions in which everyone is invited to share their thoughts and feelings takes a lot of time and expertise. For this reason, more and more companies are moving toward using personalised communication tools and advanced data analytics to improve their organisational learning. In their study examining how personalised communications affect customer-company relationships, Dantas and Carrillat (2013) found that perceived effort has a positive impact on calculative commitment, while the degree of relevance of the message increases affective commitment. Today, personalization algorithms are helping companies like Amazon, Uber, Airbnb, and Netflix personalise their products and services to improve the customer experience and drive higher conversion rates (Deloitte, 2023). According to an online survey of 1000 consumers aged 18 to 64 conducted by Epsilon (2018), 80% of respondents prefer to do business with companies that offer personalised experiences. According to a survey of 30,000 small and medium-sized businesses in 18 countries conducted by Deloitte (2021), small businesses that use personalised advertising are 16% more likely to increase sales than those that do not.

Implementation of integral communication within business organisations improves efficiency and quality of their presentation, employee mapping, talent recruitment and identification, human resource management, including employee training and career management, group management and teamwork, market research, quality management, organisational learning, marketing, procurement, sales, and business reporting (see Fig. 4). All business users can create a personal map of their own organisation, as well as personal maps of their employees, by defining all the tags that will identify employees and organisations within the integral communication network. The integral communication methodology helps business users identify compatible and complementary organisations and audiences, not only in their local community, but also globally, regardless of their first language or location. In addition to displaying maps in

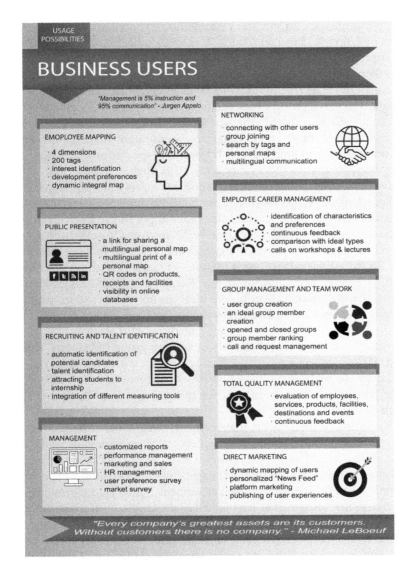

Fig. 4 Usage possibilities of integral networking in business dimension. (Source: Made by authors)

multiple languages, an integral communications framework can use QR codes or Universal Product Codes (UPCs) to collect feedback about different products, services, events, employees, and organisational characteristics. For example, a downtown restaurant operator has decided to display the code QR on its receipts as a link to its integral map. In addition to an invitation to join a group of restaurant customers, diners are asked to rate restaurant offerings based on tags set by the manager and/or group administrator. Within the user interface, a restaurant manager can easily determine quality by tracking which features of specific products, services, employees, locations, and events receive the highest ratings and which receive the lowest. Using this information, managers can easily adjust their market campaigns, personalise restaurant menus to their customers, improve employee training, and make other important strategic decisions. When used optimally, Management by Objectives (MBO) can improve the performance of any group or organisation (Hoffmann-Burdzińska & Flak, 2016). All a manager needs to do to set goals for a group of employees in ICF is to create a group (e.g., "Receptionist") and assign integral tags to that group that describe the ideal group member (e.g., problem solving, communication, empathy, organisation, etc.). The people in this group will clearly identify the goals, and those who evaluate this group (mutual evaluation within the group or another group of "Guests" evaluating this group) will evaluate them in accordance with these tags, i.e., the objectives. To make his job even easier, the manager can download and use a predefined ideal set of tags for the group (e.g., "Receptionist"), which he can change later at will.

In addition to total quality management, integral networking for business users also facilitates the hiring process. Recruitment is optimised through the use of various measurement tools that allow automatically identifying all interested candidates who have the required talent. For example, the HR manager of the IT company has created a group called "Web designer", in which he has defined all the characteristics that describe an ideal group member or employee for this position. If necessary, the vertical dimension of each specific characteristic can be determined by specific tests that measure the competencies of the applicants. If the group is open, anyone interested can join, and if it is closed, it is accessible only to those who have been invited. In both cases, the HR manager effectively identifies the best candidates and simply narrows down the selection. On the other hand, all potential candidates see how far they are from the characteristics of an ideal employee, which facilitates the process of personal improvement and provides insight into what one needs to know to meet the required conditions. When a group is designated as open, the platform sends notifications to potential performers and users who might be interested in joining that group (e.g. web designers.). In closed groups, members are invited by administrators. In both cases, group administrators or managers are given a list of people most similar to an ideal group member created by the group administrator. Those who get a job are transferred to a new group called Employees and asked to regularly update their personal integral map of knowledge, skills, and preferences, as this helps managers motivate, train, and manage the careers of their employees. Of course, one should not be fooled by the notion that an integral communication framework will solve all problems of motivation and management. As Appelo (2011) points out, motivation is non-linear and sometimes unpredictable, so it cannot always be successfully defined or modelled.

Nevertheless, there is no doubt that all the information about employees and customers that managers can obtain and use to improve their organisations is an extremely valuable resource. Empirical studies show that only 13% of workers are engaged at work (Crabtree, 2013). In rough numbers, this means that 900 million workers worldwide are disengaged and 340 million workers are actively disengaged (Crabtree, 2013). Effective communication is key to employee motivation and high performance. An integral framework captures the characteristics and preferences of all users and helps managers harmonise organisational processes. Over time, people's interests, experiences and preferences change. To be best informed, every management needs a communication tool that can regularly capture these changes. Many employers complain about a skills gap and believe that university graduates do not have sufficient skills to be effective (Cedefop, 2015).

Potential applicants should know how far they are from the ideal job candidate and have easy access to educational materials that facilitate learning the required knowledge and skills. Empirical findings show that organisational climate is highly correlated with organisational commitment and perceived organisational performance (Berberoglu, 2018). Nearly one-third of employees report that their managers do not effectively communicate goals and objectives for their teams (Blair, 2012). More than 40% report that they do not receive clear and regular feedback from their managers about how well they are doing their jobs (Blair, 2012). Considering that effective communication in organisations increases their competitiveness (Stacho et al., 2019), every employee should be actively listened to, and familiar with the key goals and objectives for their position. The purpose of employee relations management is to reinforce honesty in various types of activities to reward desirable behaviour and sanction undesirable behaviour. Employee relations should be measured frequently and continuously, and adjustments should be made when results do not show continuous improvement or satisfactory performance levels. The same is true for quality control of products and services. Sixty-six percent of consumers have switched providers in the past year due to poor customer service experiences, while 81% indicated that the company could have done something differently to prevent the switch (Accenture, 2013). Dynamic and integral user mapping offers many opportunities to improve quality, collaboration, and personalised user experience. In the experience economy, where companies help individuals find meaningful experiences, the ability to improve user experience becomes a key competitive advantage (Boswijk et al., 2012). Today, the most successful companies in the market are not those that sell the most products, but those that meet and exceed the expectations of their own customers. Every organisation needs to develop and use different communication channels, methods and techniques to identify the motivational structure of their users and show them what their customers feel, need and want. Companies developing a new product or service should find out what their existing and potential users think about it. To reach their target audiences and test their attitudes toward existing and potential products at minimal cost, all organisations need tools that improve user mapping and feedback exchange. If the communication strategy is not supported by applications that enable efficient identification and visualisation of user characteristics and preferences, management is forced to invest a lot of time, money and energy to gather this information, which is why enterprise resource planning and customer relationship management (ERP and CRM) tools have become so popular in recent decades (Hawking, 2008; Prakash Nunna, 2020). The latest upgrade to these systems comes in the form of an integral communications app that enables integral dynamic mapping of customers and users to ensure a new set of capabilities to improve the user experience. By using reports on the structure of relationships and dynamic changes in the attitudes and characteristics of different groups and teams, management can improve strategic decision making and coordinate all activities of the organisation. In addition, some of these reports, especially those that highlight the overall positive attributes of the organisations, can be used very successfully in public presentation and marketing.

Educational Dimension

Integral networks in education are considered as a separate dimension, since education is realised in practice through the three specific spheres. The private sphere (what subjects need and want independently of others), the public sphere (what society needs and wants), and the economic sphere (what the economic sector needs and wants). Integral networks in education are designed to meet all three spheres. Since the private and business spheres have been discussed in previous chapters, special attention is given here to the possibilities of integral networking in the public sphere of educational organisations. As shown in Fig. 5, integral networking in educational organisations can be used for the following purposes: Assignment of students and staff, development of educational programmes, linkage with enterprises, career counselling, vocational education and training, improvement of student employability, quality management, attraction of students and participants, scientific research and management. Implementing integral communication allows educational institutions to identify the interests and developmental preferences of all stakeholders and link them to an integrated information system that facilitates communication, collaboration, and organisational management. Although feedback is an extremely important component of learning and personal development, various surveys around the world have shown that students are dissatisfied with the feedback they receive on their coursework (Nicol, 2010; Mulliner & Tucker, 2015). Students complain of a lack of appropriate, timely feedback, and their teachers claim that students do not act on the advice given (Orrell, 2006). These findings clearly suggest that educational institutions and lecturers should rethink the process of giving feedback. Nowadays, there are more and more authors, such as Al Bashir et al. (2016), who suggest that lecturers should avoid the traditional methods of giving feedback to students and try new approaches supported by modern technologies.

By creating their own information network for key competencies (of educational staff and students), educational institutions create a basis for automatic networking with companies not only in a local context, but also in a global context. Without effective communication with companies that hire their students, educational institutions cannot easily adapt their educational programmes to the needs of the market. A solution to this problem can be found in an integral communication framework that improves the identification of desirable skills and attributes for different user groups.

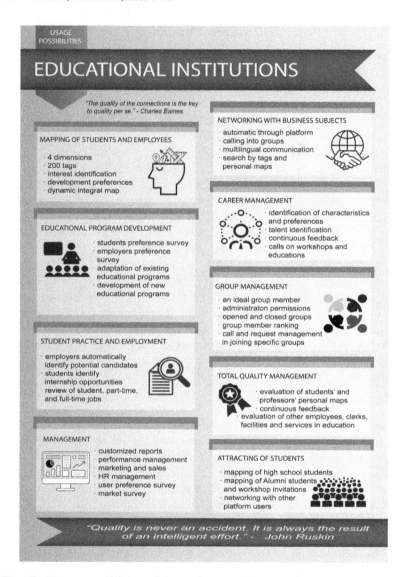

Fig. 5 Usage possibilities of integral networking in educational dimension. (Source: Made by authors)

Without information about student characteristics and preferences, teachers and career counsellors cannot provide personalised advice and suggestions. Dynamic, integral, and personalised mapping improves communication and adds value for everyone involved in the educational process. If they want to ensure the employability and competitiveness of their students in the labour market, today's educational institutions need to increase communication and collaboration with the companies that employ their students. Although this networking has mainly taken place through workshops and bilateral face-to-face meetings, there is a growing need for information systems that facilitate communication between educational and business sectors, regardless of their physical location. To improve teamwork and collaboration, educational institutions need to adopt integral information sharing. Students usually have to invest a lot of time and energy to find professors and colleagues who have similar interests. Automatically identifying users who share compatible and complementary positions (characteristics and interests) greatly improves the ability to collaborate.

Without integral solutions that enable continuous feedback, educational institutions are forced to invest significant time and resources in quality management. Dynamic evaluation of student facilities, educational programmes, professors and project staff opens a space for quality improvement and personal mastery. Standard lectures, materials, and tests offered to all students are often insufficient for those who want to learn more about a particular subject. All students, and especially the best, need direct connections to mentors, experts, instructors, advisors, workshops, tests, and instructional materials that support personalised learning and personal skills. By defining tags and other criteria that describe an ideal member of a group, administrators of integral networks make it easy for group members to see how close they are to the ideal member of that group (e.g., an ideal professor) and what characteristics they should achieve or improve upon to become better. Here are some other examples. Through integral student mapping, professors and/or career counsellors can easily identify workshop topics, professional field trips, and lectures that have the greatest demand. Another example would be an educational institution that wants to collaborate with foreign partners in research and student exchange. Despite language barriers, organisational managers easily identify compatible and complementary tags and negotiate further collaboration. After looking at evaluation reports from the university's own student affairs office, university leaders determine that several administrators are performing poorly in the areas of communication and feedback and invite them to attend a special workshop that provides additional training in this area.

In addition, faculties and vocational schools that have cooperation agreements with various companies and organisations can facilitate the search for and contact with students who are interested in an apprenticeship or job. As part of integrated educational networks, students automatically identify opportunities for apprenticeships and student jobs. By combining dynamic information about student and employer preferences, educational institutions can effectively adapt and update their own educational programmes. Integral networking need not be limited to students, professors, and business partners, but can also be applied to many different educational products (e.g., educational programmes), services (e.g., student office), locations (e.g., cafeteria, library), and events (e.g., workshop, conference, career day). In addition, ICF can also be used to conduct scientific research. By simply identifying the target sample and allowing random sampling according to the specified criteria, the ICF greatly facilitates the conduct of scientific research. The main advantage of the ICF is that it gives researchers access to a larger number of independent variables that they do not have to collect themselves (e.g., age, gender, place of birth, etc.), which greatly simplifies the conduct of research and facilitates the interpretation of the dependent variables. Since such a framework allows for the integration of a wide range of different audiovisual measurement tools, observation of specific individuals over different time periods, and advanced visualisation capabilities of the results, there is no doubt that integral digital identity within ICF will represent a major breakthrough in scientific research.

Career counselling is one of the most important tasks that educational institutions perform. Because these organisations usually have hundreds of staff members (teachers and administrators) and thousands of students, the process of career counselling is enormously challenging. Over time, people's interests and preferences change. An integral communication framework can efficiently track these changes and suggest possible solutions. Unlike the business sector, which has been using similar tools for several decades, educational institutions have until recently been rather uninterested in adopting information systems that enable effective human resource management, collaboration, guidance, personal mastery, and enhancement of the user experience. The main reason for this was that the available solutions were not adapted to their specific needs. The economic crisis, the decline in the number of young people, and increasing competition have forced educational institutions to improve communication and collaboration with employers, as well as the overall quality of their services. Such examples simply confirm that quality is always the result of an intelligent effort based on intensive communication (Ruskin, 2022). The best solutions are those that integrate, in the simplest way possible, different functions, such as: personal mastery, organisational learning, career guidance, market and scientific research, promotion of educational programmes, workshops and content that help attract new students and participants. There is no doubt that integral networking can improve the overall quality of education. However, special care must be taken when interpreting and using e-evaluation results. Unlike standardised tests, which offer a somewhat higher degree of objectivity, evaluations involving individuals (with their own limitations) are not always objective and therefore should not be the sole criteria for hiring, firing, and promotion. In other words: If we ask incompetent and biased evaluators to evaluate something they are not experts in, there is a high probability that we will not get a qualitatively satisfactory answer. As Boring et al. (2016) explain, nowadays student assessment tests (SET) seem to measure student satisfaction and grade expectations rather than teaching effectiveness. For this reason, the integrated communication framework seeks to distinguish different types of assessments (e.g., tests and other measurement instruments), groups of raters, assessment periods, and other parameters that can reduce bias and increase the accuracy of the information provided.

Public Dimension

In the public sector, integral networking and personalised communication based on digital identity could also bring about quite significant improvements. One of the most important benefits of integral networking in the public sector is the ability to collect, present, and use information about the characteristics and preferences of all citizens. Intelligent application of these insights can be used in planning, decision-making, and overall quality management of all public services and operations. When information is collected and presented in a simple, transparent, safe and understandable way, and when it can be used by anyone who needs it, it becomes an extremely valuable public resource that enables overall socioeconomic development. Today, for example, it still takes too much time and energy to report to a public service that a bench or slide in the park is broken.

Applied to the public sector, integral communication takes quality management and collaboration to a whole new level. The main obstacle in the implementation of integral communication in the public sector is a low level of trust in the way public organisations manage personal data of citizens. A World Risk Poll conducted in 2021 among 125,000 people in 121 countries found that 68% of Internet users worldwide are concerned about how their personal data is being used by their government (Gallup, 2022). In a survey conducted by McKinsey in 2019 among 1000 respondents in the North American market only 11% of the participants believe that the public sector handles users' data responsibly (Anant et al., 2020). Although trust in how the public sector deals with personal data depends on many different aspects such as, political decision, integrity of politicians, level of corruption, one part of this problem is certainly hidden in the methodology and design of communication tools used to collect this data. Recent research conducted by Gesk and Leyer (2022) in April and May 2020 among 329 respondents in Australia shows that AI solutions for general public services are preferred to human-delivered services, but that specific services at the local level remain a human domain, mainly due to fear of failure.

When there is transparency and trust, when users know exactly what personal data is being used for what purpose, they are more likely to share that data. In other words, citizens would be more willing to share the information that they have a car if that information was used to ensure a sufficient number of parking spaces in their neighbourhood. For this reason, integral communication tools should give users the greatest possible control over the personal data they are willing to share with others, as well as information about how that data will be used. Although some data will always be beyond their control for legal and practical reasons, end users should have a clear view of what kind of information is used for personalization and/or shared with other users of the network. When user data and preferences are linked to platform security protocols that support anonymous feedback sharing and/or blockchain technology, there is very little room for abuse or false reporting, even if someone has such intentions. Integral assessment (e.g., of public officials, services, places, and events) and presentation improve user experiences and optimise the use of public resources. Although public opinion should not always be used as a deciding factor in decision making, in many situations it can be a good guide in the design of public policies.

In learning organisations, knowledge is the result of an open exchange of information, while important group decisions are made by those who are qualified and directly affected by a particular public issue. Someone can be a qualified voter because of their citizenship, residency, knowledge, skills, qualifications, age, gender, income status, vocation, integral score, etc. Therefore, it is desirable to develop integral communication networks at the national, regional, and local levels of government that enable secure, transparent and efficient exchange of personal information and feedback with all users of public services. As Fig. 6 shows, integral networking improves the quality and efficiency of public organisations in various domains. One of the benefits of integral networking in the public sector is improved presentation of public facilities and services. Many residents, as well as many non-residents and tourists, face problems in determining the availability and location of public facilities and services. Integral mapping on a multilingual basis improves personalised searching and finding of all offers available at the destination. Through the use of web links, QR codes on accounts and physical facilities (e.g., parks, beaches, museums), and/or barcodes, tourists are encouraged to rate their own experiences so that destination management can continue to work on the quality of public services. For example, the ICF can help tourists and residents find a city park where the fitness equipment they are looking for is located, while park visitors can rate the cleanliness of the park with low scores, signalling to public services that the park needs to be cleaned. When there is an effective and transparent framework for the exchange of personal data, the provision of public services can be more accurately tailored to the needs of citizens, significantly reducing costs and increasing long-term environmental sustainability. To prioritise their activities, policymakers need a communication framework that helps them measure and analyse public opinion on various social issues. ICF enables organisational learning and sustainable governance based on transparent, efficient, and effective monitoring of public opinion. Since they are funded by public resources, the quality of all public products and services should be transparently assessed and monitored. In addition, the integral communication framework enables efficient and transparent evaluation of all public offices, products, services, events, and places.

Integral connectivity can also be applied to healthcare, from information and management, to the evaluation of the cleanliness of the waiting room. One of the areas where integral networking is very useful is psychological counselling. Anonymity, simplicity, and low cost of use are some of

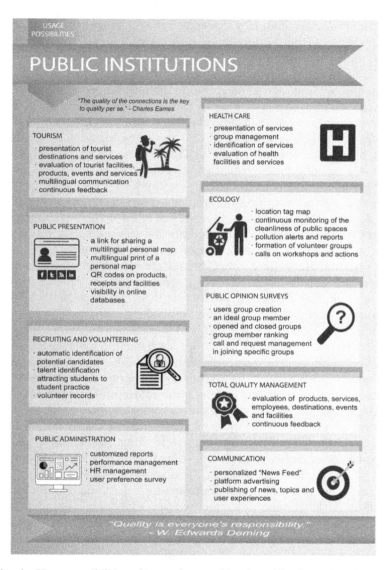

Fig. 6 Usage possibilities of integral networking in public dimension. (Source: Made by authors)

the key benefits that integral networks offer in psychological counselling. Gibson and Cartwright (2014) examined young people's experiences of using mobile text messaging in counselling and concluded that the use of digital technologies can help young people balance their needs for autonomy and connectivity and increase their engagement in counselling. Integral connectivity also helps protect the environment. Integral mapping of different sites facilitates the introduction of labels and forms for reporting different types of pollution, which opens the possibility of systematic monitoring and environmental protection. In such and similar situations, public administration often has to rely on temporary workers and volunteers. An effective answer to this challenge is hidden in integral networking, which greatly facilitates employment and volunteer work in the public service.

In addition to automatically identifying potential candidates, ICF enables the evaluation of public servants and the services they provide, which in turn improves the overall quality of public services and reduces costs. Finding the best candidates for various public roles, including volunteer positions, is a time-consuming and costly process. If our society is to reduce costs and improve transparency in the employment of public employees, it needs a framework in which anyone who is qualified can apply and/or vote for the best candidate. All public products and services are created through some form of collaboration. If our society is to be sustainable, it needs a collaborative framework that encourages the sharing of resources. To improve the quality of life and reduce the cost of living, all social individuals should join together in an integral network that fosters their cooperative skills. In recent years, the idea of optimising public administration and services through digital technologies has gained popularity. This support stems from the successful examples that show that the implementation of e-management models in the public sector leads to lower costs, higher levels of innovation and greater citizen participation. Following an analysis of South Korea's open source e-government initiative, Sojung and Thompson (2013) identified six key lessons for managing development framework ecosystems, as shown in Table 1. According to Fishenden and Thompson (2012), the implementation of e-governance in the public sector can be seen as the dissolution of tightly integrated, proprietary systems traditionally organised around vendors and service providers, and restructuring in the form of services around the citizen, taking advantage of the utility economy of rapidly evolving service markets. According to the 2014 United Nations

Table 1 Six lessons for managing development framework ecosystems

Number	Lesson
1.	Focus on collective stakeholder benefits to ensure buy-in.
2.	Evolve from open sourcing to open outputs.
3.	Operate openly but under strong formal governance.
4.	Develop horizontal infrastructures and vertical areas at the same time.
5.	Build trust and open source software mindset for ecosystem cohesion.
6.	Extend the development framework for use with new technologies and in other countries.

Source: Sojung and Thompson (2013)

e-government rankings, South Korea and the Netherlands were the top countries in the "e-participation" category (UN, 2014). In its report titled " E-Government Survey," the United Nations highlights the seven key criteria that enable e-participation: archived information; public data on government performance (e.g., education grades), access to government websites in more than one language; social networking features; e-consultation mechanisms; online surveys and consultation tools; and e-decision tools (UN, 2014). In half a decade, things have changed somewhat. According to the OECD report (2019), South Korea is still the leader, but the United Kingdom has moved up to second place in implementing e-government strategies, and these two countries were followed by Colombia, Denmark, and Japan. In its research OECD uses slightly different criteria to measure digital government maturity and these are: digital by design, data-driven public sector, government as a platform, open by default, user-driven, proactiveness.

Figure 7 shows how the implementation of integral communication in the public sector could improve the overall quality of public services. Given that digitization of the services may bring certain security risks with it, not all countries are equally decisive in implementing these advanced solutions. From one perspective it is quite clear that e-government data are in many cases confidential and too sensitive to be publicly available. On the other hand, actual information systems and organisational policies in the public sphere are often so outdated, that it is no surprise that the public sector often shows substantially lower efficiency than the private sector which strongly relies on the newest digital information systems to achieve its goals. The fact is that there are still a substantial number of political leaders who are not interested in organisational

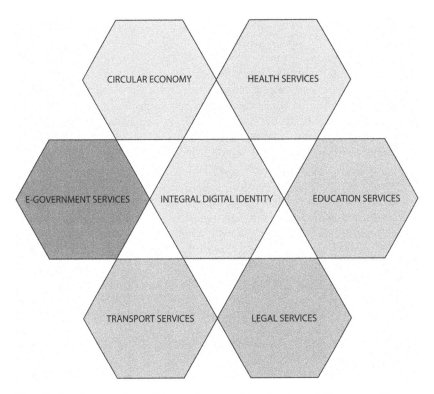

Fig. 7 Implementation of integral networking in the public sector. (Source: Made by authors)

improvements that could improve transparency and reduce their actual political power. Unfortunately, practice shows that advanced, digitally-enabled organisational models are often not on the priority list of today's policymakers, especially in less developed countries. Apart from the short-term burden of extra work for the same salary from launching such projects, in the long run such solutions would lead to laying off between 30% and 70% of the public sector workforce, and this is what most politicians want to avoid at all costs. This thesis is confirmed by the examples of governments trying to ban and regulate in detail various Internet services and technologies in their own markets. Despite the resistance of those who refuse to change, these new open and flexible organisational cultures will continue to change the world we live in. But even if the public sector tries to follow the path of digital transformation, sooner or later it will face the problem of incompatibility between the solutions created by different entities. To solve this problem, it is necessary to develop a digital integral identity that can be used simultaneously in different applications for specific purposes. Despite the fact that the public sector is somewhat slower in accepting new communication technologies that have already become popular among contemporary individuals and private companies, it is undeniable that the implementation of integral networking in the public sector will lead to savings and improvements in the quality of public services. To ensure transparency and objectivity in public networking, integral communication platforms should remain protected from political pressures and particular interests. ICF supports sustainable development and follows the European Union's guidelines on creating value through open data. The direct economic benefits of open data policies in the public sector are financial benefits such as VAT revenues, an increase in the number of new jobs related to the production of newly created products and services, and significant resource savings (EC, 2015). Indirect economic benefits of open data policies in the public sector are new goods and services, time savings for users, transparent reporting, development of the knowledge economy, higher organisational learning capacity, increased efficiency and quality of public services, environmental protection, and growth of all related markets (EC, 2015).

User Attitudes Toward Integral Networking

Considering that integral networking can be applied in different ways and in different domains, users' attitudes regarding the different application modes of integral networking can certainly vary. In this research, the authors focused on the two main types of users: end users and organisational users. End users were represented by students and regular individuals, while organisational users were represented by owners, managers, directors, mayors, executives, or employees of various business, public, and educational organisations who completed questionnaires on behalf of their organisations. The main objective of this study was to investigate the extent to which selected user types show interest in various functionalities of integral networking.

Methodology

To analyse users' attitudes toward integral networking, the authors conducted an empirical survey among a sample of 772 (N) respondents between May 2019 and February 2022. Through random sampling methods, the researchers were able to reach 577 students, 88 individuals, 37 representatives of educational institutions, 37 representatives of business organisations, and 33 representatives of public organisations in the Republic of Croatia. The instruments used for the study were (printed and an online) questionnaires that allowed respondents to answer the questions anonymously. This method was used to collect as many relevant responses as possible. Students were invited through a variety of channels, including physical flyers with a link to the survey, email invitations sent to randomly selected student committees and faculty professors, and invitation links posted on student social networking pages. In 2021, 155,627 students were enrolled in higher education institutions in the Republic of Croatia (DZS, 2021). The conducted study included 0.37% of the total student population in the Republic of Croatia. Natural persons 18 years of age and older were invited mainly through invitation links posted on public social network pages (LinkedIn and Facebook), as well as physical flyers placed in public places in the city of Rijeka with a link to the survey. In addition, randomly selected individuals over the age of 18 were asked for their email addresses in public places in the city of Rijeka, to which invitations to the survey were sent. In 2021, there were 1,816,000 of the active population older than 18 years in the Republic of Croatia (DZS, 2022). The conducted study included 88 physical persons, which corresponds to 0.005% of the total active population in the Republic of Croatia. The contacts of 500 public organisations that received an invitation to participate in this survey were ensured by random selection from various sources that publish information about public organisations, such as the web portals https://zdravlje.gov.hr, https://mpu.gov.hr, https://upisnik.mdc.hr, https://www.parkovihrvatske.hr, etc. The exact number of public organisations in the Republic of Croatia is very difficult to determine. Of the approximately 273,000 people working in the public sector in the Republic of Croatia, 33 people were included in the survey, which corresponds to 0.01% of the total population (EC, 2015). The response rate among public organisations was 6.6%, and such a response rate can be considered quite normal for web surveys in social sciences in the EU (Žmuk, 2018). The contacts of 500 educational organisations that received an invitation to participate in this survey were ensured by random selection from various sources that publish information about educational organisations, such as the web portals https://www.isvu.hr, https://www.azvo.hr and by unstructured search for contacts on the Internet. In the academic year 2019/20, there were 18,167 faculty and staff in higher education institutions in the Republic of Croatia, which means that this survey covered 0.20% of the total population. The response rate among higher education institutions was 7.4%. An invitation to participate in the survey was sent by e-mail to 900 randomly selected e-mail addresses of companies operating in the Republic of Croatia. The contacts of the 900 companies that received an invitation to participate in the survey were ensured by random selection from various sources that publish information on business topics, such as the portals www.digitalnakomora.hr, www.rgfi.fina.hr, www.fininfo.hr and by unstructured search for contacts on the Internet. Due to political restrictions on the disclosure of economic indicators, some business organisations declined to participate in the survey. The response rate among companies was 4.1%. Originally, the research instrument consisted of 29 questions divided into three different sections. This chapter contains the results of the most important questions from the first, second and third sections. The first section consisted of basic questions used to describe the respondents. The second section contained 21 statements about different activities in integral networking that correspond to the main functions of the ICF. Using the Likert scale with scores ranging from 1 (strongly disagree) to 5 (strongly agree), respondents were asked whether they agreed or disagreed with a particular statement. The third section consisted of two additional open-ended questions asking respondents to comment on the survey and leave their personal contact if they would like to try integral networking. The first step of the empirical research was to apply the questionnaire to the student population. Since the student population had the largest number of respondents ($N = 577$), this data was used to apply factor analysis. Using the Cronbach's Alpha statistical method, a reliability coefficient of 0.70 was determined for the instrument. Application of factor analysis to common axes with oblique rotation revealed the existence of 3 factors: integral presentation ($\alpha = 0.85$, $N = 6$), integral assessment ($\alpha = 0.91$, $N = 8$), and integral development ($\alpha = 0.85$, $N = 7$). Particles that exhibited double saturation were associated with the factor to which they meaningfully belonged (see Table 4 in Appendix I). The factor structure determined on the larger sample of students was then adopted for the smaller sample of individuals. In addition, the same factor structure was used for organisational users, with statements slightly adjusted for organisational context (see Table 5 in Appendix I). Descriptive statistical analysis was used to describe the profile of respondents and the frequency of respondents' attitudes toward integral networking. The Shapiro-Wilk test was used to test the normality of the distribution of the data across different factors of integral networking. The Mann-Whitney U test was used to analyse whether there were statistically significant differences between students and natural persons in their interest in three different factors of integral networking. In addition, the same test was used to compare the differences between male and female respondents regarding their interest in integral networking. In addition, the Mann-Whitney U test was used to analyse whether there are statistically significant differences between public and educational institutions in their willingness to apply integral presentation and integral development. The Kruskal-Wallis test was used to analyse whether there were statistically significant differences among three different types of organisational users in terms of their interest in three different factors of integral networking. In addition, the Mann-Whitney U test was used to analyse whether there are statistically significant differences between public and educational organisations in their willingness to apply integral presentation and integral development. In addition, the same test was used to compare the differences between three different fields of study from which the students come in terms of their interest in integral networking. Kendall's tau-b correlation was used to determine the relationship between users' attitudes regarding integral presentation, integral assessment, and integral development. In this chapter, user attitudes toward integral networking are discussed in more detail in relation to the three basic factors – integral presentation, integral assessment and integral development. The Integral Communication Framework (ICF) that can be used for integral networking has two basic types of users. The first group are end users who use this framework for themselves. The second group are organisational users who use this framework on behalf of their organisations. Although the questions used to measure interest in integral networking were almost identical, the final results are elaborated separately. Tables 6 and 7 in Appendix I show the detailed structure of the research sample.

End Users

This study included 665 (N) potential end users of ICF represented by 577 students and 88 individuals. Using a Likert scale where 1 represents "strongly disagree" and 5 represents "strongly agree," respondents rated their agreement with various statements measuring their readiness to use integral presentation, integral assessment, and integral development in their daily activities. Table 2 shows the median and interquartile range (IQR) of the three main factors of integral communication for two different types of end users. In Table 2, it can be seen that in all cases the median values are slightly higher than the means, indicating that the distributions are negatively skewed. The Shapiro-Wilk tests performed showed that the end-users' attitudes toward the integral communication factors were not normally distributed, so non-parametric tests were applied. To analyse the relationship between the different integral communication factors, Kendall's tau-b test was applied to the sample of 665 end users. The analysis revealed a statistically significant positive relationship between end-users' willingness to use integral presentation and integral evaluation, (τb = 0.484, p < 0.01). In addition, the analysis found a statistically significant positive relationship between end users' willingness

Table 2 Median and interquartile range (IQR) of the three main factors of integral communication for two different types of end users

Type of respondent / Factor		Integral presentation	Integral assessment	Integral development
Students	N	577	577	577
	Mean	3.5822	3.3239	3.6362
	Median	3.6667	3.3750	3.7143
	St. Deviation	0.85018	0.99574	0.82679
	IQR	1.17	1.25	1.14
Physical persons	N	88	88	88
	Mean	3.7576	3.4773	3.7955[a]
	Median	3.8333	3.7500	4.0000
	St. Deviation	1.02208	1.27300	0.87272
	IQR	1.33	2.47	1.00

Source: Made by authors

[a]One particle is missing: I want to find out my position in a group given the closeness of my personal characteristics and the characteristics of a desirable group member

to use an integral presentation and integral development, (τb = 0.533, p < 0.01) and a statistically significant positive correlation between end-user willingness to use integral development and integral assessment, (τb = 0.479, p < 0.01). These correlations are statistically significant at 1% a risk (p < 0.01), and the relationship is strong if the coefficient τb > 0.30 (Botsch, 2009; Walker 2003).

Integral presentation represents a set of activities that allow respondents to make their positive attributes and preferences publicly visible on the Internet through a consistent set of keywords and symbols in multiple languages. The integral presentation enables a comprehensive representation of users in all dimensions and aspects of their personality. The final purpose of integral presentation is to improve presentation, collaboration, and identification of compatible and complementary positions among different types of users. It is important to note that the integral presentation includes all quadrants and levels of a person's personality, which means that users can indicate not only their current characteristics but also their preferences. Figure 8 shows that integral representation is quite a useful functionality among end users, as 37.8% of students and 48.9% of physical users agree and strongly agree that they are willing to use integral

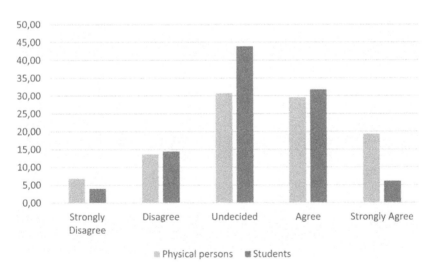

Fig. 8   The relative number of end users interested in an integral presentation, by end user type (N = 665). (Source: Made by authors)

presentation in their online communication. The results presented in Table 2 and Fig. 8 directly confirm the first hypothesis, which states that members of a network society want to present themselves in an integral way in an online environment so that other members can find them for collaboration.

To assess the difference between students and natural persons in their attitudes toward various integral networking factors, the Mann-Whitney U test was applied. The test revealed that statistically significant differences existed between students (Mdn = 3.66, n = 577) and natural persons (Mdn = 3.83, n = 88) only in their attitudes toward integral presentation, U = 21562, z = -2.28, p = 0.022, r = 0.08. Although these differences are statistically significant, according to Cohen (1988), it is a rather small effect. The Kruskal-Wallis test was used to compare the differences among three different majors from which the students came in terms of their interest in various factors of integral connectivity. The analysis showed that there were no statistically significant differences between students of technical, social, and other sciences in their attitudes toward integral assessment, H (2) = 2.21, p = 0.33, integral presentation, H (2) = 4.16, p = 0.12 and integral development, H (2) = 0.845, p = 0.65.

Integral assessment consists of a series of activities that improve the accuracy and confidence of the information presented. It is a process of multidirectional anonymous evaluation carried out between friends, team members, users and/or third parties specialised in such activities. The goal of integral assessment is to provide a truthful and unbiased description of various users and objects, and to enable an efficient exchange of feedback. Respondents' interest in integral assessment is the combined score of eight different statements that measure their willingness to participate in assessment and feedback exchange (see Table 4 in Appendix I). Integral assessment can be very helpful not only for teamwork and personal development, but also for raising awareness of the attitudes and feelings of different users and groups.

Given that about one-third of end-users are interested in integral assessment, the results in Table 2 and Fig. 9 show that the second hypothesis is also confirmed. Interestingly, 37.4% of the students are undecided whether they want to participate in an integral assessment. It is quite normal that all those who have never learned about the importance of feedback exchange and/or have never participated in such activities are suspicious. Nevertheless, about one-third of end users are not interested in integral assessment. Dishonest individuals, as well as those who do not give their

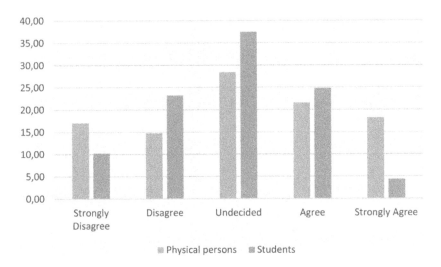

Fig. 9 The relative number of end users interested in an integral assessment, by end-user type (N = 665). (Source: Made by authors)

best at work and in relationships, are generally opposed to any type of assessment. One of the possible reasons for students' disinterest in integral assessment may be their current curricula, which are already overloaded with exams and knowledge tests. Last but not least, some think that assessment is time-consuming, or they simply have an aversion to any kind of assessment. Nevertheless, it is quite obvious that a significant number of potential end users would like to apply integral assessment in their communication and collaboration with others.

Integral development consists of a series of activities that develop the potential of users. These activities include obtaining content and materials that support personal development, conducting tests at specific time intervals that help monitor developmental dynamics, and identifying characteristics that are desirable in different groups. In addition, the ICF allows users to determine their position in relation to other group members. The ultimate purpose of integral development is to provide automatic insight into what end users should improve, as well as provide automatic links to materials and educators qualified to teach these topics. The results presented in Table 2 and Fig. 10 confirm the third hypothesis, which is that contemporary individuals are willing to participate in

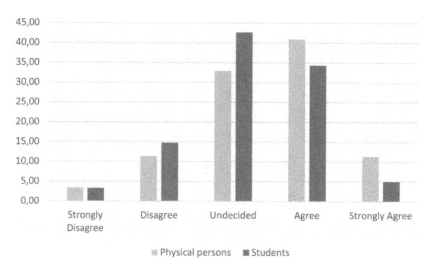

Fig. 10 The relative number of end users interested in integral development by end user type (N = 665). (Source: Made by authors)

integral development. Figure 10 shows that 52.3% of individuals and 39.4% of students are willing to participate in integral development.

The Mann-Whitney U test was used to assess the difference between male and female respondents in terms of their attitudes toward three different factors of integral networking. The test revealed that statistically significant differences between male (Mdn = 3.66, n = 295) and female respondents (Mdn = 3.85, n = 368) exist only in their attitudes toward integral development, U = 46642.5, z = -3.12, p = 0.002, r = 0.12. Although these differences are statistically significant, they are a small effect according to Cohen's (1988) criteria, since a moderately strong effect starts at 0.3. In the penultimate question, about 23% of respondents, 154 end users, provided their own email address through which they could receive an invitation and try ICF. In the last question, respondents were asked to write down their personal thoughts about the research conducted. A total of 14 responses were collected. In their comments, most respondents praised the project, supported the initiative, and felt that implementing these features was good for sharing opinions and contributed to digital socialisation. One respondent stated that he would like to use these functions mainly for business interactions. The same respondent argues that special attention must be paid to data confidentiality, as there will certainly be information that users do not want to share with others. The next interviewee supports the project, but states that he is not willing to express his opinion publicly. One of the respondents says that this is a very interesting idea, especially in terms of obtaining content that promotes personal development. The same respondent claims that it would be very useful if the assessment could be done only by those who are qualified to do it. In addition, one of the comments states that effective information sharing allows for the improvement of education and the realisation of personal needs with as few constraints as possible. Another comment states that of all the features listed, testing and insight into the proximity of the desired group member are considered the best. One respondent stated that she wanted complete privacy regarding her own thoughts. Two respondents stated that nothing needs to be anonymous. One respondent claims that it would be desirable to identify users by geographic location and suggest live meetings. Another student respondent claims that it is better to rate products than people. The same respondent argues that evaluating people is a complex process that can sometimes be very biassed. One of the comments was that a traditional evaluation is better than one done online. One of the respondents wrote that it is important to allow deletion of the account if users are not satisfied with the service.

Organisational Users

Unlike end users, who use different features of the integral communication framework to satisfy their own needs and interests, organisational users use the same framework to satisfy the operational needs and interests of their organisations. To measure the extent to which different types of organisational users are interested in integral networking, 18 different statements were defined (see Table 5 in Appendix I). The research sample included $107(N)$ organisational users from the corporate, educational, and public sectors in the Republic of Croatia (see Table 7 in Appendix I). This section elaborates on organisational users' interest in three factors of integral networking taken from the larger student sample, namely integral presentation ($\alpha = 0.87$, $N = 8$), integral assessment ($\alpha = 0.86$, $N = 5$), and integral development ($\alpha = 0.86$, $N = 5$). As shown in Table 7 (see Appendix I), a significant number of respondents were (co-)owners, managers, or held executive positions in their organisations. Using a Likert scale where

1 means "strongly disagree" and 5 means "strongly agree," respondents rated their agreement with various statements that measure their organisations' readiness to apply integral presentation, integral assessment, and integral development. Table 3 shows the median and interquartile range (IQR) of the three main factors of integral communication for three different types of organisations.

As expected, the analysis revealed a statistically significant positive correlation between organisational users' willingness to use integral presentation and integral assessment, (τb = 0.542, p < 0.01). In addition, the analysis found a statistically significant positive correlation between organisational users' willingness to use the integral presentation and integral development, (τb = 0.624, p < 0.01) and a statistically significant positive correlation between organisational users' willingness to use integral

Table 3   Median and interquartile range (IQR) of the three main factors of integral communication for three different types of organisational users

Type of respondent / Factor		Integral presentation	Integral assessment	Integral development
Business	N	37	37	37
organisations	Mean	4.1506	4.1189	3.8189
	Median	4.4286	4.2000	3.8000
	St. Deviation	0.85352	0.79925	0.98709
	IQR	1.06	0.80	1.30
Public organisations	N	33	33	33
	Mean	3.9080	4.1455	3.7980
	Median	3.8750	4.6000	3.8000
	St. Deviation	0.72586	0.94508	0.78590
	IQR	0.94	1.40	1.17
Educational	N	37	37	37
organisations	Mean	4.3769	4.2703[a]	4.2595
	Median	4.5000	4.6667	4.6000
	St. Deviation	0.65296	0.78896	0.87922
	IQR	0.94	1.33	1.20

Source: Made by authors

[a]Two particles are missing: We want to reward clients and customers who have anonymously evaluated our products, services and employees and We want our employees to be able to anonymously evaluate each other

development and integral assessment, (τb = 0.467, p < 0.01). These correlations are statistically significant at 1% a risk (p < 0.01), and the relationship is strong if the coefficient τb > 0.30 (Botsch, 2009; Walker, 2003). The Kruskal-Wallis test was used to compare the differences between three different types of organisational users in terms of their interest in various factors of integral networking. The Kruskal-Wallis H-test showed that there was a statistically significant difference in willingness to use integral presentation among the different types of organisational users, H (2) = 8.188, p = 0.017, with a mean rank value of 55.31 for private, 42.18 for public, and 63.23 for educational organisations. In addition, the same test showed that there was a statistically significant difference in willingness to use integral development among the different types of organisational users, H (2) = 7.601, p = 0.022, with a mean rank value of 49.73 for private, 46.30 for public, and 65.14 for educational organisations. Willingness to use integral assessment did not differ statistically among the different types of organisational users.

Educational organisations are particularly interested in integral presentation and integral development. Figure 11 shows that 78.4% of education respondents, 48.5% of public sector respondents, and 67.6% of private sector respondents agree or strongly agree that their organisations want to use integral presentation in communicating and collaborating with their stakeholders. In addition to enabling organisations to easily identify complementary and compatible positions with other users in their network, integral presentation enables organisations to identify a dynamic set of information about clients and customers that can help them personalise their products and services. In addition, integral presentation enables organisations to specify the attributes they are looking for in a particular job and post them as open positions to find potential candidates who best match that job. The Mann-Whitney U test was used to analyse whether there are statistically significant differences between public and educational organisations in their willingness to apply integral presentation and integral development. The Mann-Whitney test indicated that there is a statistically significant difference in the willingness to apply integral presentation between public organisations (Median = 3.87, n = 33) and educational organisations (Median = 4.50, n = 37), U = 370, z = -2.842, p = 0.004. The same test showed that there was no statistically significant difference in the willingness to use the integral presentation between public and private organisations and between private and educational

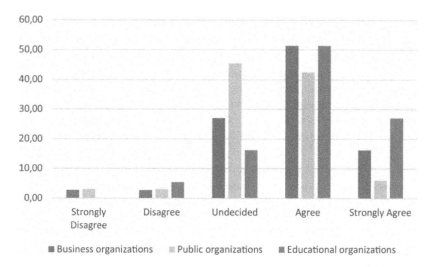

Fig. 11 The relative number of organisational users interested in an integral presentation, according to the type of organisation (N = 107). (Source: Made by authors)

institutions. In addition, the Mann-Whitney test showed that there was a statistically significant difference in willingness to use integral presentation between end users (Median = 3.67, n = 665) and organisational users (Median = 4.38, n = 107), U = 22202, z = -6.256, p < 0.05. In addition, the same test showed that there was a statistically significant difference in willingness to use integral assessment between end users (Median = 3.43, n = 665) and organisational users (Median = 4.40, n = 107), U = 18601, z = -7.936, p < 0.05, and that there was a statistically significant difference in readiness to use integral development between end users (Median = 3.71, n = 665) and organisational users (Median = 4.00, n = 107), U = 27747.5, z = -3.661, p < 0.05. Figure 12 shows that 62.14% of businesses, 60.6% of public institutions, and 72.84% of educational institutions agree or strongly agree that they want to use integral assessment in their daily work.

Integral assessment can help organisations initiate the process of total quality management in a very effective and efficient way. This is because integral assessment features enable activities such as anonymous evaluation of products and services, mutual evaluation of team members according to predefined characteristics, and regular use of various measurement tools (e.g., tests) to evaluate employees, products, services, events, and places.

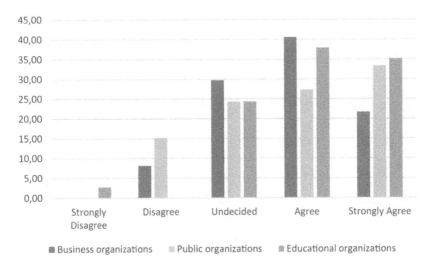

Fig. 12   The relative number of organisational users interested in an integral assessment according to the type of organisation (N = 107). (Source: Made by authors)

Interestingly, only 9.41% of organisational users disagree or strongly disagree that their organisations want to use integral assessment in their regular operations. To fulfil their purpose, organisations need to know what their users, workers, and all other stakeholders think and feel. For this reason, such results are entirely to be expected. An integral development means that organisations can create, receive, and share content (e.g., articles, web links, etc.) that can help other stakeholders develop. In addition, integral development means that organisations are willing to create or join various groups created for the purpose of learning, collaboration, and development. Within the framework of ICF, members of these groups have the opportunity to find out how close their characteristics are to those of a desirable (ideal) group member so that they can strengthen and develop as a member of that group. For example, by specifying the characteristics of a job through a series of symbols, the ICF helps potential job applicants identify which specific characteristics are required and shortens the time it takes to adapt to new jobs.

Figure 13 shows that 75.68% of educational organisations, 48.65% of business organisations, and 39.99% of public organisations agree or strongly agree that they want to apply integral development in their

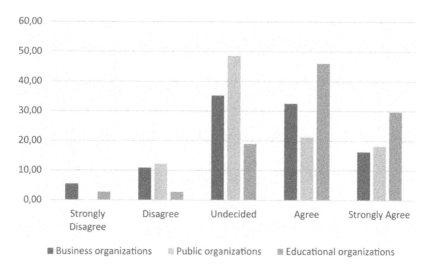

Fig. 13 The relative number of organisational users interested in integral development according to the type of organisation (N = 107). (Source: Made by authors)

operational activities. The Mann-Whitney test showed that there is a statistically significant difference in the willingness to apply integral development between public organisations (Median = 3.80, n = 33) and educational organisations (Median = 4.60, n = 37), U = 400, z = -2.500, p = 0.012. As expected, the results collected show that educational organisations are more interested in integral development than public organisations.

Interestingly, only 11.21% of organisational users are not interested in integral development. This means that an extremely large number of the organisations surveyed that participated in this research recognised that their organisations needed solutions to help them learn and develop to their full potential. These results were also expected. As technological and social complexity increases, more organisations are realising that they need a broader range of expertise than they currently have in their organisation, which means they need to collaborate more effectively with their stakeholders to capitalise on opportunities in their ecosystems. In order to analyse possible differences between smaller and larger organisations in terms of their interest in integral communication, two separate groups were formed. The first group (N = 51) included micro and small organisations and the second group (N = 19) included medium and large organisations. The Mann-Whitney test series showed that there were no statistically significant differences between smaller and larger organisations in their willingness to use integral networking.

In the penultimate question, 34.57% of organisational users left their email address through which their organisations can receive an invitation to participate in the platform. In the last question, four comments were collected. The first respondent advised extra caution in regulating the exchange of information between educational institutions and employers, especially in light of the General Data Protection Regulation. Another respondent concluded that new dynamic assessment methods that take into account a broader range of personal qualities, such as creativity, rather than just memorization of commonly known facts, are more than welcome. The third comment also praises the fact that assessment will be done not only through questionnaires, but also through interaction and teamwork. There is no doubt that nowadays students are overwhelmed with the classical exams. It is clear from the responses that it is very desirable to offer and develop new ways of interactive teaching and assessment. It seems that ICF could play an important role in this change. One of the public sector respondents notes that in addition to new digital tools that would help improve the management of HR, there is a need to hire additional staff for human resource management tasks, as most public sector organisations are understaffed in terms of human resource management experts, while existing staff are overwhelmed with mandatory administrative tasks.

SOLUTIONS AND RECOMMENDATIONS

To be better embedded in its environment, today's society needs to adopt a smart way of networking that improves communication, collaboration and trust in various social and economic activities. The solution can be found in a new way of networking based on a unified set of symbols (e.g., keywords or tags) used to connect social actors on different bases and preferences. Since integral networking enables significant resource and energy savings, it will play an important role in the implementation of a sustainable Internet. Integral networks connect individuals in interactive groups that seek to improve information sharing, social perception, learning, quality of life, collaborative experience, and time and resource efficiency of their members. Integral communication methodology strives to apply all available knowledge from the social, humanistic, technical, and biotechnical sciences that can be helpful in improving communication and the ability to collaborate among social actors. The main challenge is how to combine this practical knowledge from psychology, sociology, computer science, technology, design, and economics, especially human resource management, into a single communication framework designed to improve the overall quality of human interactions. The further development of the information society is closely linked to the development of communication solutions that ensure the efficient exchange and evaluation of information. Without a communication framework that allows for easy assessment, identification, and comparison of the views and opinions of group members based on various criteria such as place of residence, age, and expertise in the field, members of the networked society will be increasingly at risk of information manipulation. It is clear that this cannot be achieved by a narrow circle of scientists, but must be supported by a broader community of researchers and organisations willing to actively participate in the ongoing development of the integral communication framework (ICF). Last but not least is the desire of end users to participate in integral networking. Without end users willing to use and evaluate the tags used in integral mapping, it is not possible to develop the full potential of integral networking. For individuals and organisations that choose to establish their own integral networks, the biggest challenge will be to provide high-quality content, including measurement tools, tests, and games, that will motivate their employees and users to participate in these networks. Recently, more and more managers are beginning to realise that the core value of their company lies not in its assets and other material resources, but in its employees and customers. To achieve synergy in communication, integral networks must be actively managed. Fortunately, this process sounds much more difficult and complicated than it turns out to be in practice. After setting their personal data and preferences, any user who can use a cell phone has the opportunity to communicate in an integral way. Integral networks that foster collaboration among users with complementary interests become one of the most important promoters of sustainable living. In most of their characteristics, integral networks are very similar to regular social networks. For example, they can be open or closed. In open networks, anyone interested can join, while in closed networks, the administrator decides to include only certain members, while the network remains invisible to everyone else (e.g., an internal control team in some companies). In addition, integral networks can be designed as bazaar networks, in which there are no specific benefits among the different organisational levels and users, or as cathedral networks, in which the specific benefits of each level (e.g., profits) are distributed mainly among the members of that level, while all others share the same core benefits (e.g., information or services) (Raymond, 2001). However, there are some characteristics that distinguish integral networks from all other social networks. Unlike normal social networks, integral networks are based on:

- **Integral Presentation**: By using tags enriched with metadata to define their digital identity, users can present themselves to other social actors and AI devices in all aspects and dimensions of their personality. This type of presentation allows different types of users to independently choose and suggest which categories (e.g., personality, education, work, etc.) and dimensions (e.g., past, present and future) they would like to present. Unlike traditional social networks that do not collect such information, ICF clearly distinguishes between user characteristics (e.g., How good is someone at something?) and preferences (e.g., What does someone want?), allowing easy observation of compatible and complementary positions.
- **Integral Assessment**: To improve accuracy and confidence in the information presented, all nodes in the network (e.g., people, organisations, products, services, events, and places) are subject to evaluation and assessment. There are different types of assessment that can be used on different occasions. The three basic types of evaluation are subjective (e.g., peer-to-peer), objective (e.g., official testing), and automatic (e.g., global positioning system- GPS).
- **Integral Development**: All ICF users are able to automatically identify, based on their characteristics and preferences, social actors that can help them in their development, as well as learning materials that can be used for the same purpose. When creating groups (e.g., janitor, bakery, etc.), administrators are able to set group goals (e.g., tags describing an ideal janitor or bakery) through built-in tags with metadata (e.g., rating points) that represent goals for those group members. If they do not want to set it themselves, group administrators can simply download the best templates of ideal types that facilitate personal development, management, and organisational learning.

- **Quality**: Because quality is about meeting and exceeding user expectations, integral networking enables a high degree of personalization. This means that users are completely autonomous in determining what content they want to see, what filters they want to apply, and what rating processes they want to participate in. ICF enables users to experience personalization not only in the digital sphere, but also in physical interactions with people and AI devices. By analysing users' characteristics, preferences, and feedback in defining their digital identity, ICF acts as an AI intermediary, advising users on how to achieve specific goals and improve the quality of their interactions.

Integral networking is based on the user's desire to improve their communication and collaboration capabilities. In integral networks, objectivity is achieved by evaluating a wide range of information that determines the position of each member or object within a given group. Integral networks consist of one or more integral groups that gather members with compatible and/or complementary characteristics. The basic benefits of integral networking are available to anyone willing to follow the group rules. From a technical point of view, integral networks are designed according to the principles of modularity, granularity and low integration cost (Benkler & Nissenbaum, 2006). In other words, the integral network architecture is based on the tight-loose approach. This means that strategic issues – platform, rules of collaboration, and licences – are tightly controlled, while everything else outside this circle is left to third parties and end users (Benkler & Nissenbaum, 2006). By providing an integrated framework, integral networks increase the efficiency of their members through standard modules and interfaces that minimise duplication of work, increase resource utilisation, and enable significant reductions in collaboration costs. Integral communication enables individuals and organisations to collectively create value through large-scale collaboration, distribute that value where it is needed, and, when revenue is generated, distribute that revenue to all participants in proportion to their contributions. Like integral communication, integral networking is based on the following principles (Rafajac & Jakupović, 2017, p. 10):

- **Openness**: This implies that an integral networking tool should be free and accessible. In other words, anyone who is willing to abide by the common rules of conduct is welcome to join and participate in its further development.

- **Adaptability**: This implies that integral networking can be applied in a wide range of activities. Compatibility with other communication tools and platforms is one of the main factors for success.
- **Mnemonics**: Implies the use of elaborative coding, retrieval cues, and images as specific tools for encoding a particular piece of information in a way that enables efficient storage and retrieval.
- **Simplicity**: The goal is to avoid duplication of effort and unnecessary communication entries whenever possible. Finally, one of the main goals of ICF is to simplify complex procedures.
- **Personalization**: Includes customization of settings and filtering options. Among other things, this option is intended to allow parental control of communications that children have via cell phones and PCs.
- **Relevance**: Users should be able to confirm or attest to the truthfulness and accuracy of other people's profiles.
- **Privacy**: Personal information should remain protected to the maximum. This means that users can specify which variables should be publicly accessible and which should remain private.

Integral networking for end users can be described in eight steps (see Fig. 14). The first step in integral networking for end users is the creation of a personal profile, i.e., filling out the registration form and entering personal tags that allow for personal mapping. Users can update personal data and the tags used in their mapping at any time. Once they have created their personal maps, physical users can proceed to the second step, personalised search. Personalised search in integral networks is performed in two basic ways:

- **Automatically**: The information presented is associated with tags in the personal map, which is a personal information filter.
- **Manually**: The user finds the content independently by entering a specific term in the search field.

The end result is a personalised networking that allows connection with other users, groups and organisations that match the user's characteristics and preferences. In the fourth step, when accessing a group, end users identify the content intended for that group and gain access to other tools and features provided by the group administrator (e.g., the "Students" group, which displays messages intended for students). The fifth step

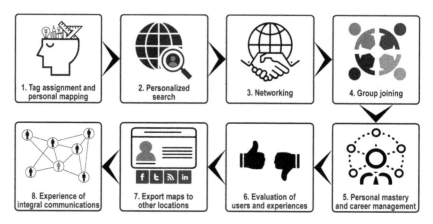

Fig. 14 Basic steps for the integral networking of end users. (Source: Made by authors)

relates to personal improvement and is closely related to the sixth step, which is about evaluating experiences and interactions. Based on their tags and ratings, end users receive content and links that allow them to improve their own attributes and identify opportunities for personal and professional development. By evaluating their own experiences and the people with whom they interact, end users support the development of other users and improve the overall quality of the integral networks in which they participate. To protect sensitive individuals from harassment, negative reviews do not always need to be directly visible to the end user. Instead of directly seeing the negative comments in the system, it is more important to give users advice on how to improve themselves and certain relationships. In this way, the ICF helps to improve personal integrity and the quality of human relationships. The seventh step refers to the ability to export the digital identity to other places, such as social networks, websites, or print, while the eighth step refers to the experience of using an integral communication framework (ICF) that enhances collaboration and the communication experience. In order to get as much feedback as possible and show their accomplishments, end users should export their digital identity or only certain tags to external entities. Through tags in their own digital identities, which they make publicly available, end users participate in Economy 5.0 and benefit from communication with robots and IoT systems that enable the creation of personalised products and services.

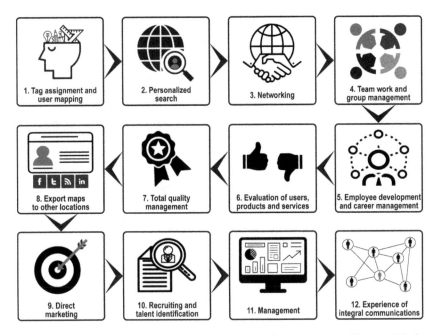

Fig. 15   Basic steps for the integral networking of organisations. (Source: Made by authors)

Integral networking for organisational users can be described in twelve steps (see Fig. 15). In addition to creating an organisational profile, which involves filling out the registration form and entering basic organisational tags, organisational users invite their employees to create their own integral maps. In this way, management obtains a dynamic integral map of all organisational characteristics. This map contains not only the existing characteristics, knowledge and skills, but also the development preferences of the employees working in the organisations. After creating the integral map of the organisation, the legal entities can start a personalised search or an automatic identification of other network users with whom they share compatible and complementary tags. The third step is networking. This means linking with suppliers and customers and automatically identifying potential customers and business partners, which significantly reduces costs and improves the efficiency of the company. The fourth step refers to teamwork and group management. To improve communication, collaboration and quality management, organisational users from different user groups are brought together. Some of these groups can be suppliers, customers, employees, work teams, clients, and business partners. In addition to being able to generate various reports on group characteristics and relationships, group management involves creating an ideal group member with the characteristics that are desirable in that specific group. ICF improves teamwork by facilitating information sharing and mutual evaluation among team members. Team members want not only to be praised but also to receive just rewards for their efforts, and this means that the evaluation system must be easy to understand and transparent. Although every team leader should encourage dialogue and discussion, things do not always go as they should in everyday life and in practice. Due to insufficiently developed communication skills or for other reasons, such as the high complexity of the work and/or lack of time, managers and their teams often fail to communicate effectively. Without appropriate tools, the complexity of organisational tasks and challenges usually leaves insufficient time for dialogue and discussion, as well as for team members to evaluate each other.

Even when there is time for open communication and leaders encourage communication, many people are often reluctant to express their opinions for fear that their comments will cause conflict. Therefore, the integral communication framework (ICF) provides tremendously important support to managers, leaders, and anyone else who seeks to improve communication and interaction within a particular group of people. While HR managers are able to use integral maps to track the characteristics and development of their people, quality managers can create integral product, service, place, and/or event maps to manage quality. For example, a quality manager decides to create an integral product map filled with tags that describe the product. Using the code QR on the product and/or the receipt, all shoppers are asked to rate the product. The product tags that receive the highest score are the ones that best describe the product. In contrast, the tags with more negative than positive ratings show the product features that need improvement. Evaluators can rate existing tags or suggest new ones, while administrators receive notifications of all comments and ratings, which can be downloaded as quality improvement reports.

An ideal member represents a role model for group members and is described by (horizontal and vertical/developmental) characteristics (e.g., tags) that members of that specific group should have according to the administrator. While the concept of ideal type is not a complete novelty, its practical application is. From 1904, when Max Weber first mentioned this

concept, until today, research on ideal types has developed rather sophisticated qualitative and quantitative models (Weber et al., 2017). Nowadays,
when human interaction can be supported by advanced artificial intelligence systems (e.g., machine learning and deep learning), it becomes
much easier to define an ideal type, find complementary partners and form
a project team. With increasing social complexity, the interdependence of
the members of a society increases (Tainter, 2017). For this reason, it is
particularly important to create a communication framework that fosters
personal development, collaboration, and organisational learning among
social actors. The concept of a desirable group member serves as a roadmap for initiating, planning, and implementing various improvement
activities (Swedberg, 2017). A group administrator not only manages
access to the group and the content that group members share with each
other, but also sets goals (e.g., in the form of tags) and time intervals at
which group members can rate someone or something (e.g., through
selected tags), which determines development dynamics. During the rating process, users can rate existing tags positively or negatively and suggest
new tags. For example, a human resources manager decided to assign tags
to employees indicating their current contribution to the organisation's
development (e.g., stars, backbones, icebergs, and problem children).
Since the ICF only wants to promote positive qualities, a negative assessment of a person or organisation does not always have to be publicly visible. Depending on the occasion, the results of ratings may be visible to
end users or only to the administrator of a group in which a particular user
has been rated. The fifth step is related to employee development and
career management and involves identifying the characteristics and preferences of each employee. Career management and employee development
imply the personalised distribution of content, tests, educational materials,
web links, and any other information that could help employees in their
professional development.

In addition, managers can use the ICF to determine relatively easily
which potential candidates best meet the requirements for a job. To do
this, they just need to create a group "Potential Employees" and define
the properties of an ideal group member. The sixth step relates to obtaining feedback. The term 'feedback' is used to describe helpful information
or criticism about a person's past actions or behaviours that is communicated to another person (or group) who can use that information to adjust
and improve current and future actions and behaviours (DeFranzo, 2015).
Dynamic insights into customer experiences when visiting events and

stores or using products and services improve perceptual capabilities and accelerate response time. In addition, strategic use of feedback enables the seventh step, which implies quality management. Quality management decides which individual and organisational characteristics are most important to measure and how they should be measured. An integral communication framework provides the opportunity to describe and evaluate many different employees, groups, products, services, places, and events through different tags, with minimal effort and cost for both the evaluators and those who want to be evaluated. The eighth step is to export an organisation's map and/or specific ratings to external locations, such as websites and social networks. If several thousand users rate product and service features positively, it is in the interest of companies to publish this information. The ninth step, called direct marketing, is based on personalised communication with users who have tags that match a topic the company wants to promote. The tenth step relates to recruiting and identifying talent. If a legal entity sets up a recruiting group and describes the characteristics of an ideal candidate, anyone who joins the group can easily identify what skills, knowledge, and other attributes are expected for that specific job. In addition, legal entities can provide educational materials and independently create tests or select existing tests that can be helpful in selecting their candidates. Of course, all of the aforementioned functions are connected to the eleventh step of integral networking for organisational users, which is management. After implementing integral networking, management is able to identify and visualise a lot of new and useful information (e.g. skills, interests and preferences) that can be used to optimise business processes, such as employee training, motivation and quality management. Most workers tend to change their own goals and preferences over time. Although there are always some exceptions, younger workers (e.g., Millennials) tend to be somewhat more likely to travel for business, in contrast to older workers (e.g., Generation X and Y) who view business travel as a necessity rather than a privilege (Castillo, 2022). While some attitudes and preferences are permanent and consistent, others change relatively frequently. In practice, there are many employees who would prefer to work in a different department or on a different project than the one they are currently assigned to. Such and similar information is very important for motivation and management of human potential. By using dynamic integral mapping, management can easily identify changes in employee preferences and propose solutions that align with employees' personal goals. Organisations that encourage their customers and users to communicate in an integral way significantly improve their social perception and organisational learning.

The human ability to recognize the actions, feelings, and intentions of others is the cornerstone of social life (Grèzes & Gelder, 2009). Organisational learning occurs when available information is used to achieve specific goals (e.g., better environmental performance, reducing costs, discovering new opportunities and perspectives, improving the user experience, etc.). Integral networking opens up many new opportunities for personalization of various products and services (e.g., restaurant menu, hotel room, web portal, medical care, etc.) and improves quality management, human resource management, and organisational development. More accurate information about customers, group members, products, services, employees, partners and citizens, means more opportunities to improve communication, collaboration and quality. Although it relies on the IT infrastructure to help improve how social actors communicate with IoT and AI devices, one of the main goals of integral networking is certainly to improve the quality of face-to-face communication. Insight into a person's emotional state, skills, and desires opens up many new opportunities to deepen live conversations. By sharing feedback on their own experiences, social actors help each other identify perspectives and uncover blind spots that would otherwise remain invisible.

Apart from the advantages and opportunities identified, integral networking certainly has some dangers and weaknesses that should be reconsidered. After analysing the problems and risks associated with integral networking, the authors identified several different weaknesses and threats using empirical results and secondary sources. The main weaknesses of integral networking are related to addictive user behaviour, privacy and security issues, filter bubbles, social distancing, and fear. The main threats are related to autocratic and unauthorised control, infrastructure issues, crime issues, and technological change. To avoid textual overlap, these topics will be discussed in detail in the next chapter, entitled "Integral Communication Framework".

FUTURE RESEARCH DIRECTIONS

An initial analysis of user attitudes toward integral networking shows that both end users and organisational users are interested in integral networking. This is especially true for educational and business organisations. Considering that integral networking can be applied in a wide range of activities not covered by this empirical study, further research is needed. In future research, it would be interesting to find answers to the following question:

- How does (sub)cultural background affect users' attitudes toward integral networking?
- In which activities does integral networking bring the greatest benefits?
- In which industries is there the greatest demand for integral networking?
- What is the impact of integral networking on social relationships?
- What measurement tools and tests are most effective in integral assessment?
- How does integral networking affect face-to-face communication?
- How does integral networking improve users' bargaining power?
- To what extent does integral networking enable cost reduction?
- To what extent does integral networking improve the reliability of the information presented?
- How does integral networking affect the quality of interpersonal relationships?
- To what extent does integral networking improve recruitment?
- How does integral networking improve the adoption of learning outcomes?
- To what extent does integral networking improve the quality of public services?

CONCLUSION

Networks in which different social actors have the opportunity to evaluate information, express their preferences, and display, measure, and improve their personal attributes provide fertile ground for overall socioeconomic development. The empirical study of users' attitudes towards integral networking, based on 772 respondents from the Republic of Croatia, identified three main factors of integral networks, namely integral presentation, integral evaluation and integral development. Although all categories of respondents showed a fairly strong interest in participating in integral networks, this interest is slightly stronger among organisational users than among end users. Such a result was to be expected. It is fairly clear that implementing integral networks, at least in the short term, may provide more tangible benefits to organisations than to end users. Given that more than one-third of end users and nearly half of organisational users were interested in integral presentation, the research findings confirmed the main hypothesis that members of a network community want to present themselves in an integral way in an online environment so that other members can find them for collaboration. The analysis showed that male and female respondents' attitudes toward integral networks did not differ significantly, with the exception that women were slightly more committed to integral development. The hypothesis that members of a network society will want to apply integral assessment in their interactions with other members was also confirmed. Considering that slightly less than one-third of end users and two-thirds of organisational users were interested in applying integral assessment in their interactions with other members, the research findings suggest that interest in integral assessment was significantly stronger among organisations than among end users. The fact that about one-third of end users recognised the benefits of integral assessment suggests that there is potential for the development and application of various tools that could facilitate feedback sharing and user assessment. The hypothesis that members of a network society want to engage in integral development was confirmed by the fact that more than one third of end users and organisational users were willing to apply activities that would promote their integral development. The analysis conducted showed that educational and private organisations were more interested in integral presentation and development than public organisations, but also that there were no statistically significant differences in attitudes toward integral assessment among selected types of organisational users. The conducted research indicates that in today's society a considerable number of social actors are interested in a priori exchange of personal characteristics and preferences and in anonymous a posteriori exchange of experiences that can qualitatively improve their interaction. The expected contribution of the conducted empirical research is reflected in the improvement of the understanding of users' attitudes towards integral networking. Integral networks can be used in civil, business, educational, and public domains. The key benefits of integral networking are improved presentation experience, better understanding of others, easy identification of personal interests, improved quality, personal mastery, time and resource savings, improved collaboration experience, improved control over personal data, improved talent search and employment experience, better communication with AI and IoT devices, and multilingualism. The main limitations of the empirical research conducted are a relatively small number of descriptive variables used to describe end users and a relatively small number of organisational users included in the research sample. Future research should attempt to describe the sample in more detail and include a larger number of organisational users from different industries. This will allow researchers to analyse which social actors have the greatest need for integral networking. Another limitation of the conducted research is the fact that respondents from different cultural environments and locations might have different attitudes towards integral networking. Despite these shortcomings, there is no doubt that the presented results of this preliminary research pave the way for future research on this interesting topic.

Key Terms and Definitions

Integral assessment: A set of procedures that improve accuracy and confidence in all information presented. There are several types of integral assessment that can be used on different occasions. The three basic types of assessment are subjective (e.g., a peer-to-peer assessment), objective (e.g., an official review), and automated (e.g., GPS) assessment.

Integral development: A set of activities that develop the potential of users in all aspects of their well-being. The ultimate purpose of integral development is to provide automated insight into all things users should improve, as well as links to materials and educators qualified to teach these topics.

Integral map: A dynamic set of information about user characteristics and preferences. These cards represent dynamic information filters that allow users to find and/or search for information that matches their personal interests.

Integral networking: A specific type of group interaction supported by an integral communication framework. Integral networking is based on the idea that integral tagging of products, services, places, events, people, and organisations is the simplest and most effective way of networking in the IoT environment.

Integral network: A set of interconnected nodes (e.g., people, organisations, products, services, locations, events, etc.) within the ICF that have complementary and compatible tags indicating some potential for collaboration.

Integral presentation: A set of activities that allow users to make their positive attributes and preferences related to all aspects of their personality publicly visible on the Internet through a unified set of keywords and symbols in multiple languages. The integral presentation enables a comprehensive representation of users in all dimensions and aspects of their personality.

Appendix 1

Table 4   Statements used to measure the three main factors of integral networking for end users

Factor	Statement
Integral assessment	I would like to invite friends to anonymously rate my personal characteristics so that I can get feedback about myself from as many of them as possible.
	I would like my friends to anonymously rate my personal characteristics several times at certain intervals so that I can monitor the dynamics of my personal development.
	I want my friends to be able to rate my personal characteristics anonymously so I can find out which characteristics I need to improve.
	I would like to anonymously evaluate the personal characteristics of my friends to help them develop and improve their personal and professional lives.
	I would like colleagues in a group I belong to evaluate me anonymously several times at certain intervals so that I can find out if my personal characteristics are changing.
	I would like colleagues from a group I belong to rate me anonymously so I know what personal characteristics I need to strengthen.
	I would like to anonymously evaluate the colleagues of the group I belong to in order to help them develop and improve their personal and professional lives.
	I would like to anonymously rate the characteristics of products, services, places, events, employers, professors, politicians, and other people I have dealt with to help others make better decisions.
Integral presentation	I want to find out how complementary I am with others so I can choose who to collaborate with.
	I want to find out how compatible (similar) I am with others so I can choose who to collaborate with.
	I would like my positive personal characteristics to be publicly visible on the Internet in several languages so that others can find me and/or choose to work with me.
	I would like to present myself on the Internet with keywords that describe my personality, knowledge, professional experience and other characteristics so that other users can find me for collaboration.
	I want to represent my preferences (desires) using keywords – personal characteristics so that others can help me achieve them.
	I want to know the positive characteristics of different subjects and objects so that I can make better decisions.

(*continued*)

Table 4 (continued)

Factor	Statement
Personal development	I would like to receive content (e.g., links, articles, educational materials, information about seminars and workshops, etc.) that will support the development of my personal characteristics.
	I would like to take tests to evaluate my personal characteristics several times at certain intervals in order to track the dynamics of my personal development.
	I would like to take tests to evaluate my personal characteristics to find out what qualities I need to strengthen.
	I want to find out what position I occupy in a group when my personal characteristics and the characteristics of a desirable group member match, so that as a member of that group I can reinforce those desirable characteristics.
	I want to find out how close my personal characteristics are to those that are desirable to group members, so that as a member of that group I can reinforce those desirable characteristics.

Source: Made by authors

Table 5 Statements used to measure the three main factors of integral networking for organisational users

Factor name	Statement
Integral assessment	We would like to give our customers the opportunity to anonymously evaluate our products and services based on a number of predefined characteristics in order to identify in which of these characteristics we excel and in which we need to improve.
	We want our clients and customers to be able to evaluate our employees (e.g., vendors, service providers, trainers, drivers, etc.) on a set of predefined characteristics so that we can motivate them and monitor their contribution to strategic goals, or to identify which employees need additional professional training and development. (For educational institutions changed to: We would like to invite students and employers to anonymously rate our services so that we can get feedback from as many of them as possible)
	We want to reward customers and clients who have anonymously rated our products, services and employees to motivate them to participate in the rating process.[a]
	We want our employees to be able to anonymously rate each other on a set of predefined characteristics (e.g., desirable attributes of a team member, etc.) so that we can monitor the quality of relationships and collaboration in our organisation, build teams of compatible and complementary people, and/or redirect employees to specific jobs that match their skills and preferences.[a]
	We intend to periodically use various measurement tools (e.g., tests) to assess characteristics of existing and potential employees, products, services, places, and events in order to increase the quality of assessment in various decisions relevant to our overall business performance.

(continued)

Table 5 (continued)

Factor name	Statement
Integral presentation	We want to have a dynamic set of information about our clients and customers (e.g., information about their personal characteristics, knowledge, work, purchases, and preferences) in order to customise and personalise our products and services.
	We would like to have access to publicly available personal characteristics and preferences of various physical persons (e.g., creative, proficient in a particular foreign language, has a particular degree, wants to work in a particular industry, etc.) in order to find and select new potential employees.
	We want to specify the qualities we are looking for in a particular job and post them as job openings in order to find potential applicants who most closely match that job and/or to help others identify the desirable qualities for that particular job.
	We want to present ourselves on the Internet using keywords (e.g., reliable, creative, user-friendly, accessible, etc.) that describe our products, services, organisational characteristics, knowledge, skills, and experience so that other users (e.g., potential customers, clients, partners, and employees) can find us to begin a business or other type of collaboration.
	We want to create/share content (e.g., news, articles, video clips, etc.) that is directly or indirectly related to our products and services and that will be sent or presented to all other users who have the same or similar interests.
	We want positive attributes of our products, services, and employees to be publicly visible on the Internet in multiple languages so that others (e.g., your potential customers, partners, and students, etc.) can find and select us as a desirable performer, partner, or employer.
	We want to know how compatible (similar) we are with others (e.g., same interests, same skills and knowledge, same work, etc.) in order to select those we want to collaborate with.
	We want to know the extent to which we are complementary with others (e.g., We have the knowledge, skills, interests, credentials that others seek, or others have what we seek) in order to select those with whom we want to collaborate with.

(*continued*)

Table 5 (continued)

Factor name	Statement
Integral development	We want to create/share content (e.g., articles, web links, etc.) that supports the improvement of desirable attributes for a particular profession to help others (e.g., students) with their personal development.
	We would like to receive content (e.g., internet links, articles, educational materials, information about seminars and workshops, etc.) that supports the development of our skills and characteristics.
	We would like to create different groups (e.g. for a specific workplace, a specific type of customer, etc.) and invite all interested parties to these groups so that we can send these members the content that is important for this type of (group) interaction.
	We would like to join various groups that we think are interesting (e.g., cluster of manufacturers, exporters association, etc.) so that we can identify and track content intended for those groups.
	We want to find out how close our own characteristics are to those of a desirable (ideal) group member, so that we can strengthen and develop ourselves as a member of that group.

Source: Made by authors

[a]Not measured for educational organisations

Table 6   The main characteristics of end users

Respondent type		Respondent characteristic	N	%
Students			577	86.8
	Gender	Male	251	43.5
		Female	324	56.2
		Undefined	2	0.3
	Faculty type	Road traffic – Polytechnic of Rijeka	44	7.6
		Management / Entrepreneurship / Marketing – Faculty of Economics in Rijeka	54	9.4
		Psychology – Faculty of Humanities and Social Sciences in Rijeka	43	7.5
		Pedagogy – Faculty of Humanities and Social Sciences in Zagreb	3	0.5
		Informatics – Polytechnic of Rijeka	58	10.1
		Medicine / Dental medicine – Faculty of Medicine in Rijeka	1	0.2
		Pharmacy / Dental medicine – University of Split	16	2.8
		Faculty of Informatics and Digital Technologies / Faculty of Humanities and Social Sciences in Rijeka	5	0.9
		Faculty of Informatics and Digital Technologies in Rijeka	119	20.6
		Department of Technical Studies – Juraj Dobrila University in Pula	7	1.2
		Entrepreneurship – Polytechnic of Rijeka	115	19.9
		Logistics and Management / Transport – Faculty of Maritime Studies in Rijeka	33	5.7
		Nutrition – Faculty of Food Technology and Biotechnology in Zagreb	6	1
		Mathematics / Geophysics / Geography – Faculty of Science in Zagreb	4	0.7
		Electrical engineering – Technical Faculty in Rijeka	1	0.2
		Telematics – Polytechnic of Rijeka	52	9
	Field of science	Technical science	148	25.6
		Social science	401	69.5
		Other	28	4.9
Physical persons			88	13.2
	Gender	Male	44	50
		Female	44	50

Source: Made by authors

Table 7   The main characteristics of organisational users

Respondent type		Respondent characteristic	N	%
Business			37	34.57
organisations	Size	Large (≥250 employees)	5	13.5
		Medium-sized (<250 employees and turnover ≤ € 50 or balance sheet total ≤ € 43 m)	8	21.6
		Small (<50 employees and turnover or balance sheet total ≤ € 10 m)	6	16.2
		Micro (<10 employees and turnover or balance sheet total ≤ € 2 m)	18	48.6
	Industry	Educational Services	1	2.7
		Accommodation and Food Services	5	13.5
		Finance and Insurance	1	2.7
		Healthcare and Social Assistance	2	5.4
		Information	2	5.4
		Manufacturing	4	10.8
		Other	2	5.4
		Professional, Scientific and Technical Services	10	27
		Retail Trade	3	8.1
		Security & Safety	1	2.7
		Utilities	2	5.4
		Wholesale Trade	4	10.8
	Respondents' functions and positions	Branch manager	1	2.7
		Chief executive officer (CEO)	7	18.9
		Consultant	3	8.1
		Finance manager	1	2.7
		HR manager	4	10.8
		Marketing manager	1	2.7
		Owner or Co-owner	12	32.4
		Procurator	1	2.7
		Project manager	1	2.7
		Quality manager	1	2.7
		Recruiter	2	5.4
		Sales manager	3	8.1

(*continued*)

Table 7 (continued)

Respondent type		Respondent characteristic	N	%
Public			33	30.84
organisations	Size	Large (≥250 employees)	5	15.2
		Medium (less than 250 employees)	1	3
		Small (less than 50 employees)	7	21.2
		Micro (less than 10 employees)	20	60.6
	Respondents'	Employee	3	9.1
	functions and	Head / Director / Mayor /	14	42.4
	positions	Prefect		
		Head of Department / Head of	11	33.3
		Organisational Unit		
		Officer	4	12.1
		Senior Officer / Inspector	1	3
	Public sector	Culture	8	24.2
		Local Government	12	36.4
		Public health	4	12.1
		State administration	2	6.1
		Tourism	7	21,2
Educational			37	34.57
organisations	Type of organisation	Business school	2	5.4
		Faculty	16	43.2
		Other	5	13.5
		Polytechnic	4	10.8
		Scientific institute	1	2.7
		University	9	24.3
	Respondents'	Career Counsellor	5	13.5
	functions and	Faculty Management	7	18.9
	positions	Head of Internship department	5	13.5
		Head of Quality Department	3	8.1
		Professors and teaching staff	17	45.9

Source: Made by authors

References

Accenture. (2013). *Accenture 2013 Global Consumer Pulse Survey.* Global & U.S. Key Finding. Accenture. Retrieved October 1, 2019, from https://www. accenture.com/t20150523T052453__w__/us-en/_acnmedia/Accenture/ Conversion-Assets/DotCom/Documents/Global/PDF/Strategy_3/ Accenture-Global-Consumer-Pulse-Research-Study-2013-Key-Findings.pdf

Aladeojebi, T. K. (2013). Planned obsolescence. *International Journal of Scientific & Engineering Research, 4*(6), 1504–1508. Retrieved May 12, 2019, from https://www.ijser.org/researchpaper/Planned-Obsolescence.pdf

Al Bashir, M., Kabir, R., & Rahman, I. (2016). The value and effectiveness of feedback in improving students' learning and professionalizing teaching in higher education. *Journal of Education and Practice, 7*(16), 38–41. Retrieved May 19, 2021, from https://www.researchgate.net/publication/ 347963917_The_Value_and_Effectiveness_of_Feedback_in_Improving_ Students'_Learning_and_Professionalizing_Teaching_in_Higher_Education

Allam, H., Blustein, J., Bliemel, M., & Spiteri, L. (2012). Exploring factors impacting users' attitude and intention towards social tagging systems. In *2012 45th Hawaii International Conference on System Sciences* (pp. 3129–3138). https://doi.org/10.1109/hicss.2012.267

Anant, V., Donchak, L., Kaplan, J., & Soller, H. (2020). *The consumer-data opportunity and the privacy imperative.* McKinsey. Retrieved July 15, 2023, from https://www.mckinsey.com/capabilities/risk-and-resilience/our-insights/ the-consumer-data-opportunity-and-the-privacy-imperative

Anderson, J. C., & Narus, J. A. (1998, November 14). Business marketing: Understand what customers value. *Harvard Business Review.* Retrieved October 5, 2022, from https://hbr.org/1998/11/business-marketing- understand-what-customers-value

Appelo, J. (2011). *Management 3.0: Leading Agile developers, developing Agile leaders.* Addison-Wesley.

Ballantyne, D. (2004). Dialogue and its role in the development of relationship specific knowledge. *Journal of Business & Industrial Marketing, 19*(2), 114–123. https://doi.org/10.1108/08858620410523990

Benkler, Y., & Nissenbaum, H. (2006). Commons-based peer production and virtue. *The Journal of Political Philosophy, 4*(14), 394–419. https://doi. org/10.1111/j.1467-9760.2006.00235.x

Berberoglu, A. (2018). Impact of organizational climate on organizational commitment and perceived organizational performance: Empirical evidence from public hospitals. *BMC Health Services Research, 18*(1). https://doi. org/10.1186/s12913-018-3149-z

Blair, J. (2012, March 23). *A positive work climate: It's the real key to organizational success.* Retrieved August 8, 2021, from https://www.tlnt. com/a-positive-work-climate-its-the-real-key-to-organizational-success/

Boring, A., Ottoboni, K., & Stark, P. (2016). Student evaluations of teaching (mostly) do not measure teaching effectiveness. *ScienceOpen Research*, 1–11. https://doi.org/10.14293/s2199-1006.1.sor-edu.aetbzc.v1

Boswijk, A., Peelen, E., & Olthoft, S. (2012). *Economy of experiences* (3rd ed.). European Centre for the Experience and Transformation Economy. Retrieved August 11, 2023, from https://www.confindustria.pu.it/$file/_id1/17/_id2/0000011665.pdf

Botha, A. (2014). Framework to enhance the mobile user experience of goal orientated interactions. In K. Rızvanoğlu & G. Çetin (Eds.), *Research and design innovations for mobile user experience* (pp. 47–75). IGI Global. https://doi. org/10.4018/978-1-4666-4446-5.ch003

Botsch, R. E. (2009). *Significance and measures of association.* Retrieved February 1, 2022, from http://polisci.usca.edu/apls301/Text/Chapter%2012.%20 Significance%20and%20Measures%20of%20Association.htm

Böhm, F., & Kamali, A. (2014). *Vitra everything is connected: Home collection.* Vitra AG.

Bracken, D. W. (2019). What is "strategic 360 feedback"? In A. H. Church, D. W. Bracken, J. H. Fleenor, & D. S. Rose (Eds.), *Handbook of strategic 360 feedback* (pp. 11–16). Oxford University Press. https://doi.org/10.1093/oso/9780190879860.003.0002

Castillo, À. (2022, June 23). *5 ways millennials are reshaping the Business Travel Industry.* Travel Perk. Retrieved August 8, 2022, from https://www.travelperk. com/blog/millennials-are-reshaping-the-business-travel-industry-heres-how/

Cedefop. (2015). *Skills, qualifications and jobs in the EU: The making of a perfect match? Evidence from Cedefop's European skills and jobs survey.* Publications Office. Cedefop reference series; No 103. https://doi.org/10.2801/606129

Chakkol, M., Johnson, M., & Finne, M. (2017). *Understanding the psychology of collaboration: What makes an effective collaborator?* Institute for Collaborative Working. Retrieved June 6, 2022, https://instituteforcollaborativeworking. com/resources/Documents/understanding_the_psychology_of_collaboration.pdf

Cohen, J. (1988). *Statistical power analysis for the behavioral sciences.* Routledge Academic.

Crabtree, S. (2013). *Worldwide, 13% of employees are engaged at work – Low workplace engagement offers opportunities to improve business outcomes.* Gallup. Retrieved May 3, 2019, from https://news.gallup.com/poll/165269/worldwide-employees-engaged-work.aspx

Dantas, D. C., & Carrillat, F. (2013). The relational benefits of Personalized Communications in an online environment. *Canadian Journal of Administrative Sciences / Revue Canadienne Des Sciences de l'Administration, 30*(3), 189–202. https://doi.org/10.1002/cjas.1254

DeFranzo, S. E. (2015, July 1). *5 reasons why feedback is important.* Snap Surveys. Retrieved June 2, 2019, from https://www.snapsurveys.com/blog/5-reasons-feedback-important/

Deloitte. (2021). *Dynamic Markets Unlocking small business innovation and growth through the rise of the personalized economy.* Deloitte. Retrieved July 5, 2023, from https://istasyon.fb.com/tr/wp-content/uploads/sites/56/2022/09/dynamic-markets-deloitte-report.pdf

Deloitte. (2023). *Connecting with meaning Hyper-personalizing the customer experience using data, analytics, and AI.* Deloitte. Retrieved July 14, 2023. from https://www2.deloitte.com/content/dam/Deloitte/ca/Documents/deloitte-analytics/ca-en-omnia-ai-marketing-pov-fin-jun24-aoda.pdf

DZS. (2021). *Studenti upisani na stručni i sveučilišni studij u zimskom semestru ak. god. 2020/2021* [Students enrolled in professional and university studies in the winter semester of the academic year 2020/2021]. Retrieved February 2, 2022, from https://podaci.dzs.hr/2021/hr/9960

DZS. (2022). *Aktivno stanovništvo u Republici Hrvatskoj u 2021* [Active population in the Republic of Croatia in 2021]. Retrieved February 4, 2022, from https://podaci.dzs.hr/2022/hr/29256

EC. (2015). *Creating value through open data: Study on the impact of re-use of public data resources.* European Commission & European Data Portal. https://doi.org/10.2759/328101. Retrieved July 14, 2023, from https://data.europa.eu/sites/default/files/edp_creating_value_through_open_data_0.pdf

Epsilon. (2018). *The power of me: The impact of personalization on marketing performance.* Slideshare. Retrieved July 11, 2023, from https://www.slideshare.net/EpsilonMktg/the-power-of-me-the-impact-of-personalization-on-marketing-performance

Fenwick, K. M., Brimhall, K. C., Hurlburt, M., & Aarons, G. (2019). Who wants feedback? Effects of transformational leadership and leader-member exchange on mental health practitioners' attitudes toward feedback. *Psychiatric Services, 70*(1), 11–18. https://doi.org/10.1176/appi.ps.201800164

Fishenden, J., & Thompson, M. (2012). Digital government, open architecture, and innovation: Why public sector it will never be the same again. *Journal of Public Administration Research and Theory, 23*(4), 977–1004. https://doi.org/10.1093/jopart/mus022

Gallup. (2022). *World Risk Poll 2021: A digital world perceptions of risk from AI and misuse of personal data.* Lloyd's Register Foundation. Retrieved July 3, 2023, from https://wrp.lrfoundation.org.uk/LRF_2021_report_a-digtial-world-ai-and-personal-data_online_version.pdf

Gesk, T. S., & Leyer, M. (2022). Artificial intelligence in public services: When and why citizens accept its usage. *Government Information Quarterly, 39*(3), 101704. https://doi.org/10.1016/j.giq.2022.101704

Getting, B. (2017, September 2). What are "tags" and what is "tagging?". *Practical Ecommerce.* Retrieved May 5, 2021, from https://www.practicalecommerce.com/what-are-tags-and-what-is-tagging

Gibson, K., & Cartwright, C. (2014). Young people's experiences of mobile phone text counselling: Balancing connection and control. *Children and Youth Services Review, 43*, 96–104. https://doi.org/10.1016/j.childyouth.2014.05.010

Golder, S. A., & Huberman, B. A. (2006). Usage patterns of collaborative tagging systems. *Journal of Information Science, 32*(2), 198–208. https://doi.org/10.1177/0165551506062337

Grèzes, J., & Gelder, B. D. (2009). Social perception: Understanding other people's intentions and emotions through their actions. In V. Reid & T. Striano (Eds.), *Social cognition: Development, neuroscience, and autism* (pp. 1–13). Essay, Wiley-Blackwell.

Hawking, P. (2008). Enterprise resource planning systems in a global environment. In C. Ferran & R. Salim (Eds.), *Enterprise resource planning for global economies: Managerial issues and challenges* (pp. 23–36). IGI Global. https://doi.org/10.4018/978-1-59904-531-3.ch002

Hoffmann-Burdzińska, K., & Flak, O. (2016). Management by objectives as a method of measuring teams' effectiveness. *Journal of Positive Management, 6*(3), 67–82. https://doi.org/10.12775/jpm.2015.016

Jones, M. (2018, September 13). *How to stop data centers from gobbling up the world's electricity.* Retrieved June 6, 2022, https://www.nature.com/articles/d41586-018-06610-y

Kelly, J. C., Maheut, P., Petiot, J. F., & Papalambros, P. Y. (2011). Incorporating user shape preference in engineering design optimisation. *Journal of Engineering Design, 22*(9), 627–650. https://doi.org/10.1080/09544821003662601

Kettle, J. (2021, June 9). *The internet consumes extraordinary amounts of energy. Here's how we can make it more sustainable.* https://theconversation.com/the-internet-consumes-extraordinary-amounts-of-energy-heres-how-we-can-make-it-more-sustainable-160639

Kliatchko, J. G. (2020). *Integrated Marketing Communication: Putting the human person at the Core.* Cambridge Scholars Publishing.

Knight, W. (2018). The importance of user experience. In *UX for developers* (pp. 13–27). https://doi.org/10.1007/978-1-4842-4227-8_2

Kuyyogsuy, S. (2019). Students' attitudes toward peer feedback: Paving a way for students' English writing improvement. *English Language Teaching, 12*(7), 107. https://doi.org/10.5539/elt.v12n7p107

Kwibisa, N., & Majzoub, S. (2018). Challenges faced in inter-organizational collaboration process. A Case Study of Region Skåne. *Journal of Sustainable Development, 11*(5), 34. https://doi.org/10.5539/jsd.v11n5p34

Leben, W. R. (2018). Languages of the world. In *Oxford research encyclopedia of linguistics.* https://doi.org/10.1093/acrefore/9780199384655.013.349

Luthra, A., & Dahiya, R. (2015). Effective leadership is all about communicating effectively: Connecting leadership and communication. *International Journal of Management & Business Studies, 5*(3), 43–48. Retrieved January 8, 2019, from https://www.mcgill.ca/engage/files/engage/effective_leadership_is_all_about_communicating_effectively_luthra_dahiya_2015.pdf

Maurer, T. J., Mitchell, D. R., & Barbeite, F. G. (2002). Predictors of attitudes toward a 360-degree feedback system and involvement in post-feedback management development activity. *Journal of Occupational and Organizational Psychology, 75*(1), 87–107. https://doi.org/10.1348/096317902167667

Mishra, S. (2020). Listening as a leadership tool: A survey of subordinates' perception towards listening skills of effective leaders. *Journal of Xidian University, 14*(6), 1410–1417. https://doi.org/10.37896/jxu14.6/170

Mulliner, E., & Tucker, M. (2015). Feedback on feedback practice: Perceptions of students and academics. *Assessment & Evaluation in Higher Education, 42*(2), 266–288. https://doi.org/10.1080/02602938.2015.1103365

Nam, H., & Kannan, P. K. (2014). The informational value of social tagging networks. *Journal of Marketing, 78*(4), 21–40. https://doi.org/10.1509/jm.12.0151

Nicol, D. (2010). From monologue to dialogue: Improving written feedback processes in mass higher education. *Assessment & Evaluation in Higher Education, 35*(5), 501–517. https://doi.org/10.1080/02602931003786559

Normore, L., & Blaylock, B. (2009). Opinions on the use and value of social tagging. *Proceedings of the American Society for Information Science and Technology, 46*(1), 1–8. https://doi.org/10.1002/meet.2009.1450460384

OECD. (2019). *The OECD Going Digital Toolkit, based on the OECD Digital Government Index.* https://oe.cd/dgi-2019

Orrell, J. (2006). Feedback on learning achievement: Rhetoric and reality. *Teaching in Higher Education, 11*(4), 441–456. https://doi.org/10.1080/13562510600874235

Papadopoulos, S., Vakali, A., & Kompatsiaris, Y. (2011). Community detection in collaborative tagging systems. In *Community-Built Databases* (pp. 107–131). https://doi.org/10.1007/978-3-642-19047-6_5

Prakash Nunna, B. (2020). A new paradigm in customer relationship management. In D. Dintsis (Ed.), *Customer relationship management and IT.* IntechOpen. https://doi.org/10.5772/intechopen.90389

Rafajac, O., & Jakupović, A. (2017). Integral communication tool: What it is, how it works, where it helps? *The International Journal of e-Collaboration, 13*(3), 1–20. https://doi.org/10.4018/IJeC.2017070101

Remtulla, K. A. (2012). Congruency in higher learning: Developing sustainable adult education program policies for the digital age. In V. Wang (Ed.), *Encyclopedia of E-leadership, counseling and training* (pp. 680–697). IGI Global. https://doi.org/10.4018/978-1-61350-068-2.ch050

Raymond, E. S. (2001). *The cathedral & the bazaar musings on Linux and open source by an accidental revolutionary* (1st ed.). O'Reilly Media.

Rogers, C. R., & Farson, R. E. (1957). Active listening. In R. G. Newman, M. A. Danziger, & M. Cohen (Eds.), *Communication in business today.* Heath and Company, 1987. https://wholebeinginstitute.com/wp-content/uploads/Rogers_Farson_Active-Listening.pdf

Ruskin, J. (2022). *Stones of Venice.* Hansebooks Gmbh.

Samuel, A. (2019, November 19). What happened to tagging? *JSTOR Daily.* Retrieved November 5, 2022, from https://daily.jstor.org/what-happened-to-tagging/

Senge, P. M. (2006). *The fifth discipline: The Art & Practice of the learning organization.* Random House Business.

Slade, G. (2007). *Made to break technology and obsolescence in America.* Harvard University Press.

Sojung, L. K., & Thompson, S. H. T. (2013). Lessons from software development ecosystems: South Korea's E-government open source initiative. *MIS Quarterly Executive, 12*(2), 93–108. Retrieved May 10, 2016, from https://aisel.aisnet.org/misqe/vol12/iss2/5

Stacho, Z., Stachová, K., Papula, J., Papulová, Z., & Kohnová, L. (2019). Effective communication in organisations increases their competitiveness. *Polish Journal of Management Studies, 19*(1), 391–403. https://doi.org/10.17512/pjms.2019.19.1.30

Swedberg, R. (2017). How to use Max Weber's ideal type in sociological analysis. *Journal of Classical Sociology, 18*(3), 181–196. https://doi.org/10.1177/1468795x17743643

Tainter, J. A. (2017). *The collapse of complex societies.* Cambridge University Press.

Tileagă, C., & Oprișan, O. (2021). Personalization – A key element in creating better customer experiences. *Expert Journal of Business and Management, 9*(2), 88–94.

Treiblmaier, H., & Pollach, I. (2007). Users' perceptions of benefits and costs of personalization. *ICIS 2007 Proceedings,* 1–15. https://aisel.aisnet.org/icis2007/141

Umoh, U. E., & Etuk, E. N. (2016). Students' involvement in social networking and attitudes towards its integration into teaching. *International Education Studies, 9*(9), 250. https://doi.org/10.5539/ies.v9n9p250

UN. (2014). *United Nations E-government survey 2014. E-government for the future we want.* United Nations. Retrieved August 22, 2021, from http://unpan3.un.org/egovkb/Portals/egovkb/Documents/un/2014-Survey/E-Gov_Complete_Survey-2014.pdf.

Valant, J. (2016). *Planned obsolescence: Exploring the issue.* European Parliamentary Research Service, PE 581.999. Retrieved August 17, 2021, from http://www.europarl.europa.eu/RegData/etudes/BRIE/2016/581999/EPRS_BRI%282016%29581999_EN.pdf

Walker, D. A. (2003). JMASM9: Converting Kendall's Tau for correlational or meta-analytic analyses. *Journal of Modern Applied Statistical Methods, 2*(2), 525–530. https://doi.org/10.22237/JMASM/1067646360

Weber, M., Shils, E., Finch, H. A., Antonio, R. J., & Sica, A. (2017). *Methodology of social sciences.* Routledge.

Wolverton, T. (2018, July 23). *Google CEO Sundar Pichai revealed a jaw-dropping fact about its translation app that shows how much money is still sitting on the table.* Business Insider. Retrieved August 1, 2020, from https://www.businessinsider.com/sundar-pichai-google-translate-143-billion-words-daily-2018-7

Xu, Z., & Dukes, A. (2019). Product line design under preference uncertainty using aggregate consumer data. *Marketing Science, 38*(4), 669–689. https://doi.org/10.1287/mksc.2019.1160

Zacharias, V., Braun, S., & Schmidt, A. (2010). Social semantic bookmarking with SOBOLEO. In S. Murugesan (Ed.), *Handbook of research on Web 2.0, 3.0, and X.0: Technologies, business, and social applications* (pp. 225–241). IGI Global. https://doi.org/10.4018/978-1-60566-384-5.ch013

Žmuk, B. (2018). Impact of different questionnaire design characteristics on survey response rates: Evidence from Croatian Business Web Survey. *Stat, 98*(1), 69–87. Retrieved July 2, 2022, from https://www.czso.cz/documents/1018 0/61266317/32019718q1069.pdf/783a5863-4bf9-4f60-800e-209200ceb 9e3?version=1.0

Integral Communication Framework

Ozren Rafajac and Alen Jakupović

INTRODUCTION

The main problem with current digital platforms and applications that support networking, collaboration, and feedback sharing is that they are incompatible with each other. When education and recruitment platforms are incompatible, educational institutions fail to align educational programs with market needs, students struggle to find jobs, and employers struggle to find new employees. Today, most applications and web platforms operate as isolated ecosystems (e.g., Airbnb is focused on renting local homes, Uber on ride-sharing, and so on). Because they do not use a single digital identity, users are forced to create their own user profile on each of these platforms and build a reputation from scratch. In other words, this personal data and the reputation that the user has built up in one IT system cannot, as a rule, be transferred to another IT system and used there. Another problem arises from the fact that most of the current social networks do not reflect the complete image of the user. Although it is quite clear that networks based on incomplete and false information

O. Rafajac (✉) • A. Jakupović
Polytechnic of Rijeka, Rijeka, Croatia
e-mail: ozren.rafajac@veleri.hr; alen.jakupovic@veleri.hr

© The Author(s), under exclusive license to Springer Nature Switzerland AG 2024
O. Rafajac, A. Jakupović (eds.), *Integral Communication and Digital Identity*, https://doi.org/10.1007/978-3-031-47460-6_3

cannot provide quality, efficiency, and reliability, most social networks and online platforms today record only distorted images or snippets of a user's character, showing only individual pieces of the puzzle. Although there are some exceptions, from an end-user perspective, it is very impractical to manage multiple virtual profiles and accounts (Ranjan & Tarasia, 2013). In the near future, most IoT devices and AI systems will require users to identify themselves, which will put additional pressure on users to apply a single digital identity. Similarly, it is fairly certain that end users will not find it convenient to use different digital profiles in the applications that control their home appliances, office equipment, and personal cars, even if they are produced by different manufacturers. The World Bank estimates that currently more than one billion people do not have official identity documents (Beduschi, 2019). For this reason, there is no doubt that at some point in the near future, each person's virtual identity and legal identity will merge into a single integral digital identity that can be used in the private, educational, business, and public domains (World Bank, 2018). The only way to overcome these problems is to develop an integral digital identity (IDI) that describes the user in all aspects of his being. Unfortunately, there is currently no consensus on how this should or will be done.

This chapter explains how to design an integral communication framework that allows users to present themselves in all aspects of their personality and to exchange all important information in the simplest possible way. In general terms, a framework represents a real or conceptual structure that is intended to serve as a support or guide for building something that extends the structure into something useful (Paulsen, 2011, p. 534). A communication framework explains how social actors should communicate (e.g., to improve their perceptual ability and understanding). In practice, there are many different physical (e.g., working at a distance), emotional (e.g., trust and fear), and linguistic (e.g., verbal and nonverbal) barriers that make communication and collaboration very difficult (Martic, 2022). Because social actors can differ significantly in terms of their communication skills and styles, character, cultural background, experiences, knowledge, and preferences, successful communicators learn to recognize these differences and adapt their own style to the people with whom they want to communicate (Oliveira et al., 2022). To successfully address this issue, companies are enlisting the services of psychologists, communications and marketing experts to help them personalise their communications with different audiences. In a cross-level field study of 31 teams and

194 members examining the relationship between leaders' communication style and subordinates' commitment to change, Luo et al. (2016) found that hope orientation, subordinate orientation, and support orientation were positively associated with subordinates' affective commitment to change. In addition, in order to improve communication with their customers, many companies today use customer relationship management (CRM) systems. Nevertheless, the process of personalised communication still does not run smoothly. The vast majority of CRM systems are one-way and reactive. This means that users have only a small degree of control over their personal data used in the personalization process, and that changes in customer preferences are usually captured indirectly (e.g., not through the direct exchange of information, but through consumer activity). Although such information systems obviously help companies create personalised experiences, end users are generally unable to view and manage the data stored by such systems and are therefore reluctant to give their consent to data processing. According to a 2019 special Eurobarometer survey, 78% of respondents are either 'concerned' or 'very concerned' about the use of their personal data online (Mildebrath, 2022). The paradox for companies investing in personalization is hidden in the fact that the consumers who value information transparency the most are also the consumers who are less willing to be profiled online (Awad & Krishnan, 2006). Another example of internet and social media users' privacy concerns is all those users who provide false information to protect their privacy (Alashoor et al., 2017). All this data clearly shows that today's people need communication solutions that protect their privacy and allow direct control over private data they share with others.

Nowadays, social actors have to re-introduce themselves each time to experience personalised communication, and this is usually done through an interview, entering data into a form, and/or monitoring the consumption process. Apart from the fact that collecting information about users is very time-consuming and energy-consuming, reactive CRM systems usually do not collect data about user activities outside of mutual collaboration and therefore provide only partially correct and incomplete images of users. Nodes in the communication system are always connected by the information available about that node. When these nodes represent people, the heart of the communication network lies in the data that defines user identity. Although it can be defined in different ways, each identity consists of information. According to Fearon (1999), an identity represents a social category defined by rules of affiliation and (alleged) characteristic attributes or expected behaviours and/or socially distinctive features that a person is particularly proud of or considers unchangeable but socially consequential. However, individual identity is more than just a record of personal transactions. According to Sullivan (2011), a person's digital identity is a collection of defined information, a subset of which is the person's transactional identity. In the last two decades, more and more authors have discussed the need to create a unique digital identity. While the International Telecommunication Union asserts that the benefits of a digital identity system are greater convenience, ease of use, reduced cost of government services, and improved citizen engagement in government actions (ITU, 2018), there are authors such as Abdelal et al. (2006) who encourage creative thinking about identity and suggest that any definition of identity must address the issues of content and contestation. A digital identity can be defined as a set of digital records about a person's identity that enhance engagement in digital interactions. An integral digital identity is a set of records that describes social actors in all aspects of their personhood and enables integral communication in digitally supported interactions. This chapter is intended for anyone who wants to design, develop, and improve integral communication solutions, as well as for those who want to understand how the integral communication framework works.

After reading this chapter, the reader will be able to:

- Recognise the challenges of designing an integral communication framework.
- Define the integral communication framework.
- Identify different ways to map and visualise the integral identity.
- Discuss strengths, weaknesses, opportunities, and threats within an integral communication framework.
- Identify important questions about integral communication frameworks that need further investigation.

BACKGROUND

Today, more than ever before, a wide range of researchers are addressing the issues related to the formation of a virtual or digital identity (Laurent & Bouzefrane, 2015; Kamberg, 2019; Windley, 2023). Some of the most popular research questions in the field of digital identity today are: how does digital IT identity influence the formation and development of online communities and society in general? How can an effective user profile be created? How can the relevance of digital identity be improved? How can digital identity be used to improve quality and sustainability? What data is most commonly used for user profiling? How can relationships between different people and groups be visualised? According to Godoy and Amandi (2005), there are three basic methods for user profiling: the content-based method, which relies on the user's past behaviour; the collaborative filtering method, which assumes that users who belong to the same group (e.g., age, gender, or location) have similar characteristics and preferences; and the hybrid method, which combines the two aforementioned approaches. Identity refers to a person's self-definition ("who I am") and places it in a specific context (Ashforth, 2014). In daily life, individuals can identify their personal, interpersonal, and collective identities. Digital identity represents the digital version of a person's physical identity (Domingo & Enríquez, 2018). As described by Bargh and McKenna (2004), selective disclosure, easy insight into the characteristics of the interlocutor, and the ease of finding compatible and complementary relationships are some of the fundamental differences between online communication and face-to-face interactions (Walther, 2007). The recent popularity of social networks clearly demonstrates the need for virtual identities. Since identities of modern people are flexible and adaptable objects of negotiation within a given context (Jenkins, 2014), the use of virtual identities requires a constant comparison between individuals, the environment in which the interaction takes place, their intentions and the context of an interaction, and their "true" (nominal) identity (Code & Zaparyniuk, 2009).

Long ago, the famous Baron Kelvin said, "To measure is to know. If you can't measure it, you can't improve it." (Thomson, 1883, p. 73). Until recently, collecting, measuring, and analysing information (outside of a digital environment) were costly and complex processes. Nowadays, advanced digital technologies have changed the way people interact with information. In addition to automatically registering activity (e.g., Amazon personalised its homepage for each user based on their past searches, views, and purchases), one of the best ways to define a person's identity is to provide a means of self-expression within the digital interface that uses consistent keywords or tags. This trend began in 2007, when technology developer and self-proclaimed hashtag godfather Chris Messina suggested using this octothorpe sign as an indicator to group tweets around a common name (Panko, 2017). Other social media sites such as Instagram and

Facebook also adopted the hashtag, making it a nearly universal Internet symbol in just a decade (Panko, 2017). Today, approximately 125 million hashtags are used every day (Molina, 2017). The usefulness of uniform symbols to describe a person's identity is related to common search methods in the digital environment, which in most cases are performed using keywords or tags (organised into different filters) (Ta'amneh & Al-Ghazo, 2021). In the last two decades, many different authors, such as Riihimaa (2004), have tried to highlight that taxonomy can be used as a science of classifying things or concepts to improve communication between people and organisations (Riihimaa, 2004; Paljak, 2018). Nowadays, semantic taxonomies represent one of the most popular methods to organise knowledge about a given topic in the form of a hierarchy of concepts connected by linking generalisation and specialisation (Holi & Hyvoenen, 2006). Semantic taxonomies are used to structure data in various fields such as biology, medicine, law, Internet communication, and software development (Razis et al., 2021). In addition, the automated creation of taxonomies from textual sources is becoming increasingly popular, as in the case of the largest lexical database in the English language – WordNet (Paljak, 2018). Computer-mediated communication systems, also known as collaborative virtual environments (CVEs), enable geographically distant individuals to conduct verbal and nonverbal interactions in a shared virtual space and time (Bailenson et al., 2004). The intertwining with technology, which is omnipresent in almost all work, entertainment and communication activities, is increasingly blurring the boundaries between personal and virtual communication. Once they try a new feature or experience added value and higher quality, people expect the same everywhere else.

To improve the experience of their users and the overall quality of their products and services and/or to reduce costs and environmental impact, 47% of companies already use personalised communications (Segment, 2022). For this reason, solutions that enable identity mapping and improve personalised communication are becoming increasingly important. The research conducted is based on the paradigm of a collaborative virtual environment that changes nonverbal and verbal behaviour during social interaction. When regular social interaction is supported by the integral communication framework, it opens many new opportunities for personal development and organisational learning that cannot be achieved in other ways. This new ability to create an arbitrary identity in different contexts, with different intentions, and in different social groups leads to a new dynamic in human communication and evolution (Koole & Parchoma,

2012). In the last two decades, the field of organisational identity has gained popularity among researchers studying management and organisational behaviour. Studies of organisational identity focus on how organisations define themselves in their relationships with internal and external stakeholders, how self-definition emerges and evolves, and the implications of organisational identity for leadership and change (Pratt et al., 2016). The exploration of organisational identity (OI) leads to the fundamental questions of human existence, such as – Who are we and what are we becoming as a collective? It is a relational construct that connects concepts and ideas that are often viewed as opposing categories, such as "us" and "them" or "similarities and differences" (Pratt et al., 2016). Furthermore, it is an integrative concept that allows the identification of individual and group characteristics and relationships. Only when all stakeholders have the opportunity to show who they are, what they want, and what they think can leaders and managers truly identify and measure OI. The dynamic adaptation of user identities in relation to the group with which they identify promotes group formation and the identification of elements that connect these members, which in turn fosters the processes of socialisation, conflict resolution, and the development of relationships (Ashforth & Mael, 1989). Therefore, open communication about the various characteristics of personal and organisational identity is an important driver of (personal) development and organisational learning, enabling the deepening of dialogue about important (personal and organisational) issues (Korte, 2007).

DESIGN CHALLENGES

Integral design means the unification of all known theories and approaches that improve communication. This means that all past and future examples of best practices in communication and collaboration are a valuable resource for designing an integral communication system. Following the discussion of the integral methodology and the attitudes of potential users presented in the previous chapters, this chapter introduces the reader to the challenges of designing an integral communication framework and its key features. To improve perceptibility and collaboration among today's social actors, it was necessary to develop a communication framework based on an integral digital identity that can be used in as many social activities as possible. The first problem is that people haven't yet developed a communication framework that could help them exchange information about their attributes and preferences automatically, or at least with minimal investment of time and energy (Batmunkh, 2022). The second problem is that an integral communication framework should perform its tasks independently of the language used by the social actors. The inability of social actors to communicate in the same language greatly reduces their ability to improve social perception and cooperation (Zhang & Zhou, 2021). The third problem is that an integral communication framework should enable the implementation of various information evaluation strategies and techniques that enhance confidence in the information presented. The fewer the options and opportunities for evaluating information, the greater the room for manipulation, error, and corrupt behaviour (Bansal & Kohli, 2019; Rogers & Niederer, 2020). The fourth problem is that user information should be presented as simply as possible, but with the ability to provide detailed insights (Buttle & Maklan, 2019). The fifth problem is related to the need to prevent unwanted and/or illegal activities that integral communication can lead to (Drury et al., 2022). The transmission of negative feedback can in some cases lead to verbally aggressive and hostile reactions towards those who give this information (Geddes & Baron, 1997). This is a rather undesirable behaviour that prevents personal development and organisational learning.

This chapter is based on the two main hypotheses:

Hypothesis One: Integral communication framework improves communication.

Hypothesis Two: Integral communication framework prevents undesirable activities in integral communication.

The main goal of this research is to develop a special type of information system called an integral communication framework. It is generally accepted that studies in the field of information systems development have two main objectives: a theoretical contribution and an impact on solving current and expected practical problems (Benbasat & Zmud, 1999; Rosemann & Vessey, 2008). One of the best methodological approaches that successfully contributes to the achievement of these two goals is the Design Science Research (DSR) methodology (Hevner et al., 2004; Purao, 2002). The DSR methodology prescribes conducting of research through six elementary steps (Hevner & Chatterjee, 2010):

1. **Problem Identification and Motivation:** Specification of a research problem and motivation. The defined problem is used to develop an artefact that provides a solution.
2. **Defining the Objectives for a Solution:** Objectives can be quantitative and/or qualitative. Objectives are set on the basis of the problem definition.
3. **Design and Development:** Creation of the artefact. In this phase, the basic functions and architecture of the artefact are specified, which is followed by the creation of the artefact itself.
4. **Demonstration:** Demonstration of the created artefacts solves the problems identified in Phase 1. This phase includes experiments, simulations, case studies, proofs, or other appropriate activities.
5. **Evaluation:** Observation and measurement of how well this artefact supports a solution to the problem. This phase compares the goals of a solution (phase 2) with the actual observed results of using the artefact in the demonstration (phase 4).
6. **Communication:** Communication of research results – the problem and its significance, the artefact, its utility and novelty, the rigour of its conception and its effectiveness.

This research is currently in the fourth phase of the methodology of DSR. Very briefly, the results can be described as follows:

1. **Problem Identification and Motivation:** The main problem is to find compatible partners, friends and people (with similar interests) with whom we can build long-term relationships in various areas of social life (business, education, leisure).
2. **Defining the Objectives for a Solution:** The authors find a solution to these problems in the development of an integral communication tool that helps in the realisation of three main goals: self-improvement, improvement of relationships, and qualitative improvement of collaboration.
3. **Design and Development:** By analysing the requirements of potential users, the authors have developed a conceptual model of an integral communication tool that effectively explains its basic functions, subsystems, and information links.
4. **Demonstration:** by writing a program code, an integral communication platform was created. In addition, a study was conducted on the usefulness of certain functionalities among potential users.

The method SWOT was used to identify the most important internal strengths and weaknesses as well as external opportunities and risks in the context of integral communication.

CONCEPTUAL MODEL

The Integral Communication Framework (ICF) is a system for personalising information exchange based on digital identities that optimises collaboration costs, quality management, and organisational learning. The user's digital identity consists of various maps (e.g., folders) through which the user creates viewing permissions. The integral data map consists of a unified set of keywords or tags that can be evaluated in different ways and additionally enriched with metadata (e.g., location, price, image). This framework allows its users to create their personal maps consisting of unified tags that facilitate the identification of compatible and complementary positions and relationships. The integral map is a dynamic set of tags that describe a user or any other subject and object within the framework. The ICF allows users to manage their own personal or organisational maps and visualise their own position in relation to other users and groups. In addition, all users can rate other users and organisations in the ICF, including their products, services, locations, and events. ICF's mission is to improve organisational and communication intelligence through integral mapping. By using a dynamic set of consistent symbols to describe people, organisations, products, services, events, and places, this framework improves the overall quality of communication and organisation. By simplifying the way users define and represent their own characteristics, needs, and interests, ICF supports personalised communication and collaboration among different types of users, including their effective connection with artificial intelligence devices in the Internet of Things (IoT) ecosystem. To accomplish these complex tasks, this framework provides virtual mapping, reporting, comparison, evaluation, and measurement of satisfaction, knowledge, skills, traits, preferences, interests, performance, and all other information that can be used in networking, management, consulting, marketing, sales, employment, and business collaboration.

The Integral Communication Framework (Fig. 1) interacts with three types of actors (Rafajac & Jakupović, 2017):

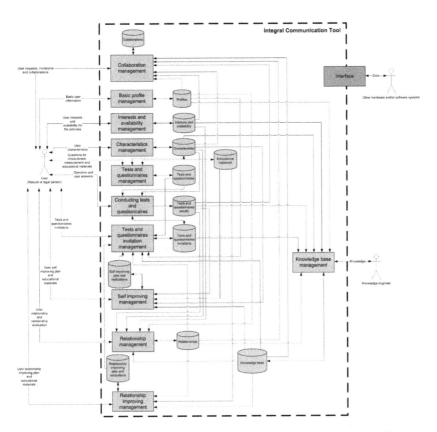

Fig. 1   Conceptual model of Integral Communication Framework. (Source: Rafajac & Jakupović, 2017)

1. **The user (natural or legal person):** is the main client of ICF, which helps to achieve three main goals: self-improvement, improvement of relationships and qualitative improvement in collaboration.

2. **Knowledge engineer:** is a type of client that manages the knowledge base in the Integral Communication Framework. The term "management"refers to the definition of the corresponding knowledge, its subsequent updating, and the recording of system information in a suitable way that allows automatically suggesting certain activities that should be performed by the user in order to achieve the above objectives.

3. **Other hardware and/or software systems**: Any hardware and/or software system with which the user can have a personalised interaction. Personalization is based on the user's personal characteristics that make up their digital identity. For example, it can be a multimedia device (various video and/or audio devices), specific software such as CRM (Customer Relationship Management), HRM (Human Resource Management), LMS (Learning Management System), etc.

The ICF consist of 12 subsystems (Rafajac & Jakupović, 2017):

1. **Basic profile management:** is part of a system that allows users to define basic personal information such as name, contact information, location, education, profile picture, etc. The personal information can be different for individuals and legal entities. All data is stored in the Profile repository. Depending on the permissions set by the user, some of this data may be publicly visible.
2. **Interests and availability management:** allows users to specify their interests and time slots in which they are available for activities related to those specific interests. For example, users can indicate their interest in PHP programming and the following activities: Tutorials (weekends) and Programming (weekends). This means that this user will be available on weekends to perform activities such as instruction and/or programming in PHP. The specified interests and availability to perform activities are stored in the Interests and Availability repository.
3. **Characteristics management:** is a part of the system that allows users to specify their own characteristics that they want to measure and improve. These can be psychological, sociological, technical, etc. Characteristics. For example, the user can specify the level of knowledge of programming in PHP as one of his technical characteristics. This means that the user wants to measure the level of his knowledge in PHP programming and improve this characteristic (if necessary). The data about the user's characteristics may be publicly available if the user selects this option. All user characteristics are stored in the Characteristics repository.
4. **Tests and questionnaires management:** allows users to define tests and questionnaires to measure certain characteristics (psychological, sociological, technical, etc.). The tests and questionnaires can be defined by any user. For example, companies can define a questionnaire to determine their customers' satisfaction with their products or

services. In addition, highly qualified users can define tests and questionnaires intended for the evaluation of some specific characteristics (e.g. psychological or professional such as the level of programming skills in PHP). Besides defining the tests and questionnaires, users can also specify the sources that can be used to improve the measured characteristics (e.g. educational materials and webinars). All tests and questionnaires are kept in the Tests and Questionnaires repository, while the sources of educational materials are stored in the Educational Materials repository. The data on the characteristics related to the test or questionnaire are kept in the Characteristics repository.

5. **Conducting tests and questionnaires:** is the subsystem through which the user completes tests and questionnaires. The type of tests and questionnaires that the user should fill out depends on the characteristics that the user has specified (and that can be managed through the Characteristics Management subsystem). For example, if the user has specified the characteristic Programming knowledge in PHP and there are tests or questionnaires for this characteristic, the user can select one or more tests or questionnaires to measure his knowledge in this area. It is also possible for a user to receive an invitation to complete a test or questionnaire. For example, a company (or an ordinary user) may send an invitation to a specific group of users to complete the test or questionnaire, which may be related to a characteristic of the user or to another object of measurement (e.g., the level of satisfaction with a product or service). All invitations to complete tests or questionnaires are kept in the Tests and Questionnaires Invitations repository. All responses to invitations are also kept there. All test results are stored in the Tests and Questionnaires Results repository.

6. **Tests and questionnaires invitation management:** allows users to send an invitation to tests and questionnaires in the Tests and Questionnaires repository. An invitation can be sent from one user to another. In this case, the user searches for information about other users stored in the Profiles repository or for information about relationships stored in the Relationships repository. For example, an organisation may develop a questionnaire for a specific group of users (measuring customer satisfaction with products and services). In addition to these user invitations, the invitations can be sent automatically by the system, which uses the rules defined in the repository knowledge base. The system automatically invites the user to check the degree of improvement of some properties of the user and/or the

user's relationship with another user. For this purpose, the system uses the repositories self-improvement plan and realisations and relationship improvement plan and realisations. For example, a user with the characteristic programming knowledge in PHP can be invited to retest or retest a questionnaire related to this characteristic (a reason for sending this invitation can be either a retest or a test after conducting the training using teaching materials specified in the Teaching Materials repository). These types of invitations are kept in the Tests and Questionnaires Invitations repository.

7. **Self-improving management:** is the subsystem that allows the user to define a plan for personal development and its implementation. This plan can also be proposed by the system itself according to the rules from the knowledge base. The plan of personal development refers to the user's characteristics (from the Characteristics repository) and is based on the results of tests (from the Tests and questionnaires results repository) and educational materials (from the Educational materials repository). The plan of personal development and its realisation are kept in the repository Self-improvement plan and realisations. If tests and questionnaires are accompanied by new educational materials, the system can automatically send them to the user (e.g., http://www.w3schools.com/php/). If he chooses to do so, the user can set a plan for working through the proposed educational material (the time needed to read and understand the material), while according to this plan the system can adjust the request for retesting.

8. **Relationship management:** helps users establish relationships with other users and evaluate those relationships. For this purpose, the system uses data from the Profile repository. In addition to creating customised relationships, the system can automatically suggest the creation of relationships based on the rules in the Knowledge base repository, user interests and availability (from the Interests and availability repository), user characteristics (from the Characteristics repository), and test results (from the Tests and questionnaires results repository). All user relationships and their evaluation are stored in the Relationships repository. For example, the user with the characteristic Programming skills in PHP can establish relationships with other users who have specified the same characteristic. Of course, this can also be done automatically with the help of rules from the Knowledge base repository.

9. **Relationship improving management:** is a subsystem similar to the Self-Improving Management subsystem, with the difference that its main goal is to improve relationships with users with whom some kind of relationship already exists. The need to improve the relationships becomes visible through the evaluation process in the Relationship Management subsystem. The results of these evaluations are stored in the Relationships repository. The plan for improving the relationships can be proposed by the system according to the rules from the repository knowledge base or defined by the user. In both cases, the system can suggest available teaching material for improving relationships (from the Teaching Material repository). This plan and its implementation are stored in the Relationship improving plan and realisations repository. Depending on these variables, the system may further prompt the user to perform various tests or questionnaires.

10. **Collaboration management:** allows system users to define the type of collaboration, an invitation to collaborate, and its subsequent evaluation. The definition of the type of collaboration refers to its description (e.g., description of the collaboration, location, duration, interests that the collaboration entails, obligations that it involves, required user properties, and other things). Depending on the type of collaboration, the user or the system may send calls for collaboration to other users that best fit in terms of location, interests, properties, etc. All collaborations are supported by the system through forums, personal chats, etc. The evaluation is performed by all users involved in the collaboration. The form of evaluation depends on the type of collaboration and its duration. The search for users best suited for the desired collaboration is based on many different variables, such as: User data from the repository Profile; User interests and availability from the repository Interests and availability, User characteristics from the repository Characteristics, User results from tests and questionnaires from the repository Tests and questionnaire results, their relationships with other users from the repository Relationships and evaluation of previous collaboration from the repository Collaboration. In addition to this data, the system uses data from the repository knowledge base for automatic invitations to collaborations. For example, the user can define the collaboration development of applications, which is in the field of

programming in PHP and requires the characteristics The level of knowledge of programming in PHP with a value of 8/10. This type of selection allows the system to propose a list of the best potential contributors.

11. **Knowledge base management:** is the subsystem used by a special type of customer – the knowledge engineer. Based on the data in other system repositories, they define the knowledge (or rules) according to which the system automatically performs a certain function (e.g., proposal for establishing relationships with other users, proposal for employees, plan for developing or improving relationships, invitations for tests, etc.). All these rules are stored in the knowledge base.

12. **Interface:** is the subsystem used to connect other hardware and/ or software systems to the ICF. The purpose of this subsystem is to provide data that can be used to personalise the user experience when interacting with external hardware and/or software systems. For example, the lighting, the video walls, the programme on TV or the music in the hotel room can be set according to the user characteristics stored in the ICF.

Integral tags describing users and other elements within ICF can be assigned: automatically by recording user activity, by tests and various measurement tools (e.g., voice tone) that users voluntarily complete, by tapping or clicking on a tag, by feedback from other users, and by voice communication with ICF or robots that use ICF. The speech interaction interface in ICF has two main goals: The first goal is to facilitate information exchange for people with visual impairments and dyslexia, and the second goal is to enable personalised communication with robots and voice-controlled IoT systems. According to Ackland et al. (2017), there were approximately 253 million people with visual impairments worldwide in 2015, while Zauderer (2023) estimates that there are 780 million people with dyslexia worldwide today, and all of these users have a need for speech interaction solutions that help them engage in digitally supported communication processes. Although more and more researchers have focused on natural language processing and human-robot interaction (HRI) in the last two decades, human-robot language interaction is still in its infancy (Sathyavenkateshwaren & Malathi, 2018; Khaewratana et al., 2020; Marge et al., 2020). The first phase of humanoid robot development focused on mimicking traditional communication methodology. At this stage, humanoid robots were developed in such a way that they had to start from scratch in every interaction with humans and use voice interaction to gather enough information to make decisions. In this simple form of human-robot interaction (HRI), commands are part of a library of words used to achieve specified goals (Naeem et al., 2023). For example, the Google Voice API can use the phone's microphone to convert a voice input into text and send it to the Arduino Node MCU in the form of a command (Naeem et al., 2023). The next phase of humanoid robot development will aim to personalise HRI and further improve the human experience when interacting with robots. To perform complex activities better, or at least as well as humans, robots will need to rely not only on spoken communication, but also on a set of predefined characteristics and preferences of the user they interact with (Collins, 2020). In order to communicate efficiently with humans, robots need to have a number of capabilities, such as feature and intent recognition, semantic understanding, and uncertainty handling (Badr & Abdul-Hassan, 2020). Although these capabilities can be efficiently achieved through various types of sensors, algorithms, and AI vision devices, the authors believe that ICF can improve personal data management so that the remaining computing power of the robot can be used for other important activities. Combined with other approaches such as the use of neural networks with noise injection, which can mitigate the negative effects of speech recognition errors in understanding robotic speech commands (Tada et al., 2020), ICF will provide a solid foundation for development of more advanced HRI systems. Although speech processing systems accompanied by intelligent speakers in robots can mimic natural conversation, the transmission and processing of speech input requires a significant amount of time (Deuerlein et al., 2021). Therefore, systems that facilitate the identification of human characteristics and preferences can significantly speed up and improve the quality of HRI processes.

As can be seen in the Fig. 2, with the help of ICF, a humanoid robot already knows which dishes correspond to the preferences and health status of the restaurant guests and is quite sure that they will enjoy eating the dishes it offers. Since, in the context of Integral Communication, everyone can simply type or vocally define their attributes and preferences, robots and AI devices will be able to enhance what Pipitone and Chella (2021) call "inner language" and provide a context for learning and decision making. Besides the fact that humans are able to easily decide and transparently define which characteristics and preferences they are willing to share with certain robots, the main benefits of ICF in HRI are: time savings, personalization of services, sustainability due to reduced direct

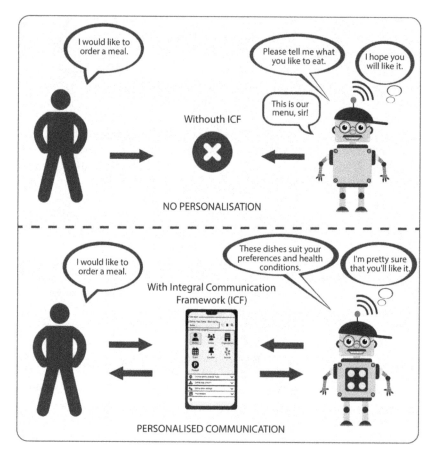

Fig. 2 Differences between human-robot interaction with and without personalization system. (Source: Made by authors)

and indirect costs in collaboration, and higher quality of communication. When information gathered in one interaction can be easily stored and used in another, a space for personalised experiences is created. All this is done through a set of tags, enriched with metadata and placed in different user maps that can be used for different purposes and activities. The proposed solution helps humans and robots avoid repetition in information exchange and take communication to a whole new level by deepening relationships in entirely new domains.

VISUALISATION OF INTEGRAL DIGITAL IDENTITY

Although in practice all communication platforms tend to collect and present specific information about their users, none of them offers users the opportunity to present all their characteristics and preferences in one place. Integral communication is not about sharing all available information, but only the information that might be useful in an interaction. However, this useful information can refer to any line of development or dimension. The basic problem of integral identity mapping is that identity is a very complex and dynamic phenomenon that often cannot be fully grasped. Other problems include identifying the key categories or perspectives that best describe an entity (e.g., a virtual person, organisation, or event), finding the right way to evaluate specific information, and the need to actively monitor the dynamics of changes in the properties, preferences, and relationships of subjects (and objects) in the network. There are many different ways to define a person's identity. The three fundamental problems with all traditional approaches to user profiling are partiality, incompatibility, and lack of developmental momentum. Partiality means the use of a limited number of identifiers, while lack of developmental momentum refers to the neglect of developmental trajectories and changes that are an important part of any identity assessment. Incompatibility means that user data created in one system cannot be transferred to another. Since user profiling is critical to improving the quality of personalization, customer satisfaction, and overall human-robot interaction, it is extremely important to develop accurate multidimensional user profiling methods (Cufoglu, 2014). In daily life, individuals can identify their personal, interpersonal, and collective identities. The study of personal identity in an organisational setting raises many interesting questions (Ashforth, 2014): How does a person's identity change and evolve? To what extent do some individuals' characteristics and preferences align with organisational identities or specific job requirements? What characteristics and preferences connect group members? What characteristics and preferences describe specific types of organisations?

Integral digital identity (IDI) is a comprehensive, flexible, shareable, numeric, textual, and visual record of users' personal characteristics and preferences. The public IDI includes all records on the private IDI map and all feedback records about that user (e.g., the results of tests used to evaluate the user). In the context of this study, the term "integral" refers to the broadest possible set of information that can facilitate various forms of identification, communication, and collaboration among users. When defined by a set of consistent integral tags, these digital records can be used not only to improve personalised communication between humans and robots, but also for motivation, performance evaluation, user experience, quality management, counselling, education, and personal development. IDI is the result of personal descriptions based on quantitative (e.g., height, weight, age, foot size, etc.) and qualitative data (e.g., interests, hobbies, preferences, occupation, education, character, etc.) and feedback collected in an integral information network (e.g., tests, evaluations from team members, customers, family, and/or acquaintances). In order to effectively personalise communication between all subjects and objects of the information network, IDI should have the following characteristics:

- **Integrity** – It refers to the wholeness, reliability, and verifiability of features describing different subjects and objects. Where appropriate, blockchain solutions can be used to ensure a high level of confidence in the accuracy of the data presented.
- **Relevance** – The closer the time interval in which it was collected is to the present and the more subjects and objects confirm it, the more accurate and relevant this information is.
- **Anonymity and Privacy** – Whenever possible, users should be able to choose whether to communicate in private or public mode. Although some data (e.g., users' personal information and tags with negative ratings) may be hidden from the public or specific users, all positive features may be displayed publicly or visible to other network members. Unless the group administrator decides otherwise, all ratings are anonymous to protect the privacy of those who provide critical feedback.
- **Adaptability** – Most of the data contained in the IDI is dynamic and can be changed either by the user or by the platform and evaluators. End users should have a high degree of control over the tags they choose to share.
- **Extensibility** – IDI can be used for a variety of activities depending on the needs of users. For example, to experience personalization of medical services, a user can create a new folder of tags that describe their personal medical characteristics and preferences.
- **Compatibility** – Since all key words can be translated into different foreign languages, mutual understanding and communication

between people is greatly facilitated. IDI data should be easily trans-ferred between different AI and IoT devices. The same set of records should be used to personalise a restaurant's menu, a car's interior, a hotel room, a web store's offer, etc.

- **Efficiency** – This is reflected in the time and resources saved by auto-matically identifying compatible and complementary items between different users.
- **Multilingualism** – IDI improves communication between people who speak different languages. Even if the interlocutors do not understand each other's language, with ICF they experience a high degree of social perceptiveness and insight into the characteristics and preferences of the audience with whom they are communicating.

Capturing a person's identity is quite a complex challenge. In discuss-ing identities in the virtual world, Chan (2007) points out that identity is much more than an identification number and a document containing a person's picture and fingerprints. This is especially evident in a virtual environment where individuals have many more opportunities to experi-ment with their own identities than is the case with a real identity (Chan, 2007). Although there are cases where the opposite is true, the avatars or identities of users in the virtual environment are usually idealised (faster, more powerful, smarter, prettier) versions of the people we encounter in the real world. Recent research has shown that participants assigned more attractive avatars in immersive virtual environments were more intimate with fellow players in a self-presentation and interpersonal distance task than participants assigned less attractive avatars (Yee & Bailenson, 2007). These results confirm that digital identity visualisation has a significant impact on human behaviour.

As shown in Fig. 3, there are different levels of user identity that coexist in the domains of privacy, education, work, public, shopping, health, lei-sure, acquisition, and anonymity. In the broadest sense, virtual persons can be defined by what they love, feel, think, and do, as well as by many dif-ferent attributes, roles, skills, and acquisitions. As can be seen in Fig. 3, each person's partial identities overlap, meaning that they can contain the same descriptive data. All users in a virtual network can be defined by what they (Anrig et al., 2006, p. 6):

Fig. 3 Different layers of user identity. (Source: Anrig et al., 2006)

1. **Are (internal roles and attributes):** For example, adventurous, sailor, the first buyer in a transaction, magazine editor.
2. **Do (external roles and abilities):** For example, the person who opened the door, the person who offended someone.
3. **Know (internal acquisitions and abilities):** For example, the one who has mastered the Italian language, the one who has circumnavigated the globe.
4. **Have (external acquisitions and attributes):** For example, the owner of a cell phone, the one who owns 51% of the shares of a company, the one who has office keys, etc.

Figure 4 shows that each person's identity contains specific elements from the past, present, and future. In defining the integral identity of a person, any attribute (e.g., the owner of the fingerprint, the highest

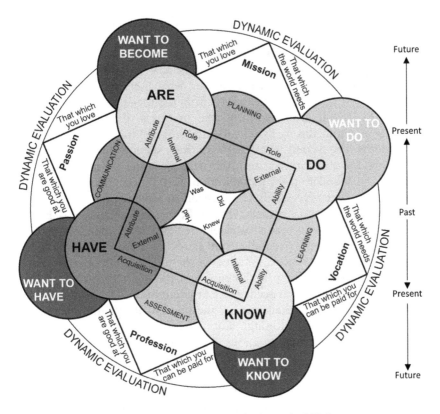

Fig. 4 Integral identity mapping. (Source: Anrig et al., 2006)

person in the world, etc.) and any ability (e.g., the person who swam the English Channel) can be used. In other words, people and organisations can be defined by their attributes, roles, abilities, achievements, preferences, habits, etc. In the context of this study, the term "integral" refers to any information that can facilitate and promote various forms of identification, communication, and collaboration among users. Integral mapping means the assignment, visualisation, and analysis of integral tags that facilitate integral communication. When used within ICF, which enables automatic analysis of integral tags in different types of integral maps (e.g., features and preferences), integral mapping facilitates automatic identification of compatible and complementary items. An integral tag is a specific type of hashtag that can be described by metadata, translated into multiple languages, and scored by users or tests. Although there are differences between a classic hashtag and an integral tag, this book uses the terms tag and integral tag as synonyms.

Figure 4 shows that virtual persons can be analysed using three specific classes and four categories, depending on what users are, do, have, and know. The first class includes elements from the user's past and is formed over time. It describes everything the user was, did, had, or knew. Information about this part of the identity is useful for measuring potential progress. The second class describes current states, while the third class represents desirable future states. Although capturing the as-is state provides a solid foundation for identification, without identifying the user's development preferences, it is very difficult to provide personalised solutions that the user actually wants. One of the main advantages of ICF over other social networks is that all available elements are included in the networking, i.e., not only past and current states corrected by dynamic feedback, but also user preferences. To reduce the total amount of information users are exposed to, the past dimension of the user's identity is usually hidden, but available when needed (e.g., to determine the user's progress).

One of the biggest challenges in the process of integral mapping is information gathering. Although automated collection of user data and recording of their activities (e.g., searching and shopping) can be practical and useful for mapping a person's identity, the easiest way to gather important information about users, and in particular their development preferences, is through their self-definition. The methodology of semantic concepts or keywords used to connect different topics improves the efficiency and overall quality of communication (Chen et al., 2008; Stojanović et al., 2006). Since they are the best way to determine preferences (what subjects want) and the quality of relationships (what subjects think about each other), self-definition and assessment are extremely important aspects of integral communication. The dynamic assessment of available information and the ability to comment on specific information creates a feedback loop that enables personal development and organisational learning. In economic theory, preferences refer to the subjective or factual granting of advantages in choosing among real options. According to their needs, tastes, social status, culture (...) all individuals or social groups form a system of preferences that is expressed in their actual choices and that can be used to predict their behaviour. Although some people tend to consider their own preferences as fixed, empirical studies confirm the opposite. An actor's preferences are based on certain 'motivationally salient' properties of the alternatives for which the preferences are thought to be (Dietrich & List, 2012). Preferences are always constructed, as context influences nearly every aspect of the judgement and decision-making process, and these constructs depend on goals, cognitive constraints, and experience (Warren et al., 2010). Within the integral communication framework, characteristics describe what users are, have, know, and work for, while preferences encompass the desired states and personal development goals that users would like to achieve in the future. Users can define their integral identity through the listed integral tags or through integral tags they write in free input mode. For network efficiency, users are encouraged to use predefined integral tags in self-presentation, and use their own input only in the case of a detailed description, and/or when the predefined tag does not exist.

The basic integral map represents the total set of data describing a person's identity. This map contains both positively and negatively rated integral tags. Although negatively rated integral tags should be displayed to users and administrators of the groups in which these labels are assigned, analysis shows that it is not desirable for such tags to be publicly visible. For this reason, the public integral maps contain only positively rated tags. Nevertheless, in the background analysis and when proposing specific activities (e.g., workshops or educational materials that can help users improve this specific feature), ICF uses all available tags in the basic integral maps. In addition to defining the identity of end users, integral maps can also be created for organisations, products, services, events, and places. Integral tags describe not only a person's horizontal dimensions (indicating an area of interest), but also their vertical dimensions, indicating expertise and skills, as well as their preferences (e.g., desires). For security and potential misuse reasons, all tags in the system are validated using artificial intelligence and then confirmed by the administrator. Tags that pass validation are translated into foreign languages. Each user group can enter their own set of tags that can only be used by their members. The tags that users enter, select, earn, approve, or gain through tests and challenges are a fundamental part of their digital identity, which is then used to create personalised user experiences. Tags can also contain metadata that describes them in more detail (e.g., GPS location, image, time frame, price). In this way, it is possible to create a digital identity of all organisations, employees, products, services, places and events, as well as an ecosystem for personalising products and services (e.g., employee training, hotel room, restaurant menu, art exhibition, etc.).

SWOT ANALYSIS

The Integral Communication Framework (ICF) offers numerous benefits, including improved social perceptiveness, control over personal data, enhanced collaboration and cooperation capabilities, automatic identification of compatible and complementary positions, time and resource savings, the ability to dynamically share feedback, and improved online trust and security. By assigning keywords to a specific subject, organisation, product, service, or event that can be assigned to different groups and then evaluated in different ways, ICF improves semiosis based on meronomy and taxonomy processes (e.g., semiosis is a sign process in which a set of signs creates a new set of signs with new meanings). While a taxonomy classifies individuals, a meronomy deals with part-whole relationships and describes the relational or functional structure of the whole (Kull, 2019). Meaning is specified semantically by the relations between signifiers and their referents, syntactically by relations between signs, and pragmatically by actions and reactions associated with their use (Morris, 1945; Thibodeau, 2021, p. 3). Personalization, which implies automatic identification of compatible and complementary positions, significantly improves sales. A study by McKinsey (2013), conducted on a sample of 418 executives from large companies in Europe, the Americas, and Asia, shows that personalization helps companies achieve up to 126% higher profits, 131% higher revenues, and 132% higher returns on investment with advanced customer data analytics. With personalization algorithms, Amazon improves conversion by 35%, and Netflix claims that 80% of users prefer to opt-in to content recommendations, while only 20% search for it on their own (Deloitte, 2023). In addition, ICF offers numerous opportunities for sustainable and inclusive development, electronic collaboration, quality management, talent identification, personal development, and organisational learning. There is no doubt that social actors who kindly ask others to assess their behaviour, knowledge, and skills will benefit from these observations. A communication framework that helps social actors identify their attributes and preferences could significantly reduce transaction costs and improve long-term environmental sustainability. Eurostat (2023) indicates that about 10% of food is thrown away in the EU, which is equivalent to 131 kilograms of food per inhabitant per year, and according to some estimates, up to 14% of food produced worldwide ends up in waste (FAO, 2019). Advanced analysis of data on the key characteristics and dietary preferences of hotel restaurant guests will reduce procurement and distribution costs, as well as costs associated with quality management, human resources, and organisational learning, and improve food quality and habits.

Unlike other personalization tools on the market, ICF does not hide personalization data in the background, but allows users to manage personalization tags they want to share with specific user groups. If the exchange of feedback does not follow scientifically proven and safe principles, it becomes ineffective, inaccurate, incomplete, and unclear. Today, the availability of solutions that enable easy, transparent, anonymous, and secure feedback sharing and personal information management is still quite limited (Masseno & Sanots, 2019), while trust in organisations that manage personal user data is quite low. In a survey conducted by McKinsey in 2019 among 1000 respondents in the North American market, 44% of them believe that the healthcare and financial industries handle users' personal data responsibly, 22% of them think the same for the pharmaceutical industry, which ranks third, while only 11% of the participants believe that the public sector handles users' data responsibly (Anant et al., 2020). A Eurostat survey (2022) shows that in the European Union, citizens of the Netherlands and Finland (91%), Portugal (89%), and the Republic of Croatia (87%) are the most willing to share personal information online, but also that only a small number of Internet users (36%) check that the websites they use are secure. The ICF allows for a higher level of transparency and security when sharing personal data and feedback.

In addition to the strengths and opportunities mentioned above, ICF still has some weaknesses and may pose several potential threats. Since any technology can be abused, it is important to talk not only about the strengths and opportunities, but also about the weaknesses and risks associated with its use. Table 1 shows the results of the SWOT analysis of the ICF. Addictive user behaviour is a weakness associated with almost any technology that stimulates brain activity. In the last decade, there is a growing body of empirical evidence showing how social networking and internet gaming can produce addictive behaviour (Andreassen et al., 2016; Pontes, 2017). As a result, research on technological addictions such as Internet addiction, smartphone addiction, and social networking addiction has proliferated (Hussain & Pontes, 2019). The solution to addictive behaviours in media and technology use is not to eliminate media and technology use, but to find the right balance (Fisher et al., 2016). This means that social actors need to find and apply solutions that reduce negative elements (e.g., time spent searching, need for duplicate input, etc.)

Table 1   The SWOT analysis of the integral communication framework

Strengths	Weaknesses
Improved social perceptivity	Addictive user behaviour
Improved control over personal information	A large amount of sensitive
Improved collaboration and cooperation capabilities	data
Automatic identification of compatible and	Filter bubble
complementary positions	Social distancing and anxiety
Time and resource efficiency	
Dynamic exchange of feedback	
Improved trust and security	
Opportunities	**Threats**
Sustainable and inclusive development	Autocratic and unauthorised
Potential for e-collaboration	control
Total quality management	Infrastructure issues
Easy identification of skills and talents	Crime issues
Personal development and organisational learning	Technological shift

Source: Made by authors

and reinforce positive elements of current digital communication patterns (e.g., sustainability, trust, creativity). As Gardner and Davis (2014) argue, contemporary society should seek ways to use technology to foster creativity, collaboration, and identity in ways that support well-being. This means that new communication solutions should try to reduce the overall time spent exchanging information with machines and AI devices. In addition, this means notifying users when their level of interaction with the technology becomes hazardous to their health and well-being. Another potential weakness of integral communications is the need to manage large amounts of sensitive data. Fortunately, there are cloud solutions available today that ensure very high standards of data security and availability. Until recently, the data economy was hidden behind a veil of secrecy for the public and legislators. The General Data Protection Regulation (GDPR) has lifted that curtain, and new laws now give users more control over the data they generate (Rahnama & Pentland, 2022). Unfortunately, in an IoT environment where everything is connected, malicious IT activities such as phishing (identity theft online) and unauthorised user tracking will not go away, but will likely continue to increase. Although GDPR legislation represents a step forward in data protection, its practical application is not without its problems. If they have a valid reason (e.g. contract, legal obligation, vital interests, public duty and legitimate interests), organisations can use all kinds of user data without their consent. Nowadays, it is still too complicated for users to define what personal information they want to share with third parties. The good news is that this unauthorised use of user data has raised awareness of the problem of surveillance capitalism, which refers to an economic system based on the surreptitious extraction and manipulation of human data (Zuboff, 2019). Even when users give consent for their private data to be used by organisations, they are usually unable to clearly and easily decide what data they want to share. To solve this problem, it was necessary to develop a tool that would simplify the management of personal data.

Despite all efforts, there will always be the possibility of malicious attacks, and for this reason it is advisable to continuously improve security standards. According to Rahnama and Pentland (2022), the 3 new rules of data security include:

1. **Trust over transactions:** Data collected with meaningful consent will soon be the most valuable data of all.
2. **Insight over identity:** Rather than moving data, algorithms instead share non-identifying statistics.
3. **Flows over silos:** The goal is to gain maximum insights from the released data for the benefit of the customer.

Although a picture is worth a thousand words, social networking based on personal photos leads to a high degree of exposure and vulnerability of users. In matters related to group management and collaboration, for example, citizens should not be interested in what their prime minister looks like in a bathing suit, nor in the picture of the sunset from her or his balcony. It is obvious that such pictures could do more harm than good to the prime minister's personal security. However, citizens should be interested in the prime minister's attitude toward pension or energy policy. In addition, citizens would probably like to know what different groups of people think about certain political decisions. In the wrong hands, whether through corrupt managers or repressive governments, any kind of personal information collected without the user's consent can be considered a security issue. In 2020, the Irish Data Protection Commission (DPC) issued an injunction to block the mechanism by which company Meta transfers EU users' data to the United States (Reuters, 2022). In 2020, the European Court of Justice annulled the pact between the European Union and the United States on data flows, called the Privacy Shield, due to concerns about U.S. surveillance practices (Manancourt, 2022). To avoid this problem, users should have direct control over the personal data they are willing to share with others. Over the past two decades, many different authors have argued that the algorithms used by search engines, social networking platforms, and other major online intermediaries can reduce information diversity by creating so-called filter bubbles (Munson & Resnick, 2010; Nagulendra & Vassileva, 2014; Bozdag & van den Hoven, 2015). This is one of the reasons why designers of new systems are emerging, trying to find more efficient, credible and secure ways for personalised information exchange. These days, there is a growing number of authors who recognize that filter bubbles (created without user consent) may increase polarisation and support false beliefs (Pariser, 2011; Papa & Photiadis, 2021). On the other hand, there are also authors, such as Burbach et al. (2019), who find that end users show a low propensity to adopt avoidance strategies despite being aware of the filter bubble phenomenon. Within ICF, two strategies are used to combat filter bubbles. The first strategy is to allow users to easily identify and independently adjust the filters (e.g., tags, groups, etc.) applied in their information framework. The second strategy involves allowing users to find out what other social actors or groups think and feel about various ideas, projects, people, organisations, products, services, events, and places. While it is quite clear that there will always be important information that should be communicated to users, even if it is not in their information filter, the decisions about the level of personalization should be made by the users themselves. Another potential weakness of ICF is social distancing. Aside from saving time and resources, ICF could reduce the number of live interactions people would normally engage in to fulfil their wants and needs. While some introverts will be happy to avoid these "unnecessary" social interactions, for some people, reducing social interaction could have a negative impact on their mental health. Others may be afraid of being evaluated or so focused on receiving positive feedback that they cannot communicate in a relaxed and natural way. While a society where no one cares what others think would be very aggressive and unpleasant, a society where everyone cares what others think can become too conservative. Social anxiety stems from worrying about what others might think about one (Leary & Kowalski, 1995). Although sharing feedback constructively can be very beneficial, worrying too much about how one will be perceived and evaluated by others can cause psychological problems. To reduce these extreme behaviours, it would be important to openly discuss positive and negative elements of feedback exchange. The same is true for addictive and aggressive behaviours that can be seen among users of various social networks. Although such things are difficult to prove, there is evidence that algorithms can be used on social networks to increase traffic and influence users' opinions. As people begin to recognise the negative impacts and threats in various communication frameworks, there is a concurrent awareness of the need for new communication solutions that reduce opportunities for manipulation and optimise the time and energy people invest in communication and collaboration. Although the fine-tuning of these operational elements may be different for each group, preliminary analysis has shown that only positive features of a person's personality should be publicly visible, while negative elements are better kept hidden from public view. Negative ratings should remain visible only to users, group administrators, and framework operators. The main goal of ICF operators is to help all users who have problems (e.g., send automatic links to learning materials and advisors) while protecting everyone else.

One of the biggest threats to ICF is the external infrastructure that supports its functioning. ICF cannot function without electricity, cloud servers, the Internet, computers and smartphones. This means that any security problem in the infrastructure elements can negatively impact this framework. Another threat comes from all those immoral individuals or organisations that might try to use this framework for various criminal activities. There will always be individuals and organisations that will attempt to use online communications to carry out socially unacceptable behaviours such as theft of private data, harassment, and other forms of crime. Applications that enhance collaboration and teamwork may be of particular interest to criminal organisations. To avoid such threats, advanced security mechanisms such as Deep Learning and suspicious behaviour tracking must be deployed. On the other hand, transparency is a means to reduce most criminal activity. Therefore, our society needs a robust communication framework that provides a high level of privacy and trust in communication. Although some popular social platforms primarily focus on publishing users' personal photos, this is certainly not the best way to protect privacy. The robust communication solutions are the ones that reduce the possibilities of harassment and abuse while allowing easy control over the sharing of personal information. The final, but certainly not least important, threat under ICF comes from autocratic and unauthorised control by the deep state. As seen in the case of China using its Social Credit System (SCS) system and the NSA surveillance scandals in the U.S., it is not unlikely that autocratic political leaders and/or intelligence agencies would want to use communications platforms to impose various undemocratic surveillance measures on their citizens (Canales, 2021). The loudest opponents of integral communication are usually those who would lose some of their interests and power with its implementation. For example, former U.S. Vice President Mike Pence has compared China's version of state-controlled SCS to an Orwellian system based on control of virtually every facet of human life (Hudson Institute, 2018). While this may not be so far from the truth in some respects, it is important to distinguish the technology from how it is used. At the same time, the Internet of Things is making its way into nearly every aspect of our lives in the Western world, and no one is much concerned about the privacy issues associated with this technology or the fact that national security agencies in the U.S. are continually violating Americans' privacy rights online (Toomey, 2018; Goitein, 2019). One of the greatest external threats related to ICF is hidden in an imminent technological change. Considering that some labs like Meta, Microsoft, and Tesla are already developing mind-reading devices that can access our thoughts and dreams using AI, these breakthroughs could eventually create new ways to communicate and share feedback. Facebook, for example, plans to offer a device that allows people to type with their thoughts (Revell, 2018). However, this doesn't mean that ICF will immediately become obsolete. With or without mind readers, the human mind will always have cognitive limits, which means that it will be necessary to store and manage all important information in some kind of app or cloud. On the other hand, new technological discoveries will likely be helpful in managing ICF without typing.

Members of today's society need a communication framework that helps them manage the personal information they share in public, business, and private interactions. Empirical results confirm that many users are willing to accept potential risks in exchange for potential benefits, as long as they have control over the information shared. Since end users of communications platforms will never be able to fully control what happens to their personal data in the backends of the applications they use and in the various communications nodes and networks over which they transmit their personal data, the best possible protection against autocratic or unauthorised control in communications is freedom of choice. Freedom of choice is one of the greatest advantages of modern Western society. When freedom of choice is given, everyone can turn away from platforms and organisations that do not meet their ethical standards. On the other hand, there are infrastructural and technical solutions (e.g., fibre optic cables) for which there are no alternative providers, and in such cases it is desirable to ensure independent public and transparent control.

SOLUTIONS AND RECOMMENDATIONS

Today, social actors need to be able to communicate in a personalised and proactive way not only with CRM systems and artificial intelligence (AI) devices, but also with other social actors. To improve their communication and collaboration in a secure and efficient way, today's social actors need a multilingual communication framework capable of identifying and analysing different aspects of their personal identity in the form of integrated tags that can be automatically shared with other social actors or artificial intelligence devices. In the context of this research, this type of information system is called Integral Communication Framework (ICF). The ICF is an information system that supports the collection, presentation, and analysis of integral data maps, which consist of integral tags. Integral data maps consist of a uniform set of keywords or integral tags that can be analysed in different ways and additionally enriched with metadata (e.g., images, time interval, GPS coordinates, assessment points, etc.). An integral tag is a specific type of hashtag that can be described by metadata, translated into multiple languages, and evaluated by users or tests. The ICF is designed to structure, collect, exchange, and evaluate information about various subjects and objects in a way that improves automated information exchange, avoids duplicate entries, and protects user privacy. By using a unique set of symbols and words that can be automatically translated into different languages to define different social actors, products, services, events, and places, the integral communication framework facilitates perceptivity and collaboration among social actors who do not know each other and do not speak the same (native) language. The ICF allows its users to automatically exchange information about their characteristics and preferences. Within this system, administrators retain the right to add new categories and convert existing user tags into new or modified tags that can later be offered to other users. The system is designed to automatically remove any user identifiers that do not comply with the ethical principles of the framework. All information entered into the system by users is considered voluntarily provided data that can be used to improve networking. ICF should allow users to see their connections to other users and rate other users with whom they interact.

The visualisation takes the form of a network in which a node represents a user and a link represents a tag (e.g., a keyword). The stronger the link, the more tags connect two nodes or users. Although the integral identity of a person and/or organisation can be visualised in many different ways, in most cases the three basic forms are used:

1. **Significance:** This perspective shows the top-rated tags in selected categories (e.g., character, knowledge, work, and acquisition). The goal is to identify the most important features of the interlocutor in the shortest possible time.
2. **Hierarchy:** This perspective provides a detailed look at the structure of tags in a specific category of integral digital identity. The purpose of this visualisation is to identify all the characteristics and preferences of the particular social actor (e.g., end user, organisation, team, etc.).
3. **Comparison:** This perspective provides detailed insight into compatible and complementary positions. The purpose of this visualisation is to easily identify ways to improve the relationship and collaboration.

The purpose of these visualisations is to identify important information about social actors that can be used to improve communication. Each tag in the integral map can be assigned additional sub-tags (e.g., metadata) for further definition, branching, and clarification. In addition to the top twenty rated tags describing a user, Fig. 5 shows how the significance perspective provides information about the importance and accuracy of tags and offers insight into the number of evaluators, number of followers, names of groups the user participates in, and personal contact information.

The second type of visualisation shown in Figure 6 is the hierarchy perspective, which provides insight into all user tags, sub-tags, and their correlation with other tags. As seen in Figure 6, each tag can be extended by a new set of tags. This tag hierarchy is not fixed, meaning users can customise it to their own needs. If needed, organisational users can use their own specific tags. In addition to the information presented in these screens, many other items can be displayed as part of the integral identity, such as the total number of tags, the lowest scoring tags, the preference tags, the test results, the dynamic changes in the values of specific tags, etc. Although group administrators should have visibility into all tags in their group (including negative ratings), the IDI should only promote positive

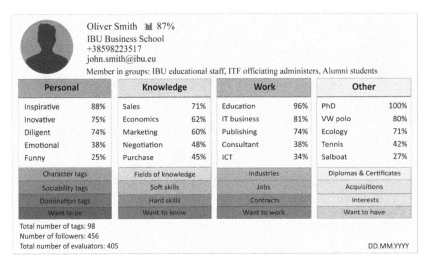

Fig. 5   Significance perspective. (Source: Made by authors)

features and properties. If the number of negative ratings exceeds the number of positive ratings, the tags should no longer be displayed publicly.

Figure 7 shows the third type of visualisation, the comparative perspective. It can be applied between two users, between two groups of users, and between a user and a particular group of users. These comparative views are used to identify compatible and complementary tags and other interesting information such as position in the group, relationship dynamics, (...) and any other comparative information that can improve the quality of relationships, personal mastery and organisational learning (e.g., nationality, age, scores in the same test, etc.). Figure 7 shows that User A and User B have 37 compatible tags and 7 complementary tags. Also, Fig. 7 shows that person A's IDI (87%) is more accurate than person B's IDI (72%) and that B could go sailing with person A while B could suggest a travel experience to person A. As can be seen from the last three illustrations, effective identity visualisation allows for a deeper and broader understanding of social individuals, which in turn enhances their self-awareness, social perceptiveness, ability to collaborate and dialogue, and facilitates the identification of specific connections between different group members.

To increase confidence in the information presented, ICF provides a full range of details about the assessment process, such as the total number

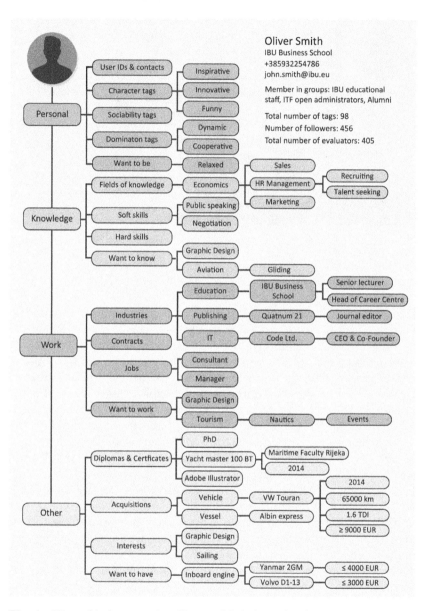

Fig. 6 Hierarchical perspective. (Source: Made by authors)

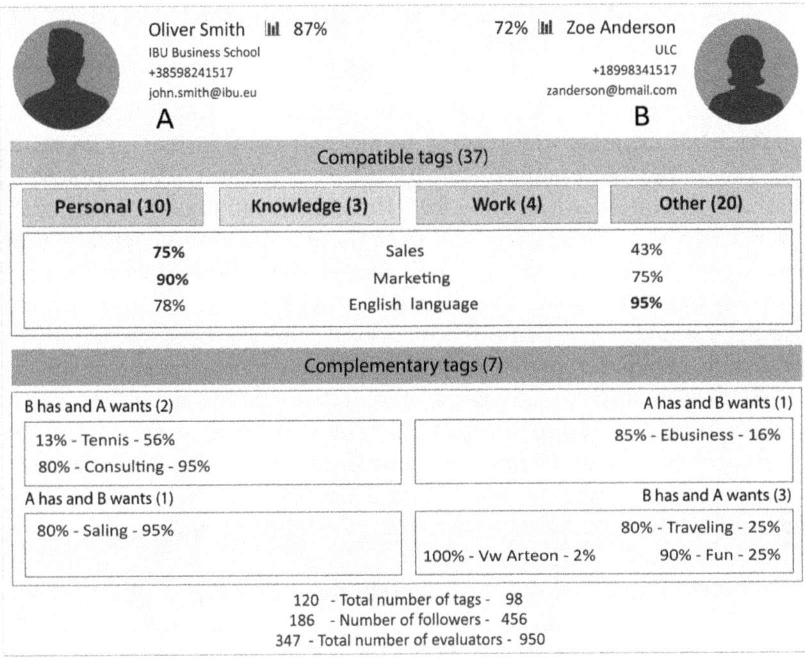

Oliver Smith ‖ 87%			72% ‖ Zoe Anderson
IBU Business School			ULC
+38598241517			+18998341517
john.smith@ibu.eu			zanderson@bmail.com
A			**B**

Compatible tags (37)			
Personal (10)	**Knowledge (3)**	**Work (4)**	**Other (20)**

75%	Sales	43%
90%	Marketing	75%
78%	English language	95%

Complementary tags (7)

B has and A wants (2)	A has and B wants (1)
13% - Tennis - 56%	85% - Ebusiness - 16%
80% - Consulting - 95%	
A has and B wants (1)	**B has and A wants (3)**
80% - Saling - 95%	80% - Traveling - 25%
100% - Vw Arteon - 2%	90% - Fun - 25%

120   - Total number of tags -   98
186   - Number of followers -   456
347   - Total number of evaluators -   950

Fig. 7   Comparative perspective. (Source: Made by authors)

of evaluators, the timing of the assessment, the evaluator's ID, the assessment history, information about the results of related tests, etc. The ICF supports diagnostic (e.g., current state of knowledge and skills), formative (e.g., progress toward learning goals), and summative assessments (e.g., final learning outcomes) (Johnson et al., 2008). In the context of the ICF, assessment of dynamic information can occur in three different ways:

1. **Subjective evaluation:** As part of this process, users can rate other users they interact with by entering a new tag into their user map or rating existing tags (e.g., with + or -) in their personal or group map.
2. **Objective evaluation:** Users can be scored through various tests that adjust the score of existing tags or assign new tags.
3. **Automatic evaluation:** Using algorithms that employ machine learning to improve information accuracy, the system automatically rates users based on their actions. If users want to apply this type of

evaluation, they can connect various IoT devices to their IDI to evaluate and measure their activities.

Although there is no direct guarantee that the information in the ICF is completely accurate, the relative accuracy of the information increases with the number of examiners and tests that confirm it. The problem of filter bubbles can be solved in at least three different ways. The first strategy is to give users direct control over the personalization settings they want to apply. The second strategy is to give users direct insight into the positions and attitudes of other users and groups with whom they interact. The third strategy is to share information of public interest, even if it falls outside the filters set by users. Within ICF, each integrated tag can be translated into different languages and have its own metadata (e.g., time, price, colour, geolocation, image, etc.). The translation of the tags can be done automatically, and administrators can adjust it manually if needed.

To prevent undesirable and/or illegal activities to which integral communication can lead, the authors suggest four specific strategies:

1. **Unified set of symbols:** To prevent the use of inappropriate expressions, group administrators should be able to customise the available set of built-in tags and symbols used in group communications when necessary. Any new category or tag proposed by a user must be approved by one or more administrators. Within the ICF, inappropriate tags can be automatically banned and/or manually removed as needed.

2. **Emphasis on positive characteristics**: To reduce the frustration and discouragement that can result from negative ratings, ICF can automatically remove tags whose sum of positive and negative ratings is negative because they no longer describe a particular topic or object.

3. **Indirect feedback of verified users:** The best strategy to avoid problems when sharing critical feedback is anonymity. Fortunately, even with anonymous ratings, the system can record all important information about the raters and monitor which of them have permission to rate different topics and objects. This means that only verified users have permission to rate information in ICF. To improve trust and objectivity, ICF should display all important information about the rating (e.g., the total number of raters, the rater's ID verified by administrators, the raters' rating, the date of the rating). On

the other hand, there are situations where it is desirable or necessary to share direct feedback (e.g., university degrees). In addition to direct and indirect feedback, there is also public and private feedback. Public feedback is visible to all, while private feedback is only visible to those who have access to a specific closed group. For this reason, ICF needs to facilitate the sharing of different types of feedback.

4. **Suspension:** Within ICF, any user may at any time report a tag, group or user for violating the rules and general terms of use. This strategy will only be used in case of gross or frequent violations of the rules and will result in exclusion from the group and/or the entire communication framework.

Today's society needs a communication framework that promotes assertiveness and inclusion by providing equal access to opportunities and resources for social actors who would otherwise be excluded or marginalised. The ICF encourages social actors to express their views and advance their own interests in a safe and controlled manner that protects user privacy. To achieve sustainability in communication, members of the network society need a communication framework that reduces the time and energy required to exchange information. Development and learning are not possible without the inclusion of all social groups regardless of their ethnicity, geographic location, and financial means. Therefore, ICF should be open and accessible to all societal stakeholders.

FUTURE RESEARCH DIRECTIONS

The future development of the integral communication framework is likely to go in several directions. The first direction relates to the ability to automatically collect user tags from various external systems and digital sources. The IoT devices and the Internet can be important sources of information for defining the integral identity. Various pieces of information in an individual's IDI, if collected in a privacy-preserving manner, can be used to introduce sustainable measures. The second direction refers to the possibilities of "mind-reading" technology, which can be used to manage and read data in integral maps. The third direction relates to the optimization of key processes within ICF. Some of the key issues related to ICF optimization are:

- How can the ICF be used to improve environmental sustainability?
- What information in the IDI should always remain private?
- How often do evaluations need to be conducted?
- Which instruments show the best results when assessing a person?
- Which instruments show the best results when evaluating a group?
- What data is most commonly used for integral mapping?
- How can relationships between different users be visualised in the ICF?
- How can weaknesses and threats in integral communication be reduced?

CONCLUSION

The proposed solution will enhance the communication capabilities of social actors and personalise their interaction with AI devices. Integral digital identity (IDI) can be designed by a unified set of identifiers used to describe subjects and objects in an information network. By facilitating the representation and exchange of feedback, the ICF enhances the quality of communication and collaboration and enables effective identification of relationships between different types of social actors on a multilingual basis. ICF reduces the need for multiple entries of personal information and optimises the time social actors spend searching and communicating online. By allowing its users to define their characteristics and preferences through integrated tags, ICF enables personalised communication and saves social actors time and resources in presenting, collaborating, evaluating, and analysing important user data. By using a unified set of digital symbols (e.g., tags) translated into different languages, ICF improves communication between social actors who do not speak the same language and improves human communication with AI machines and IoT devices. By assessing integral tags used to define qualities and characteristics of different people, organisations, products, services, events, and places, the ICF aims to improve trust, the experience of collaboration, personal mastery, and organisational learning. Like any other technology, ICF has certain weaknesses and poses specific risks, in addition to strengths and opportunities. The analysis conducted has shown that social perceptibility is the main strength, sustainable and inclusive development is the main opportunity, addictive behaviour is the main weakness, and autocratic and unauthorised control is the main threat related to integral communication. When used properly, ICF improves the quality of communication and dialogue and lowers transaction costs; when misused, ICF becomes a means of control and surveillance. How it is used depends primarily on the morality and intentions of those who use it, but also on the laws that govern the activities in which it is used. Open networks, freedom of choice and transparency are often the best antidote to the tyranny of those with autocratic tendencies.

Key Terms and Definitions

Basic Integral Map: A set of data that contains all the records of the personal integral map and all the records that other users and third parties have written about this user (e.g. the results of the tests used to evaluate the user).

Digital Identity: A set of digital records about a person's identity that improves engagement in digital interactions.

Integral Communication: An automatic exchange of all information that might be useful in an interaction. The goal is not to exchange as much information as possible, but only that which the communicators consider most important.

Integral Communication Framework: An information system that provides a personalised communication experience using tags placed in various maps. A digitally supported environment that promotes human perceptiveness and collaboration.

Integral Design: A design approach that uses all available knowledge and insights to optimise product use and interaction with stakeholders.

Integral Data Map: A unified set of tags that can be evaluated in different ways and enriched with metadata (e.g., location data, images, prices, time, dates, etc.).

Integral Digital Identity: A comprehensive, flexible, shareable, numeric, textual, and visual record of users' personal characteristics and preferences in information networks. A set of digital datasets that describes social actors in all aspects of their personalities and enhances integral communication in digitally supported interactions.

Integral Mapping: A process of assigning, visualising, and analysing integral tags that facilitates integral communication and enables automatic identification of compatible and complementary items.

Integral Tag: A specific type of hashtag that can be described by metadata, translated into multiple languages, and rated by users or tests.

Personal Integral Map: A flexible, shareable, numeric, textual, and visual record of personal characteristics and preferences that users write down about themselves to improve their own efficiency in presenting, communicating, collaborating, and searching content on information and communication networks.

References

Abdelal, R., Herrera, Y. M., Johnston, A. I., & McDermott, R. (2006). Identity as a variable. *Harvard Business Review, 4*(4), 695–711. https://www.hbs.edu/ris/Publication%20Files/Identity%20as%20a%20Variable_15cfe909-8570-4669-8e11-480c95e8a885.pdf

Ackland, P., Resnikoff, S., & Bourne, R. (2017). World blindness and visual impairment: despite many successes, the problem is growing. *Community Eye Health, 30*(100), 71–73. PMID: 29483748; PMCID: PMC5820628.

Alashoor, T., Han, S., & Joseph, R. C. (2017). Familiarity with big data, privacy concerns, and self-disclosure accuracy in social networking websites: An APCO model. *Communications of the Association for Information Systems, 41*, 62–96. https://doi.org/10.17705/1cais.04104

Anant, V., Donchak, L., Kaplan, J., & Soller, H. (2020). *The consumer-data opportunity and the privacy imperative.* McKinsey. Retrieved July15, 2023., from https://www.mckinsey.com/capabilities/risk-and-resilience/our-insights/the-consumer-data-opportunity-and-the-privacy-imperative

Andreassen, C. S., Billieux, J., Griffiths, M. D., Kuss, D. J., Demetrovics, Z., Mazzoni, E., & Pallesen, S. (2016). The relationship between addictive use of social media and video games and symptoms of psychiatric disorders: A large-scale cross-sectional study. *Psychology of Addictive Behaviors, 30*(2), 252–262. https://doi.org/10.1037/adb0000160

Anrig, B., Benoist, E., & Jaquet-Chiffelle, D. O. (2006). Virtual persons applied to authorization, individual authentication and identification. In D.-O. Jaquet-Chiffelle, E. Benoist, & B. Anrig (Eds.), *FIDIS: Future of Identity in the Information Society – Identity in a Networked World: Use Cases and Scenarios.* VIP – Virtual Identity and Privacy Research Center, Berne University of Applied Sciences. http://www.fidis.net/fileadmin/fidis/deliverables/booklet/fidis.booklet.Identity_in_a_Networked_World.d26.pdf

Ashforth, B. E. (2014). Identity, personal; role transitions. In P. C. Flood & Y. Freeney (Eds.), *Wiley encyclopedia of management* (Organizational Behavior) (Vol. 11, 3rd ed., pp. 1–2). Wiley. https://doi.org/10.1002/9781118785317.weom110163

Ashforth, B. E., & Mael, F. (1989). Social identity theory and the organization. *The Academy of Management Review, 14*(1), 20–39. https://doi.org/10.2307/258189

Awad, N. F., & Krishnan, M. S. (2006). The personalization privacy paradox: An empirical evaluation of information transparency and the willingness to be profiled online for personalization. *MIS Quarterly, 30*(1), 13–28. https://doi.org/10.2307/25148715

Badr, A., & Abdul-Hassan, A. (2020). A review on voice-based interface for human-robot interaction. *Iraqi Journal for Electrical and Electronic Engineering, 16*(2), 1–12. https://doi.org/10.37917/ijeee.16.2.10

Bailenson, J. N., Beall, A. C., Loomis, J., Blascovich, J., & Turk, M. (2004). Transformed social interaction: Decoupling representation from behavior and form in collaborative virtual environments. *Presence: Teleoperators and Virtual Environments, 13*(4), 428–441. https://doi.org/10.1162/1054746041944803

Bansal, H., & Kohli, S. (2019). Trust evaluation of websites: A comprehensive study. *International Journal of Advanced Intelligence Paradigms, 13*(1/2), 101. https://doi.org/10.1504/ijaip.2019.099946

Bargh, J. A., & Mckenna, K. Y. (2004). The internet and social life. *Annual Review of Psychology, 55*(1), 573–590. https://doi.org/10.1146/annurev.psych.55.090902.141922

Batmunkh, A. (2022). Carbon footprint of the most popular social media platforms. *Sustainability, 14*(4), 2195. https://doi.org/10.3390/su14042195

Beduschi, A. (2019). Digital identity: Contemporary challenges for data protection, privacy and non-discrimination rights. *Big Data & Society, 6*(2), 205395171985509. https://doi.org/10.1177/2053951719855091

Benbasat, I., & Zmud, R. W. (1999). Empirical research in information systems: The practice of relevance. *Management Information Systems Quarterly, 23*(1), 3–16. https://doi.org/10.2307/249403

Bozdag, E., & van den Hoven, J. (2015). Breaking the filter bubble: Democracy and design. *Ethics and Information Technology, 17*(4), 249–265. https://doi.org/10.1007/s10676-015-9380-y

Burbach, L., Halbach, P., Ziefle, M., & Calero Valdez, A. (2019). Bubble Trouble: Strategies Against Filter Bubbles in Online Social Networks. In: Duffy, V. (eds) *Digital Human Modeling and Applications in Health, Safety, Ergonomics and Risk Management*. Healthcare Applications. HCII 2019. Lecture Notes in Computer Science, vol 11582. Springer. https://doi.org/10.1007/978-3-030-22219-2_33

Buttle, F., & Maklan, S. (2019). *Customer relationship management: Concepts and technologies*. Routledge.

Canales, K. (2021, December 24). *China's 'social credit' system ranks citizens and punishes them with throttled internet speeds and flight bans if the Communist*

Party deems them untrustworthy. Business insider. Retrieved May 3, 2023, from https://www.businessinsider.com/china-social-credit-system-punishments-and-rewards-explained-2018-4

Chan, M. J. (2007, June 14). *Identity in a virtual world.* CNN. Retrieved May 15, 2023, from http://edition.cnn.com/2007/TECH/06/07/virtual_identity/index.html

Chen, L., Stankovski, V., Shi, Z., & Watson, P. (2008). Semantic-enabled and agent-based environment aware agile service utilities. In *2008 fourth international conference on semantics, knowledge and grid, Beijing* (pp. 461–464). https://doi.org/10.1109/SKG.2008.109

Code, J. R., & Zaparyniuk, N. E. (2009). Social identities, group formation, and the analysis of online communities. In S. Hatzipanagos & S. Warburton (Eds.), *Handbook of research on social software and developing community ontologies.* IGI Global. https://doi.org/10.4018/978-1-60566-984-7.ch086

Collins, G. R. (2020). Improving human–robot interactions in hospitality settings. *International Hospitality Review, 34*(1), 61–79. https://doi.org/10.1108/ihr-09-2019-0019

Cufoglu, A. (2014). User profiling – a short review. *International Journal of Computer Applications, 108*(3), 1–9. https://doi.org/10.5120/18888-0179

Deloitte. (2023). *Connecting with meaning Hyper-personalizing the customer experience using data, analytics, and AI.* Deloitte. Retrieved July 14, 2023. from https://www2.deloitte.com/content/dam/Deloitte/ca/Documents/deloitte-analytics/ca-en-omnia-ai-marketing-pov-fin-jun24-aoda.pdf

Deuerlein, C., Langer, M., Seßner, J., Heß, P., & Franke, J. (2021). Human-robot-interaction using cloud-based speech recognition systems. *Procedia CIRP, 97*, 130–135. https://doi.org/10.1016/j.procir.2020.05.214

Dietrich, F., & List, C. (2012). Where do preferences come from? *International Journal of Game Theory, 42*(3), 613–637. https://doi.org/10.1007/s00182-012-0333-y

Domingo, A. I. S., & Enríquez, Á. M. (2018). *Digital identity: The current state of affairs – BBVA research.* BBVA Research, Retrieved January 14, 2023, from https://www.bbvaresearch.com/wp-content/uploads/2018/02/Digital-Identity_the-current-state-of-affairs.pdf

Drury, B., Drury, S. M., Rahman, M. A., & Ullah, I. (2022). A social network of crime: A review of the use of social networks for crime and the detection of crime. *Online Social Networks and Media, 30*, 100211. https://doi.org/10.1016/j.osnem.2022.100211

Eurostat. (2022). *How do EU citizens manage their personal data online?* European Commission. Retrieved July 12, 2023, from https://ec.europa.eu/eurostat/web/products-eurostat-news/-/edn-20220127-1

Eurostat. (2023). *Food waste and food waste prevention – estimates.* European Commission. Retrieved July 18, 2023, from https://ec.europa.eu/eurostat/

statistics-explained/index.php?title=Food_waste_and_food_waste_prevention_-_estimates

FAO. (2019). *2019 the state of food and agriculture - moving forward on food loss and waste reduction.* Food and Agriculture Organization of the United Nations. Retrieved July 20, 2023, from https://food.ec.europa.eu/system/files/2019-10/fw_lib_fao-2019_en.pdf

Fearon, J. D. (1999). *What is identity (As we now use the word) (draft)?* Department of Political Science Stanford University, Stanford, Retrieved January11, 2023, from http://www.web.stanford.edu/group/fearon-research/cgi-bin/wordpress/wp-content/uploads/2013/10/What-is-Identity-as-we-now-use-the-word-.pdf

Fisher, J. H. N., Caldwell, J., Price, B, Price, E. (2016). *Technology addiction: Concern, controversy, and finding balance. Common sense media.* Retrieved November 11, 2022, from https://www.commonsensemedia.org/sites/default/files/research/report/csm_2016_technology_addiction_research_brief_0.pdf

Gardner, H., & Davis, K. (2014). *The app generation: How Today's youth navigate identity, intimacy, and imagination in a digital world: With a new preface.* Yale University Press.

Geddes, D., & Baron, R. A. (1997). Workplace aggression as a consequence of negative performance feedback. *Management Communication Quarterly, 10*(4), 433–454. https://doi.org/10.1177/0893318997104002

Godoy, D., & Amandi, A. (2005). User profiling in personal information agents: A survey. *The Knowledge Engineering Review, 20*(4), 329–361. https://doi.org/10.1017/s0269888906000397

Goitein, E. (2019). *How the FBI violated the privacy rights of tens of thousands of Americans.* Brennan Center. Retrieved June 10, 2023, from https://www.brennancenter.org/our-work/analysis-opinion/how-fbi-violated-privacy-rights-tens-thousands-americans

Hevner, A., & Chatterjee, S. (2010). Design research in information systems. In *Theory and practice.* Springer. https://doi.org/10.1007/978-1-4419-5653-8

Hevner, A. R., March, S. T., Park, J., & Ram, S. (2004). Design science in information systems research. *Management Information Systems Quarterly, 28*(1), 75–105. https://doi.org/10.2307/25148625

Holi, M., & Hyvönen, E. (2006). Modelling uncertainty in semantic web taxonomies. *Soft Computing in Ontologies and Semantic Web,* 31–46. https://doi.org/10.1007/978-3-540-33473-6_2

Hudson Institute. (2018, October 4). *Vice president Mike Pence's remarks on the Administration's policy towards China.* Hudson. Retrieved June 5, 2023, from https://www.hudson.org/events/1610-vice-president-mike-pence-s-remarks-on-the-administration-s-policy-towards-china102018

Hussain, Z., & Pontes, H. M. (2019). Personality, internet addiction, and other technological addictions: A psychological examination of personality traits and technological addictions. In I. Management Association (Ed.), *Internet and technology addiction: Breakthroughs in research and practice* (pp. 335–361). IGI Global. https://doi.org/10.4018/978-1-5225-8900-6.ch020

ITU. (2018). *Digital identity roadmap guide*. International Telecommunication Union. Retrieved February 5, 2023, from Applications/Documents/Guides/Digital_Identity_Roadmap_Guide-2018-E.pdf

Jenkins, R. (2014). *Social identity*. Routledge.

Johnson, D. W., Johnson, R. T., & Holubec, E. J. (2008). *Cooperation in the classroom*. Interaction Book.

Kamberg, M.-L. (2019). *Digital identity: Your reputation online*. Rosen Publishing.

Khaewratana, W., Veinott, E. S., & Ramkumar, S. M. (2020). Development of a generalised voice-controlled human-robot interface: One automatic speech recognition system for all robots. In *2020 3rd international conference on control and robots (ICCR)* (pp. 38–42). https://doi.org/10.1109/iccr51572.2020.9344123

Koole, M. L., & Parchoma, G. (2012). The web of identity. *Digital Identity and Social Media*, 1–15. https://doi.org/10.4018/978-1-4666-1915-9.ch002

Korte, R. F. (2007). A review of social identity theory with implications for training and development. *Journal of European Industrial Training, 31*(3), 166–180. https://doi.org/10.1108/03090590710739250

Kull, K. (2019). Steps towards the natural meronomy and taxonomy of semiosis: Emotin between index and symbol? *Sign Systems Studies, 47*(1/2), 88–104. https://doi.org/10.12697/sss.2019.47.1-2.03

Laurent, M., & Bouzefrane, S. (2015). *Digital identity management*. Elsevier Science.

Leary, M. R., & Kowalski, R. M. (1995). *Social anxiety*. Guilford Press.

Luo, W., Song, L. J., Gebert, D. R., Zhang, K., & Feng, Y. (2016). How does leader communication style promote employees' commitment at times of change? *Journal of Organizational Change Management, 29*(2), 242–262. https://doi.org/10.1108/jocm-11-2014-0204

Manancourt, V. (2022, July 7). *Europe faces a Facebook blackout*. Politico. Retrieved June 10, 2023, from https://www.politico.eu/article/europe-faces-facebook-blackout-instagram-meta-data-protection/

Marge, M., Espy-Wilson, C. Y., & Ward, N. G. (2020). Spoken language interaction with Robots: Research Issues and Recommendations. *Report from the NSF Future Directions Workshop*. https://doi.org/10.48550/arXiv.2011.05533

Martic, K. (2022). *Top 13 communication barriers and how to tackle them*. Haiilo. Retrieved March 5, 2023 from https://haiilo.com/blog/communication-barriers/

Masseno, M. D., & Santos, C. T. (2019). Personalization and profiling of tourists in smart tourism destinations - a data protection perspective. *International Journal of Information Systems and Tourism (IJIST)*, 4(2), 7–23. http://www.uajournals.com/ijist-tourism/journal/4/2/1.pdf

McKinsey. (2013). *Using customer analytics to boost corporate performance*. Key insights from McKinsey's DataMatics 2013 survey. McKinsey. Retrieved July 3, 2023. from https://www.mckinsey.com/~/media/McKinsey/Business%20Functions/Marketing%20and%20Sales/Our%20Insights/Five%20facts%20How%20customer%20analytics%20boosts%20corporate%20performance/Datamatics.pdf

Mildebrath, H. (2022). *The future of data protection and privacy. How the European Parliament is responding to citizens' expectations.* Members' research service, PE 729.396. European Parliament. Retrieved May 15, 2023 from https://www.europarl.europa.eu/RegData/etudes/BRIE/2022/729396/EPRS_BRI(2022)729396_EN.pdf

Molina, B. (2017). *Want to feel #old?* This is the first tweet with a hashtag. USA Today. Retrieved May 20, 2023, from https://eu.usatoday.com/story/tech/talkingtech/2017/08/23/twitter-hashtag-turns-10/592868001/

Morris, C. W. (1945). *Foundations of the theory of signs.* University of Chicago Press.

Munson, S. A., & Resnick, P. (2010). Presenting diverse political opinions. In *Proceedings of the 28th international conference on human factors in computing systems* – CHI '10 (pp. 1457–1466). https://doi.org/10.1145/1753326.1753543

Naeem, B., Hassan, S. U., & Yousuf, N. (2023). *An AI Based Voice Controlled Humanoid Robot* [Unpublished manuscript]. https://doi.org/10.21203/rs.3.rs-2424215/v1

Nagulendra, S., & Vassileva, J. (2014). Understanding and controlling the filter bubble through interactive visualization. In *Proceedings of the 25th ACM conference on hypertext and social media* (pp. 107–115). https://doi.org/10.1145/2631775.2631811

Oliveira, N., Argyres, N., & Lumineau, F. (2022). The role of communication style in adaptation to Interorganizational project disruptions. *SSRN Electronic Journal.* https://doi.org/10.2139/ssrn.4090335

Paljak, I. (2018). *Modeli za izgradnju semantičke taksonomije iz debatnih rasprava [Semantic Taxonomy Learning from Online Debates] (thesis).* University of Zagreb, Faculty of Electrical Engineering and Computing. https://urn.nsk.hr/urn:nbn:hr:168:399034

Panko, B. (2017, August 23). *A decade ago, the hashtag reshaped the internet.* Smithsonian magazine. Retrieved January 11, 2023, from https://www.smithsonianmag.com/smart-news/decade-ago-hashtag-reshaped-internet-180964605/

Papa, V., & Photiadis, T. (2021). Algorithmic curation and users' civic attitudes: A study on facebook news feed results. *Information, 12*(12), 522. https://doi.org/10.3390/info12120522

Pariser, E. (2011). *The filter bubble: What the internet is hiding from you.* The Penguin Press.

Paulsen, K. (2011). *Moving media storage technologies: Applications & workflows for video and media server platforms.* Elsevier.

Pipitone, A., & Chella, A. (2021). What robots want? Hearing the inner voice of a robot. *iScience, 24*(4), 102371. https://doi.org/10.1016/j.isci.2021.102371

Pontes, H. M. (2017). Investigating the differential effects of social networking site addiction and internet gaming disorder on psychological health. *Journal of Behavioral Addictions, 6*(4), 601–610. https://doi.org/10.1556/2006.6.2017.075

Pratt, M. G., Schultz, M., Ashforth, B. E., & Ravasi, D. (2016). *The Oxford handbook of organizational identity.* Oxford University Press. https://doi.org/10.1093/oxfordhb/9780199689576.001.0001

Purao, S. (2002). *Design research in the Technology of Information Systems: Truth or dare.* Semantic scholar. Retrieved June 13, 2022, from https://www.semanticscholar.org/paper/Design-Research-in-the-Technology-of-Information-or-Purao/2cad8bcab1990dd536724bbc97331d67b25cf4ed

Rafajac, O., & Jakupović, A. (2017). Integral communication tool: What it is, how it works, where it helps? *The International Journal of e-Collaboration, 13*(3), 1–20. https://doi.org/10.4018/IJeC.2017070101

Rahnama, H. & Pentland, A. (2022, February 25). *The new rules of data privacy.* Harvard Business Review. Retrieved July 6, 2023, from https://hbr.org/2022/02/the-new-rules-of-data-privacy

Ranjan, P., & Tarasia, N. (2013). Challenges in password memorization for multiple accounts of single user. *International Journal of Science and Research, 2*(3), 284–286.

Razis, G., Anagnostopoulos, I., & Zhou, H. (2021). Identifying dominant nodes in semantic taxonomies. In *16th international workshop on semantic and Social Media Adaptation & Personalization (SMAP).* https://doi.org/10.1109/smap53521.2021.9610779

Reuters. (2022). *Irish regulator moves closer to ban on Facebook EU-U.S. data flows.* Reuters. Retrieved July 12, 2023, from https://www.reuters.com/technology/irish-regulator-moves-closer-possible-ban-facebook-instagram-eu-us-data-flows-2022-07-07/

Revell, T. (2018, September 26). *Mind-reading devices can now access your thoughts and dreams using AI.* New Scientist. Retrieved July 14, 2023, from https://www.newscientist.com/article/mg23931972-500-mind-reading-devices-can-now-access-your-thoughts-and-dreams-using-ai/

Riihimaa, J. (2004). *Taxonomy of information and communication technology system innovations adopted by small and medium sized enterprises*. University of Tampere. Department of Computer Sciences. https://trepo.tuni.fi/bitstream/handle/10024/67404/951-44-6027-8.pdf?sequence=1

Rogers, R., & Niederer, S. (2020). The politics of social media manipulation. *The Politics of Social Media Manipulation*, 19–70. https://doi.org/10.2307/j.ctv1b0fvs5.3

Rosemann, M., & Vessey, I. (2008). Toward improving the relevance of information systems research to practice: The role of applicability checks. *Management Information Systems Quarterly*, *32*(1), 1–22. https://doi.org/10.2307/25148826

Sathyavenkateshwaren, S., & Malathi, S. (2018). Humanoid robot: A survey on communication, tracking and voice recognition. In *3rd international conference on inventive computation technologies (ICICT)* (pp. 555–560). https://doi.org/10.1109/icict43934.2018.9034329

Segment. (2022). *The State of Personalization 2022*. Segment. Retrieved January 28, 2023, from https://segment.com/pdfs/State-of-Personalization-Report-Twilio-Segment-2022.pdf

Stojanović, N., Mentaz, G., & Apostolu, D. (2006). *Semantic-enabled agile knowledge-based e-government*. American Association for Artificial Intelligence. https://www.aaai.org/Papers/Symposia/Spring/2006/SS-06-06/SS06-06-022.pdf

Sullivan, C. (2011). *Digital identity: An emergent legal concept*. University of Adelaide Press.

Ta'amneh, I. M., & Al-Ghazo, A. (2021). The importance of using hashtags on raising awareness about social issues. *International Journal of Learning and Development*, *11*(4), 10–24. https://doi.org/10.5296/ijld.v11i4.19139

Tada, Y., Hagiwara, Y., Tanaka, H., & Taniguchi, T. (2020). Robust understanding of robot-directed speech commands using sequence to sequence with noise injection. *Frontiers in Robotics and AI*, *6*, 1–12. https://doi.org/10.3389/frobt.2019.00144

Thibodeau, K. (2021). Discerning meaning and producing information: Semiosis in knowing the past. *Information*, *12*(9), 1–21. https://doi.org/10.3390/info12090363

Thomson, W. (1st Baron Kelvin). (1883). *"Lecture on electrical units of measurement", in popular lectures and addresses* (Vol. 1). Macmillan.

Toomey, P. (2018, August 22). *The NSA Continues to Violate Americans' Internet Privacy Rights*. ACLU. Retrieved March 1, 2023, from https://www.aclu.org/blog/national-security/privacy-and-surveillance/nsa-continues-violate-americans-internet-privacy

Walther, J. B. (2007). Selective self-presentation in computer-mediated communication: Hyperpersonal dimensions of technology, language, and cognition.

Computers in Human Behavior, 23(5), 2538–2557. https://doi.org/10.1016/ j.chb.2006.05.002

Warren, C., McGraw, A., & Van Boven, L. (2010). Values and preferences: Defining preference construction. *Wiley Interdisciplinary Reviews: Cognitive Science, 2*(2), 193–205. http://leeds-faculty.colorado.edu/mcgrawp/pdf/ warren.mcgraw.vanboven.inpress.pdf

Windley, P. J. (2023). *Learning digital identity: Design, deploy, and manage identity architectures.* O'Reilly Media, Inc.

World Bank. (2018). *Technology landscape for digital identification.* World Bank. Retrieved February 14, 2023, from https://documents1.worldbank.org/ curated/en/199411519691370495/Technology-Landscape-for-Digital-Identification.pdf

Yee, N., & Bailenson, J. (2007). The Proteus effect: The effect of transformed self-representation on behavior. *Human Communication Research, 33*(3), 271–290. https://doi.org/10.1111/j.1468-2958.2007.00299.x

Zauderer, S. (2023, June 30). *33 dyslexia statistics & facts: How many people have dyslexia?.* Life-changing ABA therapy – Cross River therapy. Retrieved July 1, 2023, from https://www.crossrivertherapy.com/research/dyslexia-statistics

Zhang, X., & Zhou, M. (2021). An exploration of Chinese students' perceived barriers to effective intercultural communication. *Journal of Language and Cultural Education, 9*(2), 11–31. https://doi.org/10.2478/jolace-2021-0008

Zuboff, S. (2019). *The age of surveillance capitalism: The fight for human future at the New Frontier of Power.* PublicAffairs.

Perspective on Integral Communication

Ozren Rafajac and Alen Jakupović

INTRODUCTION

In order to transform its policies and activities towards sustainable development, modern society urgently needs a communication methodology that promotes the exchange of feedback, coordination, cooperation and collaboration. In fact, each of the above processes plays an important role in socio-economic development. Although all organisations strive to develop these processes, not all organisations are equally good at them. When leaders strive to develop communication, they improve understanding and information sharing. Unfortunately, there are still a large number of leaders and managers today who are unfamiliar with the importance of active listening, dialogue, and organisational learning. In addition, workshops where they could learn more about communication skills such as sharing feedback are expensive and require a lot of time and effort. Even when there are leaders who practise and support professional development and training, dialogue, effective sharing of feedback, and active listening, they face significant problems in applying these processes to large groups.

O. Rafajac (✉) • A. Jakupović
Polytechnic of Rijeka, Rijeka, Croatia
e-mail: ozren.rafajac@veleri.hr; alen.jakupovic@veleri.hr

Although advanced communication frameworks can be helpful, implementing such systems is not an easy or cheap task. Due to the economic crisis, lack of funding, and/or a shortage of engineers to develop such solutions, many organisations still do not use communication frameworks that integrate human resource management, customer relationship management, and quality management. When seeking to improve coordination, organisations focus on improving efficiency. To achieve coordination, managers inform each unit (e.g., employee, group, etc.) or part of the whole about how and when they need to take action (Denise, 1999). Coordination is the ability to use various sources of information and organisational elements smoothly and efficiently. The basic function of the coordinator in an organisation is the same as that of an orchestra conductor who directs the activities of the orchestra group to produce harmony in the music (Havinal, 2009, p. 84). Coordinating a large number of people without advanced information systems that rely on complex algorithms and machine learning to propose potential solutions is a major challenge. Therefore, nowadays there are more and more researchers advocating the adoption of integral information systems and cloud solutions that improve organisational intelligence (Merletti de Palo et al., 2015; Nedjah et al., 2018). Although the idea that IT systems should be used to improve communication in organisations is not particularly new, the wider application of such solutions is still in its infancy. For example, coordination languages and models such as Linda and Reo, which were developed in computer science to coordinate the interaction between components and objects, are now also being used to model and analyse organisations (Boella & van der Torre, 2006). Through learning and self-adaptive functions, such systems have the potential to significantly improve the organisational and coordination potential of modern organisations in an organic and flexible manner (Groenewegen et al., 2006). By studying the formation and dissolution of ties between individuals in Social Coordination Dynamics (SCD) scholars today seek to explore how self-organisation occurs and how the loss of stability of a self-organising system is associated with the transition to another phase (Oullier & Kelso, 2009). While coordination refers to the joint establishment of goals (Castañer & Oliveira, 2020), cooperation and collaboration refer to the implementation of these goals. Although these two processes are an integral part of any teamwork or group project, there is a key difference between them. While in cooperation all actors are free to decide what to do, how to do it, and to what extent to self-organise their behaviour (e.g., bottom-up management), in collaboration there is a clear hierarchy of relationships and it is known who makes the decisions (e.g., top-down management). In a jazz band, for example, each musician can improvise (e.g., This is a cooperation.), but all must follow the rhythm of the drum (e.g., This is a collaboration.). Nowadays, there is still considerable confusion in the literature about the definition and distinction between collaboration and cooperation (Axelrod, 2000; Moseley, 2020). According to Axelrod and Keohane (1985, p. 226), cooperation occurs when actors adjust their behaviour to the actual or expected preferences of others. Cooperation is a process of joint neutral action with mutual satisfaction based on the principle of self-organisation (Merletti de Palo et al., 2015). Self-organisation refers to the ability of a complex system to find a new equilibrium after a severe shock, which may be far from its starting point (Rupasingha et al., 1999). Given that social actors in cooperation may or may not have the same goal, outcome, or mission, cooperation is usually based on a small number of informal rules and does not have a strict hierarchy. It takes place when a teammate suggests to others how to improve their performance and when a neighbour helps someone find an exact address. Therefore, leadership by personal example predominates in cooperative behaviour. In the context of this research, cooperation represents a process in which social actors work independently on various activities that help them achieve a common goal or task. Cooperation is based on voluntary help and sharing of resources, without strict hierarchy or rules that must be followed. It leads to the best results when it comes to promoting creativity and integration. While cooperation has its own advantages when organising large groups, collaboration is usually the better option when dealing with fast-paced, confidential, and/or highly dependent activities in small teams. According to Castañer and Oliveira (2020), collaboration is the process of co-creation in which two or more people with complementary skills work together based on a specific agenda and timeframe to achieve desired goals. According to Moseley (2020), collaboration is when a group of social actors come together and work on a project to achieve a common goal, outcome, or mission. A plumber collaborates with an architect to build a house or a swimming pool. In the context of this research, collaboration is defined as a process in which social actors work together on a set of dependent activities that help them achieve a common goal or task. This type of interaction usually involves a deep hierarchy, clearly defined roles, and strict rules that must be followed to achieve a particular goal or task. It produces the best results when it comes to acting quickly and in a coordinated manner. Although there are no clear boundaries, when there are a larger number of people and when working on very complex tasks, collaboration often becomes ineffective in achieving the set goals. Since collaboration and cooperation have their advantages and disadvantages, modern organisations tend to combine both approaches. But how do the most successful companies in the market strike an optimal balance? These companies usually apply the so-called tight-loose principle, in which the most important processes and tasks are handled by relatively small teams with strict rules and a flat hierarchy, while everything else is attempted through voluntary self-organisation. When they strive to develop cooperation, organisations rely on creativity and voluntary support to create an environment in which each actor is free to work toward its own goals, as long as they are consistent with the goals of the organisation. As important as it is to encourage freedom of choice and creativity, there are tasks that are easier to accomplish through collaboration than cooperation. A good example of such a task is waste disposal. Groups that do not apply collaboration in waste disposal usually fail to make their environment pleasant and clean.

The balance between cooperation and collaboration is not easy to find. In practice, it is possible to identify groups that communicate, coordinate, and cooperate, but do not collaborate (Denise, 1999). This is true, for example, of any meeting where specific conclusions and time frames have not been agreed upon. On the other hand, there are situations in which social actors communicate and collaborate, but do not cooperate. This refers to any situation in which social actors are unwilling to share their opinions in order to avoid possible conflict with those who do not like such an opinion. There are many different reasons why social actors do not cooperate and collaborate better than they currently do. Sometimes social actors simply do not want to interact because they have opposing goals, but even more often, problems in interpersonal interaction arise from poorly developed communication skills, cultural differences, language barriers, and from inaccurate conclusions based on a small number of observations. Since complex goals cannot be achieved without interacting with other actors, people are forced to improve their abilities to communicate, coordinate, cooperate, and collaborate. To optimise their digital communication, contemporary researchers and innovators are constantly working on new methods of information exchange (Khanna, 2018), ethical standards in defining algorithms (Ananny, 2015; Mittelstadt et al., 2016), and solutions that ensure high levels of privacy and trust (Carminati et al., 2014). Integral communication implies an automated exchange of all information that could be useful in an interaction. The Integral Communication Framework (ICF) is a digitally supported environment that enhances the integral representation, assessment, and development of individuals and organisations. By using integral tags that can be evaluated and enriched with metadata to describe different aspects and dimensions of people, groups, organisations, products, services, events, and places, the ICF creates a new set of opportunities for improving communication, collaboration, cooperation, and learning. This chapter explains how integral communication enhances personal development and organisational learning, and how ICF can be used to create personalised experiences in the IoT ecosystem.

After reading this chapter, the reader will be able to:

- Explain the importance of feedback for personal development and organisational learning.
- Explain the difference between direct and indirect feedback.
- Explain the benefits of capturing feedback digitally.
- Recognise the importance of integral communication in digital communication.
- Explain why integral communication enhances communication with artificial intelligence devices in the IoT ecosystem.

BACKGROUND

Information and communication technologies are greatly changing social, economic, and political relations in modern society. These changes are visible in many different areas, such as communication, networking, dating, family relationships, shopping, business, public service delivery, and education. The popularity of various online platforms such as Uber, Airbnb, Facebook, WeChat, Netflix, Twitter, Instagram, LinkedIn, Reddit, and ResearchGate clearly shows that social actors have a strong interest in online collaboration and cooperation. Even though whoever offers the optimal solution can benefit, the online market is a very risky environment. What seems optimal today may not be good enough tomorrow. Unlike other markets, participants in the online market feel particularly strong pressure to conduct their interactions through a single provider. According to Brandl and Ellis (2023), in June 2022, 42.9% of websites built with an identifiable content management system used WordPress, while all other competitors had less than 5% market share. Google now dominates the global search engine market with 91.88% of all search queries worldwide (Kinsta, 2022; Oberlo, 2022). In comparison, its closest competitor, Microsoft's Bing, handles only a fraction of Google's volume, with a market share of 3.33% (Oberlo, 2022). These examples show that the provider who offers the simplest and most efficient solution to a problem wins in the online market, at least for a while. In addition to behavioural patterns, today's technologies are also changing the overall picture and experience of the world in which social actors live. These extremely rapid technological and social changes have been particularly surprising for all individuals and organisations that have failed to adapt to the latest trends due to their own inertia and/or lack of motivation. In many cases, even those who do their best do not always manage to keep up with all these innovations and changes. This means that being a teacher today is much more difficult than it was a century ago. The modern teacher is forced to constantly learn and acquire new skills in order to remain relevant and competitive in the job market. The same is true for all other jobs and professions. Cab workers have been unpleasantly surprised by the emergence of ride-sharing companies like Uber and Lyft. A significant number of low- and mid-priced hotels, especially those that have failed to develop their digital skills, saw their revenue decline when Airbnb emerged. Since its launch in 2008, this online platform for shared accommodation has registered over 300 million guest arrivals to date (Savolainen, 2018). Although information technology can make a significant contribution to reducing environmental pressures and organising human resources efficiently, policy makers and political parties do not seem interested in implementing advanced cooperative and collaborative solutions for public service delivery.

A large number of social actors manage their resources quite poorly (Lu, 2018; OECD, 2019). From an environmental perspective, this assertion is supported by numerous reports on ecological footprints, which measure how many natural resources society possesses and how many natural resources it consumes. According to UN Secretary-General António Guterres, climate change is progressing faster than efforts to combat it (WMO, 2018). Since 1970, humanity has been in an ecological overshoot with annual resource demand exceeding its annual regenerative capacity. Today, humanity consumes the equivalent of 1.7 planet Earth to secure resources and absorb wastes (Nace, 2017). If humans continue on this business-as-usual path, it is projected that human demand on the

Earth's ecosystem will exceed its regenerative capacity. This means that a modern society urgently needs new methods of communication and organisation that enable social actors to cooperate in a resource-limited environment. Apart from the environmental perspective, the problems of suboptimal resource use are also evident in the economic dimension. The tendency for the rate of return on capital to exceed the rate of economic growth threatens to create extreme inequalities that generate considerable discontent and undermine democratic principles (Piketty, 2014). According to the findings of the Global Inequality Report, inequality has increased in all regions of the world from 1980 to the present, with the fastest increases in North America, China, India, and Russia (Alvaredo et al., 2017, p. 9). Although a number of different reasons for inefficient resource use can be found in practice (e.g., administrative problems, inertia, incompetent government, corruption, etc.), in many cases these reasons are related to low levels of organisational intelligence and lack of organisational learning. In the last two decades, there are more and more scholars proposing how to use advanced IT solutions and AI for social good (Hager et al., 2019; Floridi et al., 2020; Singer et al., 2022). For example, Boella and van der Torre (2006) propose value-based rather than information-based coordination languages to model the coordination of autonomous agents and organisations, arguing that a balance between enforced control and trust-based anticipation is needed. On the other hand, policymakers show no particular interest in implementing advanced information systems that facilitate communication and cooperation. One of the reasons why political leaders and parties rarely talk about efficient public administration based on advanced IT systems is probably the fact that many of them would lose their jobs and influence by implementing such solutions. Despite this inertia, in recent years the public sector has increasingly addressed ethical issues in the implementation of algorithms and artificial intelligence, which at least provides a solid foundation for further socio-economic development. Today, there is a growing debate about the principles and criteria that should underlie the design and governance of algorithms and digital technologies more broadly, with the explicit goal of social good (Tsamados et al., 2021). According to Pennington (2008), effective governance requires leaders who act as facilitators and are able to orchestrate effective environments and interactions. Recognising that every technology has its limitations, Broussard (2018) notes that too much enthusiasm in the application of computer technology can be dangerous and produce an enormous amount of poorly designed systems. Undoubtedly, there are limits to what social actors can (and should) do with technology. Nevertheless, today's society should continue to develop solutions that promote personal development and organisational learning for all social actors regardless of their background and income status.

DEVELOPMENTAL CHALLENGES

Communication is the foundation for creating awareness, building consensus, making informed decisions, resolving conflicts, and fostering participation in change and development processes (Tabugbo & Okafor, 2021, p. 233). According to Lunenburg (2010), any organisation can promote communication in four basic directions, upward, downward, horizontal, and outward. There are at least five particular communication challenges related to personal development and organisational learning. The first problem is related to the fact that many social actors are unwilling to give and receive feedback. Unlike in private conversations, where people tend to talk about negative rather than positive experiences, many social actors in business and in public are unwilling to share negative feedback. According to Booher (2016), employees do not communicate with the boss about bad news for fear of reprisals or for fear that they will have to deal with the problem if they point it out. This tactic of non-confrontation creates a false atmosphere in which individuals and groups significantly limit their ability to grow and learn. Nevertheless, upward communication has a positive impact on employee performance (Ogundipe & Adelugba, 2022). The second problem is related to the fact that organisations that do not promote dialogue provide fewer opportunities for organisational learning and personal development than organisations that promote dialogue and open information sharing (Litman & Forbes-Riley, 2006; Lunenburg, 2010; Sadia et al., 2016). Usually, the main brake on upward communication is trust (Roberts & O'Reilly, 1974), but there may be other reasons, such as lack of understanding of the importance of sharing feedback, poorly developed communication skills, or an autocratic leadership style that does not allow for other opinions. The third problem is related to the fact that it is extremely difficult for managers of large organisations to optimise the process of organisational learning without information systems that can dynamically record and measure the quality of various human interactions (Kariuki, 2021). According to Al-Dmour and Al-Zu'bi (2014), the benefits of a human resource information system

(HRIS) are faster response time, more accurate information, less paperwork and manpower, and more efficient tracking and control, while the main obstacles are cost and insufficient knowledge in implementing the system. Nowadays, HRIS is used by all companies, regardless of their size or the industry they belong to, helping with common workplace issues such as employee turnover, workplace diversity, employee dissatisfaction, lack of recognition, etc. (Arun, 2020). No matter how hard organisations try to create a framework for more successful organisational learning, the main responsibility lies with each individual who should work on their personal development. Recently, social actors are increasingly interacting with robots and smart devices that help them improve their personal well-being. Unfortunately, these devices often do not communicate with each other and do not provide a way to process their data on a larger scale. The fourth problem is related to the fact that it is not possible to optimise communication with AI devices without an open-source communication framework that enables the automatic exchange of data about users' characteristics and preferences. Along with the linguistic aspects, human-robot interaction (HRI) can include psychological, sociological, and practical aspects, making these interactions more complex than human-computer interaction (HCI) (Bonarini, 2020). Although there are more and more organisations trying to offer personalization through their own information systems, most of these systems are not compatible with each other. The fifth problem is related to the fact that those who need the ICF solution the most often have the lowest income. Because people in low-income households have less access to Internet services (e.g., 1 in 6 households does not have Internet access), many of the online public services may remain out of their reach (Swenson & Ghertner, 2020). For the same reason, Kodransky and Lewenstein (2014) suggest that shared mobility and public transit planning must be coordinated to better address the needs of low-income communities. Although poor countries do not necessarily need more IT (Eden & Gaggl, 2020), it is quite clear that low-income people should have free access to the Internet if they want to use a wide range of online public services (e.g., health care, employment, vocational education and training, etc.). To successfully solve the problems acquired, modern society needs inclusive communication and collaboration frameworks that promote personal development and organisational learning.

Hypothesis One: Integral communication framework enhances personal development.
Hypothesis Two: Integral communication framework enhances organisational learning.

This chapter explains why it is necessary to improve the ability of individuals and organisations to work together and how an integral communication methodology promotes personal development and organisational learning. In addition, this chapter explains why personalised information sharing and trust are such important elements for the further development of the Internet of Things ecosystem.

Personal Development

Although Western civilization was built on the belief that every individual seeking well-being should have a high degree of rights and freedoms, today these rights are often out of reach for all lower-income people. It is widely known that in the United States, most top public universities are not affordable for low-income students (Marshall, 2019). Low income not only makes access to education more difficult, but also negatively impacts health and life expectancy. According to Braveman et al. (2010), U.S. residents of all income levels are less healthy than the wealthiest and most educated. While Groot and van den Brink (2010) suggest that significant savings in the social costs of crime can be achieved by investing in education, Interpol (2022) reports that various crimes such as money laundering, ransomware, and online fraud are on the rise. Transparency International (2022) report states that even the most developed countries such as Germany, the United Kingdom, and Austria face serious corruption scandals. All of these examples suggest that today's society should be more concerned with the personal development of individuals. While in many cases personal growth and personal development are used as synonyms, there are authors who note some differences between these two concepts. According to Irving and Williams (1999), personal development is a process that deals with specific aspects of an individual (e.g., something that can be planned, accomplished, and evaluated), whereas personal growth is a general process that is related to the totality of an individual and is always evaluated in terms of personal values (e.g., ethical values such as fairness, truthfulness, loyalty, etc.). Despite this subtle difference, both processes are considered as personal development in the context of the conducted research. Since both personal development and growth are related to a whole range of intertwined phenomena such as mindfulness, learning, and ethics, it is not useful from the perspective of integral communication to make a strict distinction. Integral personal development is a positive, comprehensive process of transformation and reflection through which individuals find their purpose, discover what character traits, knowledge and skills they need to improve in their interactions with others, and learn how to do so. During the integral development process, each individual has the opportunity to develop in various psychological, emotional, intellectual, social, economic and/or spiritual areas.

When discussing skills that enable personal development, the literature distinguishes between two types of skills: soft skills and hard skills. Although there is no clear boundary between them, hard skills are usually defined as skills that are easier to learn and measure, while soft skills are defined as less tangible skills that are more difficult to measure and quantify (Lumague, 2017). Examples of hard skills are work skills such as writing, arithmetic, reading, and the ability to use certain software, the ability to speak different languages, (...). Soft skills, also defined by some authors as general skills (Badcock et al., 2010), focus more on personality and include skills such as active listening, empathy, compassion, kindness, sincerity, reliability, communication, public speaking, cleanliness, etc. Although some authors debate which of these skills are more important, it is clear that it always depends on a specific context. The fact is that some companies pay more attention to soft skills during the hiring process because they believe that it is not so important how much someone knows about something, but rather how well that person will fit into an existing team in the organisation. This is especially common in the service industry and sometimes even in IT (e.g., engineering), as companies, in order to be competitive, try to create effective teams and a cooperative work atmosphere (Cimatti, 2016). As expected, there are also empirical analyses in manufacturing that confirm that there are no significant differences between hard and soft skills in recruitment (Lumague, 2017). Figure 1 shows four dimensions of soft skills. Various sources confirm that employers from all parts of the world have considerable problems finding employees who possess the appropriate qualities and competencies (WEF, 2014; Cukier et al., 2015; SHRM, 2016; Patacsil & Tablatin, 2017; OECD, 2017; Kulkarni & Kulkarni, 2019). The further optimization of ICT interaction will significantly change market relations. For this reason,

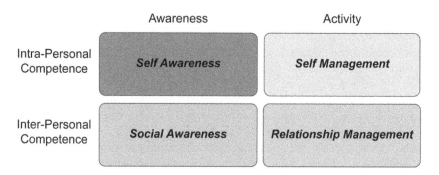

Fig. 1   Four dimensions of soft skills. (Source: Cimatti 2016)

many people will be forced to change their profession and learn new skills. Due to rapid technological development, an extremely large number of people will need lifelong learning and career guidance services. Since any learning process requires a lot of time and resources, people with low incomes are in a worse position, which further exacerbates social inequalities and inequities. While hard skills can be assessed relatively easily through standardised tests (e.g., writing, communication in a foreign language, proficiency in a programming language, and mathematics), soft skills can only be assessed in some social interactions (Cukier et al., 2015). These examples clearly show that today's society needs new solutions that facilitate communication, collaboration, learning, and assessment. The ICF simplifies and reduces the cost of these rather complex activities and helps its users to improve their self-awareness and social perceptiveness. Although a person's communication style and character tend to remain relatively constant throughout life (Manning et al., 2015; Atherton et al., 2020), a study of 13,278 college students from 55 countries conducted by Baranski et al. (2021) found that 60.40% of participants were still trying to change their personality. The highest percentage of those seeking change was in Thailand (81.91%), the lowest in Kenya (21.41%), the United States was somewhere in the middle (48.53%), while the most common goals were to increase emotional stability (29.73%), conscientiousness (19.71%), extraversion (15.94%), and agreeableness (13.53%) (Baranski et al., 2021). The ICF helps users recognise the characteristics and preferences of their interlocutors and identify those who have similar interests. In the information age and network society, integral digital identity (IDI) becomes a central point through which an individual interacts with other elements in the information network. Since networking based on incorrect or incomplete information leads to suboptimal results, the IDI of each node in the network should be as accurate as possible, and this can only be achieved through continuous multidimensional feedback exchange. As shown in Fig. 1, soft skills include intrapersonal and interpersonal competencies that can be developed by improving self-awareness, social awareness, self-management, and relationship management (Cimatti, 2016).

Everything they know people learn through instructions, research and feedback. Although critical feedback is a gift that can greatly improve a person's performance, if not shared optimally, it can lead to open conflict and/or other negative consequences (e.g., anger, disappointment, sadness, disintegration, etc.) (Heffer & Willoughby, 2020). On the other hand, when instructions and feedback are clearly directed and shared at the right level, they can assist people to comprehend, engage, or develop effective strategies to process the information intended to be learned (Hattie & Timperley, 2007). To avoid potential problems in the exchange of critical feedback, a specific communication framework had to be developed that could ensure a high level of privacy, accuracy, and security. For this reason, the feedback exchange process in ICF is highly structured by uniform tags approved by administrators and defined by profile users, who can independently decide which audiences can evaluate specific tags and at what intervals. To reduce potential conflicts, the exchange of feedback is anonymous by default. Aside from being more accurate because it comes from a larger group of stakeholders who are not afraid to voice their opinions, feedback collected through the ICF is also more targeted because it immediately points out specific things that can be improved. Although anonymity is the default option in feedback exchange, feedback results in ICF can be presented in different ways. For example, it is possible to display only the identity of those who have given a positive rating and hide the identity of those who have given a negative rating, or to display both.

The ICF helps individuals openly articulate their own goals and preferences. Goal setting shows stronger positive effects on performance when combined with some form of performance feedback or progress monitoring (Barends et al., 2016). In goal-directed learning, decisions about what, whether, how, and when to learn are determined by explicit deliberations about the learner's information needs (Ram & Leake, 1995, p. 31). The ICF can provide not only educational materials, tests, and links to potential mentors, but also real case study scenarios that can be used as a hands-on learning environment. The importance of integral communication for the personal development of modern man can be described by a well-known proverb spread by William Warde Fowler, a scholar at Oxford, and Nicholas Murray Butler, an American philosopher, diplomat, and president of Columbia University: An expert is someone who knows more and more about less and less until he knows absolutely everything about nothing (Mackay, 2017). Modern society does not need experts who know everything about nothing, but balanced and responsible individuals who, in addition to knowing their profession, practise a high level of ethics and personal integrity. Since no one likes to work with social actors who exhibit low integrity, ethical leaders rely heavily on personal integrity and trust to create a work climate that fosters employee engagement (Engelbrecht et al., 2017). The term integrity evolved from the Latin adjective integer, meaning "whole" or "complete," and describes a person who exhibits consistency and coherence of principles and values (Montefiore & Vines, 1999, p. 9). Integrity is the consistency of accountability, competence, and ethical behaviour without corruption (Integrity Action, 2015; Chennattu, 2020). In the public sphere, integrity is about the moral quality of behaviour in the process of governance, not about the content of decisions and social outcomes (Huberts, 2018). Today, many individuals, politicians, business leaders, and organisational leaders demonstrate low levels of integrity. Integral communication methodology can be used to measure and improve the integrity of these individuals. Awareness cannot be developed in isolation. To become more self-aware, one must interact with others (Bolden, 2020). Successful collaboration is based on a wide range of activities, such as: identifying opportunities for collaboration, building a team that has appropriate skills and attributes, sharing roles and responsibilities, conflict resolution, rewards, learning, etc. All of these activities require intense communication and a willingness to give and receive feedback. Only through active interaction with others individuals become aware of their weaknesses and strengths. By combining their names, psychologists Joseph Luft and Harrington Ingham developed the Johari Window in 1955 as a model that allows social individuals to better understand themselves and their social relationships. Johari is a communication model used to improve self-perception and the perception of others, based on two principles (Luft & Ingham, 1955):

- **Learning:** Individuals can learn about themselves and develop through the feedback they receive from others.

Fig. 2 Johari window.
(Source: Blackbyrn, 2022)

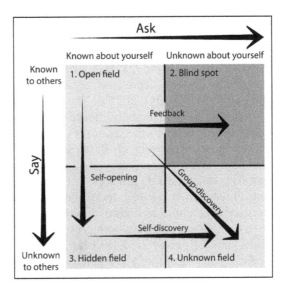

- **Trust:** Individuals can strengthen mutual trust by disclosing information about themselves.

Figure 2 shows how the exchange of feedback allows individuals to discover unknowns about themselves. Feedback is positive or negative information that social actors voluntarily exchange with each other to describe their experiences in interacting with each other. The ability to receive feedback is critical to uncovering the 'blind spot' and learning how others perceive and interpret a person's actions, intentions, and behaviours (Bolden, 2020). The purpose of feedback exchange is personal or organisational development. It is in people's best interest to get as much feedback as possible from everyone else they interact with. Of course, this does not guarantee that every exchange of feedback will automatically lead to progress and improvement. However, if the person giving the feedback is completely honest and well-meaning, the chance that the feedback will lead to improvement increases.

In addition, the ICF can be successfully used in the treatment of mental disorders. Although mental disorders encompass a wide range of problems with different symptoms, some of them, such as depression, can be successfully treated in an online environment. This is the main reason why the World Health Assembly adopted a comprehensive mental health action

plan in 2013 for the period 2013–2020, in which strengthening information systems that could improve mental health is one of the most important global goals (WHO, 2018b). Depression is the leading cause of illness
and disability worldwide (WHO, 2018a). More than 300 million people
are now living with depression, an increase of more than 18% between
2005 and 2015 (WHO, 2018a). The problem is that the majority of people suffering from mental disorders do not seek professional help (Bédard
et al., 2002). Unlike other countries, counselling is quite popular in the
United States. According to Barna Group (2018), 42% of adults in the
U.S. have seen a counsellor, while 36% are open to doing so. One of the
reasons young adults do not seek care may be because they view the mental health system negatively and feel disconnected from these services. To
reduce young adults' feelings of powerlessness and isolation, efforts should
focus on creating and developing resources and services that allow young
adults to feel connected and empowered (Marcus et al., 2012).
Unfortunately, according to Mallen et al. (2005, p. 811), there are currently no structured resources for training future counselling psychologists to work in an online setting in undergraduate counselling psychology
programmes. Having said all of the above, it is quite clear that online
counselling should become accessible to everyone. Almost everyone has at
least one personal characteristic that can be improved, or blind spot.

Personal mastery is a process of continuous improvement based on
learning and receiving feedback in various types of social interactions. It is
not something that is easy to achieve, but something that each individual
strives for in his or her life's journey (Baker, 2012). Through the integral
mapping process, which includes the exchange of feedback, ICF users gain
metaknowledge about their qualities and characteristics. The feedback
received in different types of relationships, groups, and organisations is a
fuel for development and mastery. Because it represents the transmission
of evaluative or corrective information about an action, event, or process
to the original or controlling source, feedback is one of the most important catalysts for learning (Merriam-Webster, 2020). While direct or personalised feedback means that the social actors know who is giving the
feedback, indirect or anonymous feedback means that the social actors do
not have this information. There is still an open debate in the literature
about the advantages and disadvantages of direct and indirect feedback.
Empirical research by Ghandi and Maghsoudi (2014) found that indirect
feedback was more effective than direct feedback in correcting students'
spelling errors. According to Romera (2022), anonymity creates a safe

environment for identifying and discussing difficult problems and challenges that can be recognised before they lead to conflict or failure. Similarly, Lu and Bol (2007) found that students who participated in an anonymous e-peer assessment performed better on the writing task and provided more critical feedback to their peers than students who participated in an identifiable e-peer assessment. In an empirical study by Westmacott (2017), students argued that indirect feedback is more beneficial because it promotes deeper cognitive processing and learning. On the other hand, there are authors such as Rotsaert et al. (2017) who state that anonymity can prevent a true two-way interactive feedback dialogue. According to Scherer et al. (2013), personalised assessments do not lead to biassed results in terms of social desirability as long as the assessment concept is characterised by a closed loop process and is transparent. When evaluated through various tests, measurement tools, or by others, including their friends, professors, co-workers, partners, colleagues, group and family members, and/or customers, users of integral communication platforms can find out how good they are at something and what others think about them and their actions. Aside from the fact that feedback can be direct or indirect, it can be communicated privately or publicly. Public feedback is visible to everyone, while private feedback is only visible to those who have access to a specific closed group. Although feedback can be collected in many different ways, collecting feedback in a digital framework based on IDI offers some particularly interesting advantages:

- **Dynamic monitoring:** Digital communication solutions enable continuous monitoring of critical information. When feedback is captured digitally, it is possible to track exactly who met the criteria for submitting information, when the information was received, and whether any changes have occurred over time.
- **Better understanding:** Advanced visualisation of feedback helps users understand what is happening and identify possible solutions. In ICF, feedback can be easily visualised in various ways, e.g., upward or downward trend, diagram, mind map, etc.
- **Higher precision:** Using digital communication channels makes it easier to reach larger audiences and identify subtle differences in the demographics of research samples. Precise targeting tools make it easier to find a target audience and conduct studies that can yield interesting new insights.

- **Faster and cost effective:** There is no easier or faster way to collect feedback than by scoring a consistent set of tags. If needed, traditional surveys can be created with questions whose answers or endnotes result in tags that can be inserted into the user's ID card. Digitally supported feedback systems allow for easy customization of evaluation methods and reporting. Although indirect feedback encourages free expression without fear of retribution in the event of negative comments, there are certain situations where public and direct feedback is more desirable (e.g., parliament, college degrees, testimonials, sales activities, etc.).
- **Reliability and trust:** Digitally supported feedback systems should be designed and managed as independent and reliable intermediaries that maximally protect user privacy and follow high ethical standards. The good news is that in the digital sphere, almost any information can be encrypted and protected by passwords at various levels of authorization. Although it is always possible to find some exceptions, the probability that a piece of information is true is higher if it is confirmed by a larger number of reliable sources. When managed by an organisation with high integrity, the ICF can improve objectivity and trust in the information presented and serve as a catalyst for electronic collaboration.

As highly distributed, heterogeneous, but interconnected technological infrastructures become the norm in conducting various social and economic activities, the concept of trust in online communications is becoming increasingly important. Despite the fact that security standards are constantly improving, online communications are still vulnerable to fraud and theft. In 2015, large e-commerce merchants lost an average of 1.39% of their revenue to fraud, despite spending approximately $115,000 annually on fraud prevention (Juniper Research, 2016, p. 12). In its Global Fraud and Identity Report, based on surveys of more than 5500 consumers and 500 businesses worldwide, Experian (2018) found that nearly three-quarters of businesses (72%) report fraud as a growing concern over the past 12 months, and that nearly two-thirds (63%) report consistent or higher fraud losses over the same period. Whenever they have a choice, buyers prefer to buy from sellers they like and trust. This applies not only to purchases, but also to all other common activities, especially those that take place in an online environment. This means that trust is the cornerstone of the digital economy. Without trust, digital businesses cannot use and share the data on which their operations are based (Terry, 2016). Improving trust and collaboration between people who do not know each other personally are becoming the biggest challenges in socioeconomic development. In their definition of digital trust, Chakravorti et al. (2018) distinguish two sides: the givers or users who are on the giving side of trust (e.g., those who order a car through a ride-sharing app, check messages on social media, or pay for an online transaction), and the guarantors or companies and organisations that build the platforms (e.g., car-sharing platforms such as Uber) and provide comprehensive trust-building measures (e.g., cybersecurity companies, GDPR regulators, etc.) that make the online experience seamless and convenient. An empirical study by Vries et al. (2018) suggests that trust in an online environment is strongly influenced by perceived capability and integrity, which are fostered by reputation, third-party perceptions, and project structure.

Trust and trustworthiness contribute to reciprocal behaviour and social relationship development (Li et al., 2017). As Fig. 3 shows, trust is a product of many different elements, experiences and interactions. To optimise their decision-making process, social actors need to evaluate others' trustworthiness. The main problem with traditional approaches to trust evaluation is that they require a significant investment of time and energy. From a traditional point of view, it is said that trust takes years to build, seconds to break and forever to repair (Smith, 2018). Digital trust on the other hand, takes an instant to build, an instant to break and is continuously adaptive (Allan et al., 2017). According to Allan et al. (2017) there are at least three different types of digital trust: transactional trust, competence trust and representational trust. According to Heldman and Enste (2018), empirical results suggest that dispositional trust determines the degree of trust in the recipient of private data, especially when the individual is unfamiliar with the recipient. These days, the pervasiveness, interoperability

Fig. 3   Trust in business and social relations. (Source: Made by authors)

and inter-dependency of digital infrastructures extends how we define the Internet beyond networks and people to the relationship between machines, virtual constructs or other entities (e.g., Groups of people, etc.) with greater or lesser degrees of autonomy and intelligence (van der Werff et al., 2018, p. 24). When individuals decide to share their IDI with other network members, they present themselves in a multidimensional way that improves confidence in truthfulness of presented information. In the proposed solution, the sharing of feedback is maximally simplified. The ICF automatically and periodically prompts users to rate each other (e.g., subjective evaluation) and perform various tests (e.g., objective evaluation). Feedback is shared via integral cards where evaluators can like or dislike existing personal tags and/or suggest new tags that describe the subject that they are evaluating. If someone receives low scores or negative tags, the system automatically suggests learning resources and/or network members that could help with learning. Although it is often considered undesirable to comment on the behaviour of other actors in their absence, the fact is that social actors do not always do so out of malice, but also because such information can reduce their potential losses and costs. Integral communication methodology enables the decentralised exchange of feedback, significantly reducing the cost of learning and trust. Rapid technological development requires further enhancement of lifelong learning and collaboration in geographically distant teams. From a holistic perspective, there is no fixed boundary between the digital and the non-digital (material) world. Strengthening trust between people (and companies) who do not know each other personally is one of the most important prerequisites for further socio-economic development. Since trust is always based on experiences in different types of interactions, it is advisable to develop a communication framework based on the Integral Digital Identity (IDI) that can dynamically collect and publicly present feedback from a variety of social interactions. The main advantage of the ICF is that it can distinguish those who are qualified to assess certain domains and issues from those who are not. The greater the number of qualified evaluators, the greater the confidence in the information that such a system provides.

ORGANISATIONAL LEARNING

In the globalised and knowledge-based economies of the digital age, there is a great need for information systems and solutions that can improve organisational learning (Remtulla, 2012). Despite the billions of dollars companies spend on training their employees, many of today's workers are incompetent in 20% to 40% of the activities that are critical to their performance (Christensen, 2018). Organisational intelligence (OI) of a system arises from an efficient flow of information and the ability to use that information to accomplish various (often complex) tasks and goals. Organisational intelligence represents the capacity of an enterprise to mobilise all of its available brain power, and to focus that brain power on achieving its mission (Albrecht, 2002, p. 10). According to Halal (2006), organisational intelligence is the ability of an organisation to create and use available knowledge to strategically adapt to its environment. Intelligent organisations are those that enable: the use of resources in an optimal (environmentally friendly) manner; the improvement of productivity and the quality of organisational processes to create new value for the organisations' owners, members, and users; the open exchange of knowledge and information to achieve synergy among members; the achievement of organisational goals with as few constraints and rules as possible; and a high level of satisfaction, support, and commitment from employees and customers (Rafajac & Pupavac, 2017).

Organisational learning results from sharing (e.g., dialogue), analysing (e.g., debate), evaluating (e.g., discussion), and systematising information into knowledge that can be used to improve different organisational processes. When analysing things in an informal way, social actors (e.g., employees, regular citizens) tend to engage in different debates. Although they are useful as an effective training strategy in which participants look for weaknesses and flaws in each other's logic (Mohammad et al., 2016), informal debates tend to be over competitive and rarely lead to concrete improvements. Whenever they need to reach a common decision or objective conclusion, social actors tend to formalise debates with a certain set of rules, and in this case such debates are called discussions. Although the term formalise should not always be taken literally, because discussion is sometimes defined broadly as an activity in which people talk about their opinions (Kasemsap, 2017), every appropriate evaluation of opinions requires a lot of time, energy and cognitive efforts. Even if they are interested in a particular topic of discussion, people are aware that participation in discussions may lead to conflict and /or reveal their opinion and point of view, which in some cases can be used against them (e.g., authoritarian superiors who interpret a different opinion as a form of insubordination, police authorities, etc.). While other types of character may react differently, empirical results confirm that narcissists show more anger than non-narcissists in the condition of negative feedback (Matsuo & DeSouza, 2016). For this reason many important information in interaction between humans remain out of their reach. To solve these problems, organisations and their leaders promote another form of communication called dialogue. Dialogue is a special form of non-competitive communication in which everyone is invited to participate in order to reach deeper insights that would otherwise remain hidden. Dialogue is based on active listening, and there is no winner, loser or need to reach a decision.

Although all forms of communication are important elements of organisational learning, it seems that many of today's social actors tend to engage in debate rather than in dialogue and discussion. To improve participation of social actors in dialogue and discussions it is necessary to devise new communication frameworks based on integral digital identity that offer adequate levels of trust and accuracy without compromising the user's privacy. Organisational learning is a collective transformation process that can be supported by a communication framework in which organisational members (e.g., owners, managers, employees, policy makers, etc.) improve their perceptual capacity, coordination, and behaviour in relation to changes in group interaction. Today, many available resources are not used optimally because misleading and/or inaccurate information is used in decision making (Lawton et al., 2013). In hiring and/or evaluating employees, for example, it is very difficult to judge people objectively because those who should do so (e.g., managers) are always strongly influenced by first personal impressions. Since people change and tend to present themselves better than they really are, only a dynamic and long-term assessment by different assessors can provide an accurate description of their character, knowledge, skills, work motivation and other specific characteristics that define their identity.

Since people are the most valuable resource of any organisation, special attention should be paid to the way people share information, develop their potential, and collaborate. Figure 4 shows that the integral communication framework contributes to organisational intelligence at five specific levels. At the first level, ICF improves communication between the organisation and all other stakeholders with whom the organisation interacts. Effective presentation and retrieval of information facilitates a variety of activities, such as finding new customers, employees, or potential partners. At the second level, ICF improves quality and user experience by personalising products and services. The methodology of integral communication enables the identification of characteristics and feelings that in

5th level ◄	Learning ►	Deep learning and big data analytics
4th level ◄	Management ►	Ideal types and decision making
3rd level ◄	Collaboration ►	Compatible and complementary positions
2nd level ◄	Quality ►	Dynamic assessment and personalisation
1st level ◄	Communication ►	Effective presentation and information searching

Fig. 4 The contribution of the integral communication framework to organisational intelligence. (Source: Made by authors)

many cases would remain invisible. At the third level, ICF promotes collaboration by intelligently mapping users and other elements in the network, allowing easy identification of opportunities for collaboration. At the fourth level, ICF helps managers set easily identifiable goals (e.g., by defining tags that describe the characteristics of an ideal group member) and identify employees who meet, miss, or exceed the set goals. At the fifth level, ICF can be used for simulations, machine learning, deep learning, and other data analytics that can provide new insights, opportunities, and answers in human psychology and organisation. It is important to note that each higher level of contribution depends on the one below it, and that the levels are connected by a feedback loop that enables improvement in organisational intelligence.

Although there is no strict consensus on how to measure organisational intelligence, the ability to communicate intelligently is a critical factor in most proposals. Albrecht (2002) suggests that organisational intelligence should be measured by seven dimensions or categories, namely strategic vision, shared destiny, readiness for change, organisational commitment, alignment and congruence, knowledge deployment, and performance pressure. The good news is that all seven dimensions can be enhanced and measured through the integral communication framework. As shown in Fig. 4, effective communication and purposeful information exchange are fundamental elements of organisational intelligence. To emphasise the importance of communication, some authors, such as Appelo (2014), argue that management is only 5% instruction and 95% communication. The integral communication methodology enables the effective identification of the organisation's cognitive subsystems.

Learning organisations are those in which people expand their capacity to achieve desired goals, in which they cultivate new and expansive patterns of thinking, in which collective aspirations are realised, and in which people continually seek to see the whole together (Senge, 2006, p. 3). To improve their organisational intelligence, modern organisations should continuously develop their own communication, collaboration, and learning capabilities. According to Garvin (1993), customers can make competitive comparisons and provide immediate feedback on services. Since organisations need such insights at all levels, from management to operations, it is necessary to implement information systems that can collect and visualise user feedback. The main goal of active listening is to understand the speaker's perspective and to communicate that understanding to the speaker. Although active listening can include negative information in some cases, it is necessary to be open to criticism (Garvin, 1993). Active listening has many different benefits. For example, active listening improves the ability to accurately assess another's communication style. In addition, active listening allows managers to gather important information about employees' experiences and preferences. By giving all team members the opportunity to express their preferences and opinions, managers and leaders can significantly improve motivation and collaboration within their teams. Active listening implies that the concerns, feelings, perceptions, and attitudes of all social actors with whom someone is communicating are valuable and important. This claim is supported by several studies showing that active listening in initial interactions increases the perception of the receiver's feelings compared to other response strategies (Bauer & Figl, 2008; Weger et al. 2014). The integral communication methodology encourages self-reflection and provides deep insights into the characteristics, preferences, and attitudes of other social actors, often leading to a change in personal attitudes about various issues and priorities. Smart societies are those that efficiently share information that helps them reduce costs and achieve a high quality of life.

A transparent flow of information is the only remedy against corruption and negative selection. Negative selection occurs when managers select and promote incompetence in order to prevent their position from being challenged. In practice, there are a number of leaders who are reluctant to hire and promote those who compete with their own strengths. Rather than hiring those who bring the most knowledge and skills to a position, many politicians and managers tend to hire only those individuals (e.g., friends, acquaintances, etc.) who are willing to show personal loyalty and blind obedience. Although many corrupt or undesirable behaviours can be identified at early stages, they are usually not identified and improved without a communication framework that allows for anonymous assessment, reporting, and provision of personal development materials. ICF can be used not only to monitor the quality of various organisational characteristics (e.g., products, services, etc.), but also to introduce trust in presented information and objectivity in reporting. In his famous book The Fifth Discipline: The Art and Practice of the Learning Organization, Senge (2006) highlights the five disciplines that facilitate organisational learning: personal mastery, mental models, building a shared vision, team learning, and systems thinking. The integral communication framework enhances processes in all five disciplines of organisational learning. Over time, more and more individuals and leaders in organisations will recognise the benefits of integral networking. Although integral communication can be applied in a variety of areas, the greatest advances are expected to be in improving personal development and organisational learning.

ICF based on digital identity can significantly improve the quality of public services. To impress and attract potential voters, most of today's politicians present themselves as experts who claim to be able to solve all of society's challenges. Considering that even the most capable people do not always have all the knowledge, insight, and skills necessary to make important decisions effectively, these foolish ideas should be rejected. Most of the things that people take for granted are the result of effective communication and interaction. Fostering dialogue and effective information sharing creates opportunities for collaboration that go beyond the possibilities of individual insights and actions. Integral communication is designed to help people, teams, and groups make smarter decisions. Social systems in which disappointed voters have to wait four long years to choose a different policy option are highly inefficient and demotivating, especially when there are solutions that enable dynamic feedback exchange.

Although a better understanding of users, customers, employees, and partners is a tangible benefit, applying the integral communication methodology does not mean that an organisation will immediately become a successful learning organisation. Learning is the process of acquiring new or changing existing knowledge, behaviours, skills, values, or preferences. Deep learning involves understanding, finding connections between different domains, and the ability to transfer knowledge to new and different contexts. When planting the seeds of synergy in different types of groups and networks, leaders and managers focus primarily on creating an optimal environment that fosters communication, collaboration, fair distribution of benefits, and the right to make mistakes. ICF creates an environment where all stakeholders are invited to contribute, build their networks and/or present and review their qualities. If they want to survive the changes in today's market, modern companies should implement communication solutions that allow them to learn from all the interactions that take place in their network. The characteristics, preferences and accumulated experiences of individual group members represent information that can be transformed into knowledge that enables the group to develop and learn.

By simplifying the way individuals and organisations can share information about their attributes and preferences, ICF enables significant savings in collaboration and cooperation costs. In the coming decades, most organisations will seek to improve their competitiveness by adopting digital communication frameworks. It seems that a sustainable future lies in e-cooperative networks. Cooperative is an ideology based on the principles of universality, fraternity, democracy, freedom, honesty, fairness, equality, unity, justice, and self-help (Emejulu, 2006, p. 10). Because they include anyone willing to abide by common rules of conduct, open electronic cooperative networks benefit from economies of scale and scope. A good example is group purchasing, where larger discounts are usually available than for small orders for individuals. While on some general issues it is desirable to hear and evaluate the opinion of the majority (e.g., human rights), on most technical decisions (e.g., building a bridge) it is far more advisable to analyse and measure the opinion of those who have the necessary expertise. A communications framework that makes it easy to determine who is authorised or qualified to participate in information sharing, evaluation, or decision making can greatly improve the efficiency of private and public organisations. In its two main documents, The Age of Digital Interdependence (UN, n.d.-a) and Transforming Our World: The 2030 Agenda for Sustainable Development (UN, n.d.-b), the United Nations emphasises the need to develop mechanisms for global digital cooperation that connects all people and societies and leaves no one behind. According to Bouras et al. (2008), e-collaboration environments must provide seamless integration of synchronous and asynchronous communication and maintain the quality of the user experience in both connected and disconnected modes. In addition, e-collaboration systems should be based on flexible service components that are applicable in different communities (Bouras et al., 2008). In their analysis of the 10 most popular e-collaboration systems, Schauer and Zeiller (2011) found that all of the products studied provided considerable support for core collaboration functions, but that most lacked support for synchronous team collaboration tasks – particularly tools for real-time synchronous editing (Schauer & Zeiller, 2011). Fortunately, things are improving so quickly these days that this functionality has become a standard. Although e-cooperatives can effectively leverage the talents, ideas, and insights of all members, whose observations often lead to innovations and improvements (Smith & Rothbaum, 2013), their efficiency and quality depend primarily on the individual quality of their members and leaders. For this reason, ICF focuses primarily on the personal development and growth of each individual.

INTEGRAL COMMUNICATION IN IOT ENVIRONMENT

Improving communication between humans and AI devices is one of the biggest challenges for society as it seeks to enter the Internet 5.0 era (Rahmawati et al., 2021). The purpose of the Internet of Things (IoT) is to create a meaningful connection between people and all the things that surround them into a functional whole (Lee et al., 2017). IoT scenarios rely on various communication protocols that enable data transmission between heterogeneous devices and users. Despite various attempts, there is not yet a general consensus on a solution that best meets the networking and service requirements (Rute, 2018; Srinidhi et al., 2019). To experience personalised communication, today's social actors need a new communication framework that enables the secure exchange of personal information with other elements of the network. For this reason, integral digital identity (IDI) is one of the fundamental components that will enable end users to communicate effectively with robots and AI devices. If a robot or other artificial intelligence device has software capable of recognizing and processing data entered by users into their IDI, the possibility of integral communication arises. Within the ICF, users independently determine which integral maps (e.g., folders) or tags are visible to which users. By simplifying the presentation, analysis, and sharing of user data, ICF enables the improvement of the efficiency and quality of various forms of interaction. Without such a framework, the quality of communication

with AI devices would be at a rather low level. It would be highly inefficient if social actors had to introduce themselves from scratch every time a
new robot (or other AI device) interacted with them. An additional challenge for robots would be to find enough memory to store all the information about the users they communicate with. The IoT environment, of
course, includes not only communication with AI devices and robots, but
also the configuration, control, and networking of all other devices or
things that until recently were not connected to the Internet, such as
motors, thermostats, pumps, lighting fixtures, etc. As more and more
devices connect to the Internet, the need for standardised and secure IDI
is increasing (Uviase & Kotonya, 2018). Although in some cases the concept of the Internet of Things completely bypasses the end user (e.g.,
direct interaction between machines and/or sensors), in cases where
humans need to interact with AI devices, it is necessary to apply user-
friendly interfaces that optimise communication and integration. For
example, when hotel guests arrive at an ICF-equipped smart hotel room,
many different things can be personalised, such as TV programmes, information websites, lighting, artwork on the wall, music, menu, etc. Similarly,
it is possible to personalise many other products and services. Of course,
this does not mean that all users' wishes are automatically fulfilled. Using
ICF, service providers can automatically identify user preferences and tai-
lor their services to meet customer needs. If some of the user preferences
stored in an enterprise database have changed over time, managers will
certainly want to know, and this can only be optimally captured through
dynamic mapping, where the user has direct control over the customization of important data in their IDI. By voluntarily sharing personal information, ICF users support sustainability and perceptiveness. According to
Lueth (2018), most IoT development projects in 2018 are smart city projects (367), followed by industrial environments (265) and IoT projects
for connected buildings (193). When looking at individual IoT segments
and regions, there are large differences. Most smart IoT city projects are
in Europe (45%), while the Americas, especially North America, lead in
implementing IoT in healthcare (55%) and automotive (54%) (Lueth,
2018). The Asia / Pacific region, on the other hand, is particularly strong
in smart agriculture projects (31%) (Lueth, 2018).

The application of integral information exchange in the IoT environment enables personalised communication. According to the Segment
(2022) report, less than half (47%) of companies personalise their communications based on real-time customer behaviour. After analysing data

from a survey in 26 countries (N = 53,314), Thurman et al. (2018) found that audiences overall believe that algorithmic selection based on a user's past consumption behaviour is a better way to receive news than editorial curation. In practise, two basic types of personalization can be distinguished: self-selected personalization, in which users actively choose what content they want to see, and preselected personalization, in which algorithms personalise content for users without them making a conscious choice (Zuiderveen Borgesius et al., 2016). Although both types of personalization can be applied in the context of ICF, the focus is on self-selected personalization. This means that each user has the right to choose which tags are used in the personalization process. The ICF is designed to be used in both digital and real-world environments. This means that even a quick look at the built-in personal maps of the people they are talking to can help users create personalised responses and suggestion. There are authors like Rainie and Anderson (2022), who argue that fully automated or algorithmic personalization can be quite problematic. While some people fear for their privacy because they do not want to be tracked while surfing the Internet, others fear missing important information and believe that they will lose insight into some views that do not match their personal preferences. Although pre-selected or fully automated personalization can lead to manipulated or distorted communications that, in the worst case, deny users access to more meaningful or diverse information, there is currently no empirical evidence to justify a strong fear of philtre bubbles (Zuiderveen Borgesius et al., 2016). Behind the positive effects that integral information exchange will bring, one of the greatest dangers in the development of IoT systems is hidden, namely data security. The fundamental problem is the IoT ecosystem itself, which is highly populated with unsecured devices. According to Hallman et al. (2017), IoT botnet armies are now capable of launching DDoS attacks on a larger scale than ever before, with rates exceeding 1 TBps. One of the most recent massive botnet attacks occurred between March and April 2019 and used more than 400,000 IoT devices to attack users of an online streaming application (Asokan, 2019). Without advanced security protocols, any compromised device on the network can be used to access sensitive data. The complexity of security and privacy issues is illustrated by the fact that any smart speaker connected to a hospital network violates privacy regulations and poses a type of security risk, as attackers can eavesdrop on or record conversations (Thales, 2021). The lack of universally applicable security and privacy standards, poor update management, dubious IoT devices, and the weak ability of users to manage their own data are some of the biggest obstacles to the further development of the network society.

Apart from antivirus, anti-malware, firewalls, data encryption, two-factor authentication, digital certificates, and biometrics, Hübschmann (2021) suggests in the context of IoT security that decentralised solutions are one of the best ways to maintain data security. Unlike centralised Application Enabled Platform (AEP) solutions, which are always exposed to potential risks (upper part of Fig. 5), decentralised AEP solutions can provide an even higher level of security. In the lower part of Fig. 5, data flows directly between the client and the IoT device, and all data is stored securely on the IoT device rather than in the cloud. This gives the user complete control over the data residing on their network and virtually eliminates the risk of third parties intercepting the data (Hübschmann, 2021). Although decentralised data processing and storage can reduce the security vulnerabilities of traditional AEPs, every device must be connected to a database at some point, and for this reason, security and privacy are always the result of a combination of methods. Overall energy consumption is increasing so rapidly that modern society must embrace any solution that optimises resource sharing and consumption. According to Hinsdale (2022), Bitcoin, the world's largest cryptocurrency, currently consumes an estimated 150 terawatt-hours of electricity per year -more than the entire country of Argentina, with a population of 45 million-and emits about 65 megatons of carbon dioxide into the atmosphere annually-comparable to Greece's emissions. Despite short-term efficiency improvements, energy demand will continue to rise in the long term. The analysis conducted shows that the ICF can be extremely helpful in achieving a

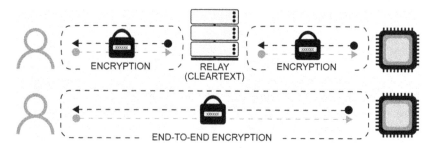

Fig. 5 Differences between centralised and decentralised AEPs. (Source: Hübschmann, 2021)

green future, especially if society transforms its current consumer culture into a culture of sharing. IT Frameworks and networks that promote social perceptivity and collaboration could play an important role in this transformation process. ICF is a sustainable solution that helps people spend less time, energy and other resources on communicating and achieving their personal goals. Optimal communication between humans, robots, and other IoT devices can only be achieved by ensuring the integrity of personal data and effective personal data management. Personal data integrity stands for rules and mechanisms that ensure the accuracy, completeness, consistency and security of personal data. On the other hand, personal data management stands for a set of activities and functions that enable control over personal data that is shared with other system participants.

Solutions and Recommendations

Today's social actors need a flexible, robust, and comprehensive communications solution that acts as an independent intermediary that determines the reliability and quality of the information shared. Through inclusive strategies and IT solutions that promote holistic personal development and organisational learning, modern society is able to reduce the problems of waste management, depression, unemployment, and increasing inequality in the availability of public services. Considering the fact that today many social actors behave unethically and socially irresponsibly (e.g. corruption, littering, etc.), it is necessary to develop a new communication framework that identifies and educates these individuals in a timely manner. To avoid the Orwellian model of society, in which autocrats control society through algorithms, the integral communication framework should be applied with special care. This means that such systems should be primarily focused on personal development and organisational learning rather than punishment and control. To improve user motivation to provide feedback, the authors suggest that group administrators should decide what type of feedback to use and during what time periods. Feedback should be solicited from authorised users who have permission to conduct evaluation (e.g., a citizen, a verified buyer, a group member, etc.). An open dialogue and the indirect exchange of feedback help to uncover blind spots that normally remain hidden. The information gained in this way is often critical to personal development and organisational learning. To save significant amounts of time and energy traditionally spent on building trust, social actors can use purpose-built information systems that provide accurate and transparent insight into the experiences of other actors who have interacted with that actor. Dialogue, exchange of feedback, and trust are much easier to foster in smaller groups where members know each other than in large groups where members rarely work on the same tasks and therefore do not even know each other. To foster dialogue, feedback sharing, and trust in larger groups and organisations, it is necessary to create IT systems designed for this purpose. Since sharing negative feedback can be quite risky and difficult (Heffer & Willoughby, 2020), direct and indirect methods of sharing feedback need to be combined. Simple insight into the different types of uniform labels assigned to people, organisations, products, services, events, and places can provide fertile ground for improvement and innovation. Without dialogue and cooperation, many technological solutions that social actors currently use (e.g., the Linux operating system) would not be as cheap, secure, and accessible. To curb environmental pressures and enable effective coordination in the use of public resources, today's society needs a communication framework that facilitates coordination, cooperation, and collaboration among social actors. New technologies encourage new patterns of behaviour. Today's people need an ICF based on an integral digital identity (IDI) that enables personalised communication with robots and AI devices. Three important factors must be considered when implementing personalised communication:

- **Positive intentions:** The way in which the ICF is applied has a significant impact on user attitudes. If this solution is used primarily for personal development, organisational learning, work, talent search, employment, public service delivery, and learning, then user attitudes will be far more positive than if this solution is used for control and monitoring.
- **Social Responsibility:** The ICF should be developed and applied according to strict ethical principles that ensure transparency, inclusiveness, privacy, security, and fairness.
- **Personal data integrity:** Today's society must apply rules and mechanisms that ensure the accuracy, completeness, consistency, and security of personal data. To communicate securely and effectively with robots and AI devices in the IoT ecosystem, individuals need solutions that give them more control over the personal data they choose to share with these devices.

To improve collaboration between actors who neither know each other personally nor speak the same language, integral communication solutions should function simultaneously in different languages.

FUTURE RESEARCH DIRECTIONS

Integral communication is a relatively new concept that is still in its early stages. This means that a variety of activities and processes related to its effective application need to be explored. For example, in order for social actors to successfully collaborate in an electronic collaboration network, the integral communication framework needs to be extended to include additional features such as electronic payment, electronic wallet, electronic meetings, document management system, etc. In future research, it would be interesting to find answers to the following questions:

- To what extent does integral communication affect integrity?
- In what areas of personal development does integral communication produce the best results?
- What functionalities within the ICF need to be improved to make it easier for people with disabilities to use?
- To what extent does integral communication affect the leader's ability to coordinate?
- In what areas of organisational learning does integral communication achieve the best results?
- In which activities is it better to use direct feedback and in which indirect feedback?
- To what extent does integral communication improve trust among social actors?
- What are the main technical challenges in connecting ICF with robots and IoT devices?

CONCLUSION

Although technology cannot solve all human problems, when used wisely and critically, it can greatly improve the quality of interpersonal relationships. The Integral Communication Framework (ICF), based on the Integral Digital Identity (IDI), will help today's society to qualitatively improve its communication, collaboration and learning processes. Using keywords translated into multiple languages that can be evaluated and enriched with metadata, the integral communication methodology creates a whole range of opportunities to enhance live conversations and digitally supported interactions that improve personal development and organisational learning. The basic functions of ICF should be free of charge so that the most vulnerable groups can also use this framework for education and empowerment. The ICF was developed to reduce the costs of communication, coordination, cooperation and collaboration, and for this very reason it is one of the best solutions to achieve long-term sustainability. The ICF is based on a unified set of symbols with varying weights that can be used as building blocks for collaboration and organisational learning. Communication frameworks that manage to improve human perceptiveness and efficiency are an extremely important factor in creating an environmentally sustainable future. Considering that the overall complexity of social interaction, including the total amount of information that social actors exchange on a daily basis, is constantly increasing, today's people need a user-friendly communication framework that optimises the management of their personal information. Without an efficient framework for information evaluation, an information society can easily become a misinformation society. Integral development occurs as a result of social tagging, group interaction, evaluation, and dialogue. When people and their interactions are assessed and described by integral tags, it is possible to identify relationships and generate reports that facilitate recognition and learning. Integral communication can be used in many different types of social and business interactions to describe and evaluate different people, organisations, products, services, events, and places. Optimising the flow of information improves quality, efficiency, trust, collaboration, and environmental sustainability. Socio-economic systems and organisations that neglect the positive sides of integral communication could lose their competitiveness on a global scale. By combining user characteristics and preferences with collected feedback, advanced algorithms can provide new opportunities and potential solutions that would otherwise remain invisible. To avoid the problem of filter bubbles, or environments where all sources of information focus on only one part of the whole picture, users must be empowered to recognize other perspectives and communicate information that is particularly relevant to the groups to which the user belongs, even if it is outside their self-imposed scope. There is no technology that cannot be abused. ICF is no exception. ICF should remain an independent and transparent intermediary in human interaction whose leaders and staff demonstrate high integrity. When ICF is used in the public sector, appropriate civilian oversight must be provided. In both cases, high ethical standards and compliance with the legal framework should be ensured. Integral communication helps modern people and organisations transform tacit knowledge into explicit knowledge. By transforming unstructured information into structured symbols that can be evaluated, social actors improve the efficiency of information sharing, save resources, improve perceptual ability, learn, and identify opportunities for new conversations. The integral communication is based on the methodology of voluntary social tagging, where tags can be structured and evaluated subjectively, objectively and automatically. The ICF is intended to provide a wide range of evaluation tools and tips that can help users find what they are looking for. This means that all end-users and third-party service providers are invited to participate and offer their products and services, especially assessment tools that help determine various human characteristics.

Key Terms and Definitions

Cooperation: A process in which social actors work independently on various activities that help them achieve a common goal or task. Cooperation is based on voluntary help and sharing of resources, without strict hierarchy or rules that must be followed. It leads to the best results when it comes to promoting creativity and integration.

Collaboration: A process in which social actors work together on a set of dependent activities that help them achieve a common goal or task. This type of interaction usually involves a deep hierarchy, clearly defined roles, and strict rules that must be followed to achieve a particular goal or task. It produces the best results when it comes to acting quickly and in a coordinated manner.

Debate: Competitive communicationv aimed at winning rather than improving relationships and learning. Participants look for weaknesses and flaws in the logic of others to challenge their ideas and theses.

Dialogue: A special form of non-competitive communication in which everyone is invited to participate in order to reach deeper insights that would otherwise remain hidden. It is based on active listening, and there is no winner, loser or need to reach a decision.

Discussion: A sophisticated form of debate based on rational arguments and aimed at reaching an objective conclusion or decision.

Feedback: Affirmative or negative information that social actors voluntarily share with each other to describe their experiences in interacting with each other.

Integral personal development: An individual transformation process supported by a communication framework in which end users improve their character, knowledge, and skills in interaction with other users.

Integral organisational learning: A collective transformation process supported by a communication framework in which organisations and their members (e.g., owners, managers, employees, policymakers, etc.) improve their perceptiveness, coordination, and behaviour with respect to information they receive through various types of interaction.

Personal data integrity: A set of rules and mechanisms that ensure the accuracy, completeness, consistency and security of personal data.

Personal data management: A set of activities and functionalities that allow control over personal data shared with other system participants.

REFERENCES

Albrecht, K. (2002). *Organizational intelligence & knowledge management: Thinking outside the silos – the executive perspective.* Karl Albrecht. Retrieved May 7, 2019, from https://karlalbrecht.com/downloads/OI-WhitePaper-Albrecht.pdf

Al-Dmour, R. H., & Al-Zu'bi, Z. M. (2014). Factors motivating and inhibiting the practice of HRIS in business organizations: An empirical analysis. *International Business Research, 7*(7), 139–155. https://doi.org/10.5539/ibr.v7n7p139

Allan, A., Zlotogorski, M., Gaehtgens, F. & Buytendijk, F. (2017, May 24). *Definition: Digital trust.* Gartner Retrieved July 7, 2020, from https://www.gartner.com/en/documents/3727718

Alvaredo, F., Chancel, L., Piketty, T., Saez, E., & Zucman, G. (2017). *World inequality report 2018. The first release.* World Inequality Lab. Retrieved June 30, 2021, from https://wir2018.wid.world/files/download/wir2018-full-report-english.pdf

Ananny, M. (2015). Toward an ethics of algorithms. *Science, Technology, & Human Values, 41*(1), 93–117. https://doi.org/10.1177/0162243915606523

Appelo, J. (2014). *Workout: Games, Tools & Practices to engage people, improve work, and delight clients.* Happy Melly Express.

Arun, T. (2020, November, 26). *Which companies use an HRIS?* Zoho. Retrieved November 18, 2022, from https://www.zoho.com/people/hrknowledge-hive/which-companies-use-an-hris.html

Asokan, A. (2019, July 26). *Massive botnet attack used more than 400,000 IoT devices*. Bank Info Security. Retrieved July 22, 2021, from https://www.bankinfosecurity.com/massive-botnet-attack-used-more-than-400000-iot-devices-a-12841

Atherton, O. E., Grijalva, E., Roberts, B. W., & Robins, R. W. (2020). Stability and change in personality traits and major life goals from college to midlife. *Personality and Social Psychology Bulletin, 47*(5), 841–858. https://doi.org/10.1177/0146167220949362

Axelrod, R. (2000). On six advances in cooperation theory. *Analyse & Kritik, 22*(1), 130–151. https://doi.org/10.1515/auk-2000-0107

Axelrod, R., & Keohane, R. O. (1985). Achieving cooperation under anarchy: Strategies and institutions. *World Politics, 38*(1), 226–254. https://doi.org/10.2307/2010357

Badcock, P. B., Pattison, P. E., & Harris, K.-L. (2010). Developing generic skills through university study: A study of arts, science and engineering in Australia. *Higher Education, 60*(4), 441–458. https://doi.org/10.1007/s10734-010-9308-8

Baker, B. (2012, August 9). *What is personal mastery – A look into personal development from a new perspective*. Start of Happiness. Retrieved September 20, 2021, from https://www.startofhappiness.com/what-is-personal-mastery/

Baranski, E., Gardiner, G., Lee, D., & Funder, D. C. (2021). Who in the world is trying to change their personality traits? Volitional personality change among college students in six continents. *Journal of Personality and Social Psychology, 121*(5), 1140–1156. https://doi.org/10.1037/pspp0000389

Barends, E., Janssen, B., & Velghe, C. (2016). *Rapid evidence assessment of the research literature on the effect of goal setting on workplace performance* (The center for evidence-based Management). Chartered Institute of Personnel and Development (CIPD). Retrieved August 8, 2023, from https://www.cipd.org/globalassets/media/knowledge/knowledge-hub/reports/rapid-evidence-assessment-of-the-research-literature-on-the-effect-of-goal-setting-on-workplace-performance_tcm18-16903.pdf

Barna Group. (2018, February 27). *Americans feel good about counseling*. Barna. Retrieved April 15, 2021, from https://www.barna.com/research/americans-feel-good-counseling/

Bauer, C., & Figl, K. (2008). Active listening in written online communication – a case study in a course on soft skills for computer scientists. In *Frontiers in education conference, FIE 2008. 38th annual, at Saratoga Springs*. https://doi.org/10.1109/FIE.2008.4720282

Bédard, M., Connolly, D., & Gravel, R. (2002). *Canadian community health survey – Mental health and well-being*. Retrieved May 15, 2021, from https://www150.statcan.gc.ca/n1/daily-quotidien/030903/dq030903a-eng.htm

Blackbyrn, S. (2022, January 9). *The JOHARI window model – the definitive guide.* Coach Foundation. Retrieved August 1, 2022, from https://coachfoundation. com/blog/the-johari-window-model-guide/#chapter2

Boella, G., & van der Torre, L. (2006). Coordination and organization. *Electronic Notes in Theoretical Computer Science, 150*(3), 3–20. https://doi. org/10.1016/j.entcs.2006.03.002

Bolden, R. (2020). *Leadership development in context.* LSW Report 3, Center for Leadership Studies, University of Exeter. Retrieved August 17, 2021, from http://www.centres.ex.ac.uk/cls/documents/LSW-report-3.pdf

Bonarini, A. (2020). Communication in human-robot interaction. *Current Robotics Reports, 1*(4), 279–285. https://doi.org/10.1007/s43154-020-00026-1

Booher, D. (2016, March, 23). *Why do so many companies have such awful upward communications?* TLNT. Retrieved August 12, 2022, from https://www.tlnt. com/why-do-so-many-companies-have-such-awful-upward-communications/

Bouras, C., Giannaka, E., & Tsiatsos, T. (2008). E-collaboration concepts, systems, and applications. *Encyclopedia of Internet Technologies and Applications,* 165–171. https://doi.org/10.4018/978-1-59140-993-9.ch024

Brandl, R., & Ellis, C. (2023, August 7). *Wordpress market share – still going strong in 2023?.* Tooltester. Retrieved August 14, 2023, from https://www.tooltester.com/en/blog/wordpress-market-share/

Braveman, P. A., Cubbin, C., Egerter, S., Williams, D. R., & Pamuk, E. (2010). Socioeconomic disparities in health in the United States: What the patterns tell us. *American Journal of Public Health, 100*(S1), 186–196. https://doi. org/10.2105/ajph.2009.166082

Broussard, M. (2018). *Artificial unintelligence: How computers misunderstand the world.* MIT Press.

Carminati, B., Ferrari, E., & Viviani, M. (2014). *Security and trust in online social networks.* Morgan & Claypool.

Castañer, X., & Oliveira, N. (2020). Collaboration, coordination, and cooperation among organizations: Establishing the distinctive meanings of these terms through a systematic literature review. *Journal of Management, 46*(6), 965–1001. https://doi.org/10.1177/0149206320901565

Chakravorti, B., Bhalla, A. & Chaturvedi, R. S. (2018, February 19). *The 4 dimensions of digital trust, charted across 42 countries.* Harvard Business Review. Retrieved August 19, 2022, from https://hbr.org/2018/02/the-4-dimensions-of-digital-trust-charted-across-42-countries

Chennattu, A. (2020). *Managing with integrity: An ethical investigation into the relationship between personal and corporate integrity.* Augsburg Fortress, Publishers.

Christensen, U. J. (2018, February 20). *How to teach employees skills they don't know they lack.* Harvard Business Review. Retrieved February 19, 2022, from https://hbr.org/2017/09/how-to-teach-employees-skills-they-dont-know-they-lack

Cimatti, B. (2016). Definition, development, assessment of soft skills and their role for the quality of organizations and enterprises. *International Journal for Quality Research, 10*(1), 97–130. https://doi.org/10.18421/IJQR10.01-05

Cukier, W., Hodson, J., & Omar, A. (2015). *Soft skills are hard: A review of literature.* Ryerson University. May 2, 2019, from https://www.torontomu.ca/content/dam/diversity/reports/KSG2015_SoftSkills_FullReport.pdf

Denise, L. (1999). Collaboration vs. C-three (cooperation, coordination and communication). *Innovating, 7*(3), 1–6. Retrieved November 7, 2022, from https://www.sccharterschools.org/assets/documents/collaboration-vsthe3cs.pdf

Eden, M., & Gaggl, P. (2020). Do poor countries really need more IT? *World Bank Economic Review, 34*(1), 48–62. Retrieved November 3, 2022, from https://openknowledge.worldbank.org/handle/10986/36070 License: CC BY-NC-ND 3.0 IGO

Emejulu, G. (2006). *Readings in co-operative economics and management.* CECTA NIG. LTD.

Engelbrecht, A. S., Heine, G., & Mahembe, B. (2017). Integrity, ethical leadership, trust and work engagement. *Leadership & Organization Development Journal, 38*(3), 368–379. https://doi.org/10.1108/lodj-11-2015-0237

Experian. (2018). *The 2018 global fraud and identity report. Exploring the links between customer recognition, convenience, trust and fraud risk.* Experian. Retrieved April 6, 2020, from https://www.experian.com/assets/decision-analytics/reports/global-fraud-report-2018.pdf

Floridi, L., Cowls, J., King, T. C., & Taddeo, M. (2020). How to design AI for social good: Seven essential factors. *Science and Engineering Ethics, 26*(3), 1771–1796. https://doi.org/10.1007/s11948-020-00213-5

Garvin, D. A. (1993). *Building a learning organization.* Harvard Business Review, July–August, 1–15. Retrieved April 22, 2021, from https://hbr.org/1993/07/building-a-learning-organization

Ghandi, M., & Maghsoudi, M. (2014). The effect of direct and indirect corrective feedback on Iranian EFL learners' spelling errors. *English Language Teaching, 7*(8), 53–61. https://doi.org/10.5539/elt.v7n8p53

Groenewegen, L. P. J., Stam, A. W., Toussaint, P. J., & de Vink, E. P. (2006). Paradigm as organization-oriented coordination language. *Electronic Notes in Theoretical Computer Science, 150*(3), 93–113. https://doi.org/10.1016/j.entcs.2006.03.007

Groot, W., & van den Brink, H. M. (2010). The effects of education on crime. *Applied Economics, 42*(3), 279–289. https://doi.org/10.1080/00036840701604412

Hager, G. D., Drobnis, A., Fang, F., Ghani, R., Greenwald, A., Lyons, T., Parkes, D. C., Schultz, J., Saria, S., Smith, S. F., & Tambe, M. (2019). Artificial intelligence for social good. *Computing Community Consortium.* https://doi.org/10.48550/arXiv.1901.05406

Halal, W. E. (2006). Organizational intelligence: What is it, and how can managers use it to improve performance? *Knowledge management review. Journal of Business & Economics Research (JBER), 1*, 20–25.

Hallman, R., Bryan, J., Palavicini, G., Divita, J., & Romero-Mariona, J. (2017). IoDDoS — The internet of distributed denial of Sevice attacks – a case study of the Mirai malware and IOT-based botnets. In *Proceedings of the 2nd international conference on internet of things, big data and security* (pp. 47–59). https://doi.org/10.5220/0006246600470058

Hattie, J., & Timperley, H. (2007). The power of feedback. *Review of Educational Research, 77*(1), 81–112. https://doi.org/10.3102/003465430298487

Havinal, V. (2009). *Management and entrepreneurship.* New Age International P Ltd.. Retrieved November 2, 2022, from http://dspace.vnbrims.org:13000/xmlui/bitstream/handle/123456789/4983/Management%20and%20Entrepreneurship.pdf?sequence=1&isAllowed=y

Heffer, T., & Willoughby, T. (2020). Sensitivity to negative feedback among children and adolescents: An ERP study comparing developmental differences between high-worriers and low-worriers. *Cognitive, Affective, & Behavioral Neuroscience, 20*(3), 624–635. https://doi.org/10.3758/s13415-020-00791-8

Heldman, C., & Enste, D. (2018). *Trust and privacy: How trust affects individuals' willingness to disclose personal information,* IW-report, no. 19/2018, Institut der deutschen Wirtschaft (IW), Köln. Retrieved November, 12, 2022, from https://www.econstor.eu/bitstream/10419/179245/1/1023107090.pdf

Hinsdale, J (2022, May 4). *Cryptocurrency's dirty secret: Energy consumption.* Columbia Climate School. Retrieved July 5, 2022, from https://news.climate.columbia.edu/2022/05/04/cryptocurrency-energy/

Huberts, L. W. (2018). Integrity: What it is and why it is important. *Public Integrity, 20*(sup1). https://doi.org/10.1080/10999922.2018.1477404

Hübschmann, I. (2021, February 19). *How to overcome IoT security & privacy challenges.* Nabto. Retrieved March 20, 2022, from https://www.nabto.com/how-overcome-iot-security-privacy-challenges/

Integrity Action. (2015, October 7). *An integrity textbook. Live and work with integrity.* You can do it! Integrity Action Retrieved November 9, 2022, from https://integrityaction.org/sites/default/files/training_materials/Integrity%20Education%20Textbook%2C%20ENG.pdf

Interpol. (2022, October 19). *Financial and cybercrimes top global police concerns, says new INTERPOL report.* Interpol. Retrieved November, 20, 2022, from https://www.interpol.int/News-and-Events/News/2022/Financial-and-cybercrimes-top-global-police-concerns-says-new-INTERPOL-report

Irving, J. A., & Williams, D. I. (1999). Personal growth and personal development: Concepts clarified. *British Journal of Guidance & Counselling, 27*(4), 517–526. https://doi.org/10.1080/03069889908256287

Juniper Research. (2016). *Online payment fraud whitepaper 2016–2020*. Experian. Retrieved April 19, 2021, from https://www.experian.com/assets/decision-analytics/white-papers/juniper-research-online-payment-fraud-wp-2016.pdf

Kariuki, M. M. (2021). The joint effect of Hris, HRM practices and differentiation strategy on competitive advantage is greater than the effect of HRIS on competitive advantage. *The International Journal of Business & Management, 9*(6). https://doi.org/10.24940/theijbm/2021/v9/i6/bm2106-030

Kasemsap, K. (2017). Advocating problem-based learning and creative problem-solving skills in global education. In C. Zhou (Ed.), *Handbook of research on creative problem-solving skill development in higher education* (pp. 351–377). IGI Global. https://doi.org/10.4018/978-1-5225-0643-0.ch016

Khanna, S. (2018). Social tagging and the enterprise: An analysis of social tagging in the workplace. *Social Tagging for Linking Data Across Environments*, 169–188. https://doi.org/10.29085/9781783303403.009

Kinsta. (2022). *Search engine market share: Who's leading the race in 2022*. Kinsta. Retrieved November 20, 2022, from https://kinsta.com/search-engine-market-share/

Kodransky, M., & Lewenstein, G. (2014). Connecting low-income people to opportunity with shared mobility. In *Report livingcities*. Institute for Transportation & Development Policy. Retrieved November 3, 2022, from https://livingcities.org/wp-content/uploads/2021/03/Can-Shared-Mobility-Help-Low-Income-People-Access-Opportunity_.pdf

Kulkarni, S., & Kulkarni, D. G. (2019). Gap analysis of soft skills in the curriculum of higher education (a case study of Management Institutes in Karnataka). *Advances in Management, 12*(1), 64–67. Retrieved May 16, 2021, from https://www.worldresearchersassociations.com/mngmntspecialissue/11.pdf

Lawton, K., Carter, C., Lee, J., Tan, A., de Prado Trigo, A., Luscombe, D., & Briscoe, S. (2013). The opportunities to business of improving resource efficiency. In *European Commission – final report*. AMEC Environment & Infrastructure UK Limited. Retrieved January 14, 2020, from https://ec.europa.eu/environment/enveco/resource_efficiency/pdf/report_opportunities.pdf

Lee, S., Bae, M., & Kim, H. (2017). Future of IOT networks: A survey. *Applied Sciences, 7*(10), 1072. https://doi.org/10.3390/app7101072

Li, D., Meng, L., & Ma, Q. (2017). Who deserves my trust? Cue-elicited feedback negativity tracks reputation learning in repeated social interactions. *Frontiers in Human Neuroscience, 11*. https://doi.org/10.3389/fnhum.2017.00307

Litman, D., & Forbes-Riley, K. (2006). Correlations between dialogue acts and learning in spoken tutoring dialogues. *Natural Language Engineering, 12*(2), 161–176. https://doi.org/10.1017/s1351324906004165

Lu, D. (2018). Rural-urban income disparity: Impact of growth, allocative efficiency and local growth welfare. *Urbanization and Social Welfare in China*, 255–268. https://doi.org/10.4324/9781351143523-13

Lu, R., & Bol, L. (2007). A comparison of anonymous versus identifiable e-peer review on college student writing performance and the extent of critical feedback. *Journal of Interactive Online Learning*, 6(2), 100–115.

Lueth, L. K. (2018, February 22). *The top 10 IoT segments in 2018 – Based on 1,600 real IoT projects*. IoT Analytics. Retrieved June 20, 202, from https://iot-analytics.com/top-10-iot-segments-2018-real-iot-projects/

Luft, J., & Ingham, H. (1955). *The Johari window: A graphic model for interpersonal relations*. University of California/Western Training Lab.

Lumague, E. A. (2017). Relative value of hard skills and soft skills for hiring employees in the manufacturing sector. *Journal of Business & Management Studies*, 3(1), 1–5.

Lunenburg, F. C. (2010). Formal communication channels: Upward, downward, horizontal, and external. *Focus on Colleges, Universities, and Schools*, 4(1), 1–7. Retrieved October 20, 2022, from http://www.nationalforum.com/Electronic%20Journal%20Volumes/Lunenburg%2C%20Fred%20C%2C%20Formal%20Comm%20Channels%20FOCUS%20V4%20N1%202010.pdf

Mackay, D. (2017, October 2). *An expert knows more and more about less and less until they know absolutely everything about nothing*. Collingwood executive Search Retrieved April 19, 2022, from https://thoughtleadership.collingwoodsearch.co.uk/post/102egvc/an-expert-knows-more-and-more-about-less-and-less-until-they-know-absolutely-ever

Mallen, M. J., Vogel, D. L., & Rochlen, A. B. (2005). The practical aspects of online counseling. *The Counseling Psychologist*, 33(6), 776–818. https://doi.org/10.1177/0011000005278625

Manning, G. L., Ahearne, M., & Reece, B. (2015). *Selling today: Partnering to create value*. Global Edition.

Marcus, M. A., Westra, H. A., Eastwood, J. D., Barnes, K. L., & Mobilizing Minds Research Group. (2012). What Are Young Adults Saying About Mental Health? An Analysis of Internet Blogs. *Journal of Medical Internet Research*, 14(1), e17. https://www.jmir.org/2012/1/e17/

Marshall, A. (2019, November 5). *Most of Nation's top public universities Aren't affordable for low-income students*. NPR. Retrieved November 20, 2022, from https://www.npr.org/2019/11/05/769465302/most-of-the-nations-top-public-universities-aren-t-affordable-for-low-income-stu

Matsuo, A., & DeSouza, E. R. (2016). The effects of anticipated negative feedback on psychological states among narcissists. *SAGE Open*, 6(2), 1–7. https://doi.org/10.1177/2158244016650921

Merletti de Palo, A., Masia, M. G., Mancinella, A., Nitti, M., Tito, I., & Singh, K. U. (2015). Cooperation: enjoying collective intelligence. In *Proceedings of the Collective Intelligence Conference* (pp. 1–4). Retrieved November, 18, 2022, from http://www.shus.unimi.it/wp-content/uploads/2017/06/170428_MerlettidePalo_VivibileSostenibileSmart_CooperationEnjoyingCollective Intelligence.pdf

Merriam-Webster. (2020). *Feedback.* Merriam-Webster. Retrieved January 8, 2020, from https://www.merriam-webster.com/thesaurus/feedback

Mittelstadt, B. D., Allo, P., Taddeo, M., Wachter, S., & Floridi, L. (2016). The ethics of algorithms: Mapping the debate. *Big Data & Society, 3*(2), 205395171667967. https://doi.org/10.1177/2053951716679679

Mohammad, N., Zohre, M., Hassanali, B. N., & Kamal, N. H. (2016). Debate learning method and its implications for the formal education system. *Educational Research and Reviews, 11*(6), 211–218. https://doi.org/10.5897/err2015.2316

Montefiore, A., & Vines, D. (Eds.). (1999). *Integrity in the public and private domains.* Routledge.

Moseley, C. (2020). *Collaboration vs cooperation: What's the difference?* Jostle Blog. Retrieved September 14, 2022, from https://blog.jostle.me/blog/collaboration-vs-cooperation

Nace, T. (2017, August 3). *Humanity has officially consumed more than earth can produce this year.* Forbes. Retrieved October 4, 2022, from https://www.forbes.com/sites/trevornace/2017/08/03/humanity-officially-consumed-more-earth-produce-year/?sh=771373aa59a4

Nedjah, N., Mourelle, L. D. M., & Lopes, H. S. (2018). *Evolutionary multi-objective system design: Theory and applications.* CRC Press, Taylor & Francis Group.

Oberlo. (2022). *Search engine market share in 2022.* Oberlo. Retrieved November 20, 2022, from https://www.oberlo.com/statistics/search-engine-market-share

OECD. (2017). *Future of work and skills.* Paper presented at the 2nd Meeting of the G20 Employment Working Group, 15th – 17th, February, 2017. Retrieved April 5, 2019, from https://www.oecd.org/els/emp/wcms_556984.pdf

OECD. (2019). *Protected sectors have dispersed productivity and low allocative efficiency.* OECD Economic Surveys. https://doi.org/10.1787/ba502649-en

Ogundipe, C. F., & Adelugba, I. A. (2022). Upward communication: A modern technique for employee participation and performance enhancement of selected hotel staff in Adoekiti. *American International Journal of Business Management (AIJBM), 5*(3), 1–6. Retrieved September 9, 2022, from https://www.aijbm.com/wp-content/uploads/2022/03/A530106.pdf

Oullier, O., & Kelso, J. A. S. (2009). Social coordination, from the perspective of coordination dynamics. In R. Meyers (Ed.), *Encyclopedia of complexity and systems science.* Springer. https://doi.org/10.1007/978-0-387-30440-3_486

Patacsil, F. F., & Tablatin, C. L. S. (2017). Exploring the importance of soft and hard skills as perceived by it internship students and industry: A gap analysis. *Journal of Technology and Science Education, 7*(3), 347. https://doi.org/10.3926/jotse.271

Pennington, D. D. (2008). Cross-disciplinary collaboration and learning. *Ecology and Society, 13*(2). https://doi.org/10.5751/es-02520-130208

Piketty, T. (2014). *Capital in the Twenty-first century*. Translated by A. Goldhammer. Belknap Press of Harvard University Press.

Rafajac, O., & Pupavac, D. (2017). Organizacijska inteligencija u Republici Hrvatskoj [organizational intelligence in the Republic of Croatia]. *Ekonomski pregled, 68*(1), 88–106. Retrieved July 7, 2022, from https://hrcak.srce.hr/179107

Rahmawati, M., Ruslan, A., & Bandarsyah, D. (2021). The era of society 5.0 as the unification of humans and technology: A literature review on materialism and existentialism. *Jurnal Sosiologi Dialektika, 16*(2), 151. https://doi.org/10.20473/jsd.v16i2.2021.151-162

Rainie, L., & Anderson, J. (2022, September 15). *Code-dependent: Pros and cons of the algorithm age*. Pew Research Center. Retrieved November 20, 2022, from https://www.pewresearch.org/internet/2017/02/08/code-dependent-pros-and-cons-of-the-algorithm-age/

Ram, A., & Leake, D. B. (1995). Learning, goals, and learning goals. In A. Ram & D. B. Leake (Eds.), *Goal-driven learning* (pp. 1–37). MIT Press / Bradford Books. https://doi.org/10.7551/mitpress%2F3314.003.0022

Remtulla, K. A. (2012). Congruency in higher learning: Developing sustainable adult education program policies for the digital age. In V. Wang (Ed.), *Encyclopedia of E-leadership, counseling and training* (pp. 680–697). IGI Global. https://doi.org/10.4018/978-1-61350-068-2.ch050

Roberts, K. H., & O'Reilly, C. A. (1974). Failures in upward communication in organizations: Three possible culprits. *Academy of Management Journal, 17*(2), 205–215. https://doi.org/10.2307/254974

Romera, J. (2022, May 10). *Anonymous employee feedback: Best methods and tools*. Office Vibe. Retrieved from November 17, 2022, from https://officevibe.com/blog/anonymous-employee-feedback

Rotsaert, T., Panadero, E., & Schellens, T. (2017). Anonymity as an instructional scaffold in peer assessment: Its effects on peer feedback quality and evolution in students' perceptions about peer assessment skills. *European Journal of Psychology of Education, 33*(1), 75–99. https://doi.org/10.1007/s10212-017-0339-8

Rupasingha, A., Wojan, T. R., & Freshwater, D. (1999). Self-organization and community-based development initiatives. *Community Development Society Journal, 30*(1), 66–82. https://doi.org/10.1080/15575339909489754

Rute, S. C. (2018). *An overview on the evolution of IoT communication approaches*. Retrieved August 2, 2021, from https://www.researchgate.net/publication/327645202_An_Overview_on_the_Evolution_of_IoT_Communication_Approaches

Sadia, A., Mohd Salleh, B., Abdul Kadir, Z., & Sanif, S. (2016). The relationship between organizational communication and employees productivity with new dimensions of effective communication flow. *Journal of Business and Social Review in Emerging Economies, 2*(2), 93–100. https://doi.org/10.26710/jbsee.v2i2.35

Savolainen, J. (2018). *Hotel industry competitive responses against Airbnb: A case study of hotels vs. Airbnb in Helsinki. (master's thesis).* Aalto University School of Business. Retrieved June 8, 2021, from https://aaltodoc.aalto.fi/bitstream/handle/123456789/32552/master_Savolainen_Javier_2018.pdf?sequence=1&isAllowed=y

Schauer, B., & Zeiller, M. (2011). E-collaboration systems: How collaborative they really are? Analysis of collaboration features of electronic collaboration systems. In *COLLA 2011: The first international conference on advanced collaborative networks, systems and applications* (pp. 16–21). Retrieved November, 12, 2022, from https://people.fh-burgenland.at/bitstream/20.500.11790/1028/1/schauer_zeiller_ecoll_systems_colla2011_50065.pdf

Scherer, T., Straub, J., Schnyder, D., & Schaffner, N. (2013). The effects of anonymity on student ratings of teaching and course quality in a bachelor degree programme. *GMS Zeitschrift fur medizinische Ausbildung, 30*(3), Doc32. https://doi.org/10.3205/zma000875

Segment. (2022). *The 2017 state of personalization report.* Segment. Retrieved November 20, 2022, from Personalization.

Senge, P. M. (2006). *The fifth discipline: The art & practice of the learning organizations* (2nd ed. edition, 1990 first edition). Doubleday.

SHRM. (2016). *The new talent landscape – recruiting difficulty and skills shortages.* A research report. Society for Human Resource Management. Retrieved May 12, 2019, from https://www.shrm.org/hr-today/trends-and-forecasting/research-and-surveys/Documents/SHRM%20New%20Talent%20Landscape%20Recruiting%20Difficulty%20Skills.pdf

Singer, J. B., Sage, M., Berzin, S. C., & Coulton, C. J. (2022). Harnessing technology for social good. *Grand Challenges for Social Work and Society,* 230–256. https://doi.org/10.1093/oso/9780197608043.003.0017

Smith, C. (2018, August 15). *Defining digital trust.* Ionic. Retrieved June 10, 2021, from https://ionic.com/defining-digital-trust/

Smith, S.C., & Rothbaum, J. (2013). *Cooperatives in a global economy: Key economic issues, recent trends, and potential for development.* Policy Paper No. 68, IZA. Retrieved May 6, 2021, from https://docs.iza.org/pp68.pdf

Srinidhi, N. N., Dilip Kumar, S. M., & Venugopal, K. R. (2019). Network optimizations in the internet of things: A review. *Engineering Science and Technology, an International Journal, 22*(1), 1–21. https://doi.org/10.1016/j.jestch.2018.09.003

Swenson, K., & Ghertner, R. (2020, April). *People in low-income households have less access to internet services.* Office of the Assistant Secretary for Planning & Evaluation, U.S. Department of Health & Human Services. Retrieved August 2, 2022, from https://aspe.hhs.gov/sites/default/files/private/pdf/263601/Internet_Access_Among_Low_Income.pdf

Tabugbo, O. P., & Okafor, C. J. (2021). Relationship between communication and performance in organisations. *International Journal of Academic Management Science Research (IJAMSR), 5*(2), 232–244. Retrieved November 3, 2022, from http://ijeais.org/wpcontent/uploads/2021/2/IJAMSR210240.pdf

Terry, H. (2016). *Digital trust: Strengthening customer relationships through ethics and security.* Accenture. Retrieved October 1, 2019, from https://www.the-digital-insurer.com/library/digital-trust_strengthening-customer-relationships-through-ethics-and-security-accenture-report/

Thales. (2021, April 9). *IoT security issues in 2022: A business perspective.* Thales Group. Retrieved June 4, 2022, from https://www.thalesgroup.com/en/markets/digital-identity-and-security/iot/magazine/internet-threats

Thurman, N., Moeller, J., Helberger, N., & Trilling, D. (2018). My friends, editors, algorithms, and I. *Digital Journalism, 7*(4), 447–469. https://doi.org/10.1080/21670811.2018.1493936

Transparency International. (2022, January 25). *2021 Corruption perceptions index reveals a decade of stagnating corruption levels in Western Europe amidst ongoing scandals.* Transparency International. Retrieved November 20, 2022, from https://www.transparency.org/en/press/2021-corruption-perceptions-index-press-release-regional-western-europe

Tsamados, A., Aggarwal, N., Cowls, J., Morley, J., Roberts, H., Taddeo, M., & Floridi, L. (2021). The ethics of algorithms: Key problems and solutions. *AI & SOCIETY, 37*(1), 215–230. https://doi.org/10.1007/s00146-021-01154-8

UN. (n.d.-a). *The age of digital interdependence. Report of the UN secretary-general's high-level panel on digital cooperation.* United Nations. Retrieved August 20, 2021, from https://www.un.org/en/pdfs/DigitalCooperation-report-for%20web.pdf

UN. (n.d.-b). *Transforming our world: The 2030 agenda for sustainable development. A/RES/70/1.* United Nations. Retrieved August 20, 2021, from https://sustainabledevelopment.un.org/content/documents/21252030%20Agenda%20for%20Sustainable%20Development%20web.pdf

Uviase, O., & Kotonya, G. (2018). IOT architectural framework: Connection and integration framework for IOT systems. *Electronic Proceedings in Theoretical Computer Science, 264,* 1–17. https://doi.org/10.4204/eptcs.264.1

van der Werff, L., Real, C., & Lynn, T. (2018). Individual trust and the internet. In R. Searle, A. Nienaber, & S. Sitkin (Eds.), *Trust.* Routledge. Retrieved August 19, 2021, from https://doras.dcu.ie/22321/1/Individual_Trust_and_the_Internet_Repository.pdf

Vries, J., Bommel, S., & Peters, K. (2018). Trust at a Distance—Trust in online communication in environmental and Global Health research projects. *Sustainability, 10*(11), 4005. https://doi.org/10.3390/su10114005

WEF. (2014). *Matching skills and labour market needs building social partnerships for better skills and better jobs.* Global Agenda Council on Employment, 22–25 January, 2014. World Economic Forum. Retrieved May 7, 2019, from https://www3.weforum.org/docs/GAC/2014/WEF_GAC_Employment_MatchingSkillsLabourMarket_Report_2014.pdf

Weger, H., Bell, G. C., Minei, E. M., & Robinson, M. C. (2014). The relative effectiveness of active listening in initial interactions. *International Journal of Listening, 28*(1), 13–31. https://doi.org/10.1080/10904018.2013.813234

Westmacott, A. (2017). Direct vs. indirect written corrective feedback: Student perceptions. *Íkala, Revista De Lenguaje y Cultura, 22*(2), 17–32. https://doi.org/10.17533/udea.ikala.v22n01a02

WHO. (2018a, 22 March). *Depression.* World Health Organization. Retrieved August 22, 2021, from https://www.who.int/en/news-room/fact-sheets/detail/depression

WHO. (2018b, 9 April). *Mental disorders.* World Health Organization. Retrieved August 22, 2021, from https://www.who.int/en/news-room/fact-sheets/detail/mental-disorders

WMO. (2018, September 27). *Climate change is moving faster than we are: UN secretary-general.* World meteorological Organization Retrieved October 9, 2021, from https://public.wmo.int/en/media/news/climate-change-moving-faster-we-are-un-secretary-general

Zuiderveen Borgesius, F. J., Trilling, D., Möller, J., Bodó, B., de Vreese, C. H., & Helberger, N. (2016). Should we worry about filter bubbles? *Internet Policy Review, 5*(1). https://doi.org/10.14763/2016.1.401

INDEX

O. Rafajac, A. Jakupović (eds.), *Integral Communication and Digital Identity*, https://doi.org/10.1007/978-3-031-47460-6